Together in Mission
The Anglican Church in Malawi and the Church of England Birmingham, 1966-2016

© the authors

All rights reserved. No part of this publication may be reproduced, stored in a retrieval system, or transmitted in any form or by any means, electronic, mechanical, photocopying, recording or otherwise, without prior permission from the publishers.

Published by

Mzuni Press

P/Bag 201

Luwinga, Mzuzu 2

Malawi

ISBN   978-99960-60-68-7

eISBN   978-99960-60-69-4

Mzuni Press is represented outside Malawi by:

African Books Collective Oxford (also for e-books) (order@africanbookscollective.com)

www.africanbookscollective.com

www.mzunipress.blogspot.com

Editorial assistance: Hope Kaombe

Cover: Josephine Kawejere

Together in Mission

The Anglican Church in Malawi and the Church of England Birmingham, 1966-2016

Richard Tucker

With a chapter by

Rt Rev James Tengatenga

MZUNI PRESS

Mzuni Books no. 45
Mzuzu
2022

Contents

Foreword by the Rt. Rev. Dr. James Tengatenga	5
Acknowledgements	7

Chapter 1
Introduction — 12

Chapter 2
A History of the Anglican Church in Malawi from 1861 — 15
The Rt. Rev. Dr. James Tengatenga

Chapter 3
The Church of England in Birmingham to 1966 — 35

Chapter 4
The Partnership's Beginnings and First Twenty Years, 1961-87 — 45

Chapter 5
The Malawian Church in Times of Stress, 1987-94 — 67

Chapter 6
New Era, New Challenges, New Dioceses, 1994-2002 — 83

Chapter 7
Bishop Christopher Boyle and the beginnings of the Diocese of Northern Malawi — 99

Photographs — 120

Chapter 8
Women in Partnership — 132

Chapter 9
The Birmingham end of the Partnership, 1966-2016 — 145

Chapter 10
Birmingham's Engagement with the Partnership, 2000-2016 — 170

Chapter 11
Developments in the Malawian Church, 2002-2016, and Birmingham's Role — 191

Chapter 12
Evaluation — 210

Appendices — 220
Bibliography — 227
Index of Names and Subjects — 230

Foreword by the Rt. Rev. Dr. James Tengatenga

Bishop of Southern Malawi 1998-2013; Distinguished Professor of Global Anglicanism, The School of Theology at the University of the South, Tennessee, USA

One of the glories of the Anglican Communion is that it is a north-south partnership, between churches which in the 'missionary era' were cast in the role of sending or receiving but are now sister churches in Christ. As a member and then as Chair of the Anglican Consultative Council I had ample opportunity both to rejoice in our unity in Christ and to feel the pain of the divisions that reflect our differing cultural and colonial heritages. Under the umbrella of that overall partnership are many local ones. The one of which I had most experience was the partnership between the Anglican Church in Malawi and the Church of England Birmingham.

As part of my work as an academic and then as bishop in Malawi I made various contributions to the history of the Anglican Church there, which now stretches for almost 160 years. One aspect of that history that has hardly been told until now (except for a pamphlet produced 20 years ago by Canon Bob Jenkins) is that of the 50-year partnership initiated in 1966 by Bishops Leonard Wilson of Birmingham and Donald Arden of Malawi. Was it serendipitous that these two bishops met over this during the Toronto Anglican Congress of 1963? It was at this Congress that the Anglican Communion spelt out its desire and intentions to live into its new reality. With its theme of "Mutual Responsibility and Interdependence in the Body of Christ" it spelt out that there are no givers/senders and receivers but that all are givers/senders and all are receivers, and all are partners in God's mission.

That gap in the story has been filled by Richard Tucker, who served as Birmingham's Malawi Partnership Officer for six years until 2017. At his request I was happy to contribute a chapter on the history of the Anglican Church in Malawi from 1861. This takes some aspects of the story up to the present day, in counterpoint to Richard's account.

Richard's work is given added immediacy by the wide range of primary sources he has drawn on to supplement his personal experience of the most recent period. Malawian voices quoted in the book help to ensure that this is a partnership history seen from both ends. He has also tried to set the partnership in its wider historical, missiological and political frameworks to enable its proper significance to be understood.

Some lessons can be drawn from this story for the wider Anglican Communion. The first and most obvious is the value to both parties of faithful friendship, through thick and thin, across different parts of the Communion. The second, linked to the first, is the valuable part that 'companion links' (the preferred term of the Church of England) can play in knitting and holding together a Communion which is being subjected to more tensions than ever before. The third lesson is the need for companion links to evolve with the circumstances of the partners: their changing strengths and weaknesses, the external challenges they face, whether from climate change, political pressure or other sources, and their mission priorities. This is a challenge to be faced both in Birmingham and Malawi, as witnessed by the outstanding agenda from the 2014 Review of the Partnership.

I commend this book as a window into a small but significant aspect of the recent past which may yet have lessons for the future.

Acknowledgements

No work of history can be written without the help of many others. As a first-time author I am especially indebted to Terry Slater, author of the centenary history of Birmingham Diocese, for invaluable advice on planning, structure, word count and style. My account of the history of the city and Diocese of Birmingham in chs. 4 and 9 relies heavily on his work. Bishop James Tengatenga has been outstandingly ready to share from his fund of knowledge of Malawian history and the Anglican Church's part in it. In addition to the chapter kindly contributed by him, he has been a spirited dialogue partner about many other points in the history. Professor Klaus Fiedler, formerly of Mzuzu University, has supported me throughout and helped me on the path to publication.

Particular thanks are due to Bishop David Urquhart, who allowed me to view and borrow the Malawi archives of the last three bishops of Birmingham – thanks too to Kate Stowe and Josephine Houghton in Bishop's Croft. I have also consulted the USPG archives and am grateful to Catherine Wakeling there. Special thanks are due to my wife Laetitia for her love, support, and patience with a hesitant first-time author.

The story told here is recent enough for many participants still to be alive. I have relied heavily on personal interviews, conducted both in the UK and in Malawi. These were supplemented by questionnaires sent both to those who served in Malawi and to Birmingham Christians, clergy and lay, whose lives have been touched by the Malawi Partnership.

Clergy and bishops who have served in Malawi have been generous in sharing their experiences with me: Revs Tony Cox, Philip Elston, Keith Gale, Len Viner and the late Bishop Humphrey Taylor. I am especially grateful to Bishop Christopher Boyle for his generous contributions to ch. 7. Jane Arden gave me valuable access to records of her husband's distinguished ministry, and Rev Dr Anne Bayley lent me papers relating to her work helping the church in Malawi. I record my thanks to the following bishops and clergy in the UK [in alphabetic order]: Paul Bracher, the late Henry Burgess, John Cooper, Peter Howell-Jones,

David Lee, David Newsome, Christopher Race, Matthew Rhodes, Bishop Mark Santer, Martin Stephenson, Philip Swan, Emma Sykes and Bishop Andrew Watson. Among lay Christians in the UK my thanks are due to: Jackie Brocklebank, Liz and the late Jim Carr, Gill Edwards, Mary Edwards, Judith Grubb, who also read and commented on a draft, Claire Laland, Alison Robinson and the late Paul Wilson. Wendy Jenkins helpfully let me have transcripts of interviews conducted by her late husband Canon Bob Jenkins and other material. Janice Price gave me access to her work on companion links in the Anglican Communion. Richard Petheram kindly prepared the map of Malawi.

In a real sense every contact I have had in Malawi has contributed to this history, so I express heartfelt general thanks. All the current bishops have given me generously of their time at every stage, and particularly as I was preparing this history: Bishops Alinafe Kalemba, Francis Kaulanda, Fanuel Magangani and Brighton Malasa. I am grateful too to Bishop Jack Biggers for his help. Special thanks are due to those clergy whose 'unfinished biographies' appear in chapter 11: Edward Kawinga, May Machemba, Baird Mponda and Eston Pembamoyo. A warm word of thanks too to lay leaders I interviewed: Mr Justice James Kalaile, Matthews Kumpolota, Bernard Mainga, Erasto M'baya, Agnes Mkoko especially, Oscar Mponda, Willy Musukwa and Jesman Seva.

Responsibility for any inaccuracies or misreading of the situation in Malawi – or come to that, in Birmingham - remains, of course, with me.

List of Abbreviations

ACM	Anglican Council in Malawi
AMECEA	Association of Member Episcopal Conferences in Eastern Africa [the RC Episcopal group for East Africa]
ARCIC	Anglican-Roman Catholic International Commission
ARV	anti-retroviral [treatment]
BCH	Birmingham Children's Hospital
CAPA	Council of Anglican Provinces in Africa
CART	Christian Africa Relief Trust
CCAP	Church of Central Africa Presbyterian
CCBI	Council of Churches for Britain and Ireland
CCMP	Church and Community Mobilisation Process
CHAM	Christian Health Association of Malawi
CLAIM	Christian Literature Association in Malawi
CMS	Church Mission Society
DfID	Department for International Development, UK
DLM	Diocese of Lake Malawi
DNM	Diocese of Northern Malawi
DSM	Diocese of Southern Malawi
DUS	Diocese of Upper Shire
HIPC	Highly Indebted Poor Countries
IGPs	Income generating projects
IMF	International Monetary Fund
LFEP	Literacy and Financial Education Programme
LKTC	Leonard Kamungu Theological College, Zomba
LTC	Lay Training Centre
MACS	Malawi Association for Christian Support
MAP	Media Awareness Project
MRI	Mutual Responsibility and Interdependence

MU	Mothers' Union
NGOs	non-government organizations
PAC	Public Affairs Committee
PIM	Partners in Mission
PWM	Partnership for World Mission
QECH	Queen Elizabeth Central Hospital, Blantyre
SPG	Society for the Propagation of the Gospel
SGR	Strategic Grain Reserve
TEE	Theological Education by Extension
TEEM	Theological Education by Extension Malawi
UMCA	Universities' Mission to Central Africa
USPG	United Society for the Propagation of the Gospel [1965-2011]; since 2016, Partners in the Gospel
WCC	World Council of Churches

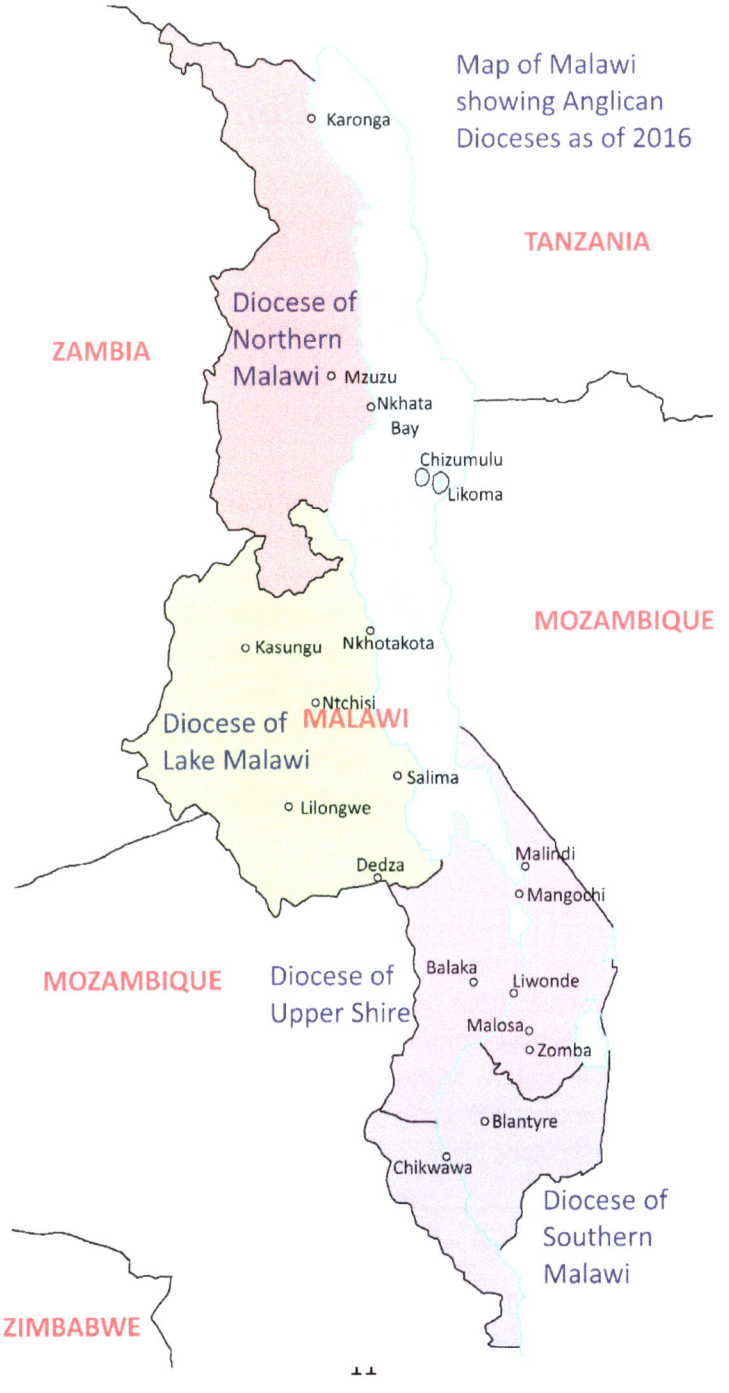

Chapter 1

Introduction

At Pentecost 2016, the festival of the Church's birthday, the four bishops of Malawi were invited to Birmingham for a week to celebrate the 50th anniversary of the Malawi Birmingham Partnership. Together with the Bishop of Birmingham they gave thanks for all the Partnership had meant in the past and recommitted themselves to its future. The visitors engaged themselves in the lives of the parishes where they stayed and visited, in church schools and at the celebration service in the cathedral.

Eleven years earlier, the then bishops of Malawi had been invited to Birmingham to celebrate the diocesan centenary. But on that occasion Birmingham was also thrilled by the singing of a young people's choir from a shanty town church in Blantyre. A motorbike, one of a gift of 58 from the Christians of Birmingham for the Malawian clergy, roared up the nave of the cathedral at a special service. Those celebrations had extra panache, and the anniversary had been more amply resourced by the diocese and parishes. The difference perhaps reflects how the Partnership continues healthy after 50 years, but has not quite the verve and vigour of its finest years.[1]

The contents of this book in some sense spill out beyond its title. It aims to tell the story of the Partnership and set it in context. The principal Christian Churches in Malawi[2] were, under God, founded by missionaries from overseas from the mid-19th century on. In each case the sending churches have continued to have close relations with their sister churches in Malawi. Malawi is a far more religious nation than the UK, and an estimated 80% or so of the population profess Christianity. Hardly any Malawians have no religion. The Roman Catholic and

---

[1] Both visits are described in more detail in chapter 10.

[2] The area now known as Malawi was known as Nyasaland from 1907 until independence in 1964. The modern name Malawi is used throughout.

Presbyterian [CCAP] Churches are now both much larger than the Anglican Church.[3] The stories of those two churches, in Malawi, Scotland and elsewhere, figure prominently, especially in chapters 2 and 5. Another larger context, which can only be hinted at in a book of this size, is Anglican mission as a whole: the work of mission societies almost worldwide, the recognition of the UK and Europe as mission fields too, the range of companion links that have grown up between dioceses and provinces in England and overseas, etc.

In an African context the partnership has been but one small part of a great wave of external influences on the Church. "History indicates that the growth of Christianity in Africa was never unrelated to its relations with the wider world; externality has always been a factor in African Christianity."[4] In earlier generations this was most visible in the presence of a substantial body of missionaries; we shall note the gradual demise of Anglican missionaries in Malawi. Parts of this book tell the story in detail, but the reader should not lose sight of the bigger picture.

To state the obvious: a partnership has two ends. Rather than being strictly chronological, the story moves from one location to another, a chapter or two at a time. I am very grateful to the Rt. Rev James Tengatenga for contributing a chapter [2] on the history of the Anglican Church in Malawi from 1861. This is balanced by one covering the earlier history of the Church of England in Birmingham. The next two chapters [4 and 5] deal with the Partnership's founding in 1966 and tell its story to 1994. These years were for the Malawian nation the Banda era, or in

---

[3] Recent estimates put the RC and CCAP on about 18% of the population each, followed by Seventh Day Adventists, Assemblies of God, Anglicans and an enormous range of other Protestant, Pentecostal, Charismatic and Independent churches. Muslims are reckoned at 13-17%. See Kenneth R Ross and Klaus Fiedler, *A Malawi Church History 1860-2020*, Mzuzu: Mzuni Press 2020, pp. 378-382.

[4] Paul Gifford, *African Christianity: Its Public Role*, London: Hurst & Co., 1998, p. 318.

Anglican terms, the era of Bishop Donald Arden and his immediate successors. Chapter 6 discusses the challenges facing the Malawian church and nation at the end of the Banda era, notably the HIV/AIDS crisis. Chapter 7 centres on the story of the Birmingham clergyman who became Bishop of Northern Malawi, Christopher Boyle. The theme of chapter 8 is women in partnership, particularly that powerhouse of the Malawian Church, the Mothers' Union.

Chapters 9 and 10 bring us back to Birmingham. Chapter 9 includes a brief sketch of the radical economic, social and religious changes of the past 50 years there and a discussion of the role of money in the partnership. This is followed by an account of the initiatives coming largely from Birmingham that renewed the partnership in the present century. Chapter 11 tells of the four Malawian dioceses that have existed since 2002, the Church's central institutions and their relations with Birmingham. I attempt an evaluation in chapter 12. I refer selectively to relevant events after the partnership's 50th anniversary, but have no wish to attempt to write its history after my retirement in spring 2017.

Chapter 2

A History of the Anglican Church in Malawi from 1861

Rt. Rev. James Tengatenga

Introduction

In Malawian culture (and indeed in most cultures) history is celebrated by feasts and/or holidays with song and dance. These commemorations have the effect of etching into the memory of the people, and in this case the church, the acts of God in the *missio Dei*. These events mark time, people and events in the history of the church. By way of introduction to the history of the Anglican Church in Malawi I outline some significant ones.

In 1980 the Bishops in Malawi led the church in dedicating the Bishop Mackenzie Chapel at Magomero, now a national monument and a shrine for Anglicans. They had first erected an iron cross a few yards from the lone grave of Fr Henry de Wint Burrup (in whose arms Bishop Mackenzie died). Since 1999 the Anglican Church has gathered annually to give thanks and remember the first missionaries of the Universities' Mission to Central Africa [UMCA] with an open-air festal Eucharist on the Saturday nearest to 2nd October. At Chikwawa the commemoration of David Livingstone, Bishop Mackenzie and the removal of the mission to Zanzibar in 1863 happen on the weekend nearest to 30th April, Livingstone's Feast Day in the Malawi calendar.

The centenary of the Church on Likoma Island was celebrated in 1987, and of the consecration of St Peter's Cathedral there in 2005. In 1994 the centenary of the establishment of the church at Nkhotakota by Fr Sim was celebrated. Just as it was a big occasion in 1957, when the Archbishop of York visited Malawi, so it was when Robert Runcie, Archbishop of Canterbury visited Malawi in 1989. In 1997 the United Society for the Propagation of the Gospel [USPG] commemorated 140 years of UMCA at Oxford and Cambridge Universities, at which Malawi was honoured by having Fr James Tengatenga as the preacher at both services. The Archbishop of York, David Hope, was the celebrant at the Eucharist at Great St. Mary's, Cambridge and gave the talk in the University Senate House that evening, attended by all the surviving UMCA missionaries and those who came as USPG missionaries in later years.

1998 was the centenary of the Malindi mission. In 2001 St Peter's Church, Lilongwe-celebrated its jubilee. 2007 marked the centenary of Kayoyo Parish, the first parish set up by the UMCA as they expanded westwards into Ntchisi from Nkhotakota. The climax in 2011 was the sesquicentenary celebrations of the UMCA at Magomero graced by the Archbishop of Canterbury, Rowan Williams, as guest of honour. Mission partners of the Malawi church including Birmingham were represented too.

The History

The Land along the River Shire and Lake Nyasa[1]

On one of missionary explorer Dr David Livingstone's furloughs in Britain, he spoke to numerous audiences about Africa and his sojourn there. His talks included the evils of the slave trade. Livingstone[2] challenged the English people and the church to help end slavery in Africa through the introduction of the three Cs, Christianity, civilization and commerce. On December 4, 1857, the missionary movement to Malawi and East Africa began, when Livingstone ended his speech at the Senate House at Cambridge University with the now-famous

---

[1] For the history before 1961 see James Tengatenga (ed), *The UMCA in Malawi: A History of the Anglican Church 1861-2010*, Zomba: Kachere, 2010. For a complete history see the three volumes of A.E.M. Anderson-Morshead, *The History of the Universities' Mission to Central Africa, 1859-1909*, London: Universities' Mission to Central Africa, 1897-1909, www.archive.org/details /historyofunivers00ande .

[2] His remains are interred in Westminster Abbey, London.

challenge: "I go back to Africa to try to make an open path for commerce and Christianity. Do you carry out the work, which I have begun? *'I leave it with you'*."[3]

The abolitionist movement had already led to the outlawing of slavery by the British Parliament in 1807, but the ban did not take full effect until 1833. The slave trade continued, however, in those parts of the world that were not under British control. In East Africa, it continued well into the first quarter of the twentieth century. The three Cs which Livingstone advocated as goals for the missionary movement in Africa, have been much debated, but they have to be understood in the context in which he was speaking. While the three Cs carry undeniable colonialist overtones, their abolitionist tenor should not be dismissed. Livingstone's idea, like that of all the missionaries of that era from Europe[4], was that the 'dark continent' needed to be opened up for Christianity and civilization, and the scourge of human trade had to be replaced with humane commerce. In response to this challenge, the Anglican UMCA, the Livingstonia Mission of the Free Church of Scotland and the Blantyre Mission of the Church of Scotland were formed and sent forth to Malawi.[5]

Bishop Mackenzie's Venture[6]

The first group to respond to David Livingstone's challenge was the UMCA with Charles Frederick Mackenzie as leader. They were sent off

---

[3] A. E. M. Anderson-Morshead, op. cit., p.4, reproduced in Tengatenga, op. cit., p. 33.

[4] See discussion and critique of the prevailing missionary consciousness and missionary method in John McCracken, *A History of Malawi 1859-1966* (Rochester NY: James Currey, 2012).

[5] The UMCA arrived in Malawi in 1861, Livingstonia Mission in 1875 and Blantyre Mission in 1876.

[6] The story of Mackenzie is told in full by Owen Chadwick in *Mackenzie's Grave*, London: Hodder & Stoughton, 1959. A shorter account may be found in

with the Eucharist from Canterbury Cathedral on October 2, 1860. Mackenzie was consecrated in St George's Cathedral in Cape Town by Bishop Gray on January 1, 1861. After recruiting a team and collecting the supplies needed, they headed for 'the Land along the River Shire and Lake Nyasa'. On the insistence of Livingstone, they tried getting there by the Ruvuma River but it proved impractical as the Ruvuma did not flow into or out of Lake Malawi. They finally did the right thing and sailed up the Zambezi and into its tributary the Shire, which is the only river that flows out of Lake Malawi (the present name of Lake Nyasa).

Their very first missionary activity was the freeing of captured people destined to be sold as slaves. As Bishop Mackenzie saw it, there was "no ruler ordained of God … to whom we could refer the matter … but we believed that being the only power in the place that could do it, we were ourselves God's ministers for the purpose."[7] David Livingstone was part of the UMCA's initial strike against the slave trade in Malawi, as he had accompanied the missionaries. When they finally settled at Magomero, in today's Chiradzulu District, the first Christian congregation was made up of freed captives.

Here they set up mission and began a regular routine of worship, work and exercise. They also built a church, the first Anglican church and also the first Christian presence in Malawi. Bishop Mackenzie's team had clergy and laymen, and was expecting lay women including his two sisters to join them within a short time. When the latter delayed in coming, the bishop and Fr Burrup set out to meet them. It was on this fateful journey that the bishop succumbed to malaria. He died at a village on the confluence of the Ruo and the Shire Rivers near Chiromo

---

Kenneth R Ross and Klaus Fiedler, *A Malawi Church History 1860-2020,* Mzuzu: Mzuni Press, 2020, pp. 29-33.

[7] Quoted in Jonathan Newell, "'There Were Arguments in Favour of Our Taking Arms': Bishop Mackenzie and the War Against the Yao in 1861," *The Society of Malawi Journal*, 45, no. 1, 1992, pp. 15–45.

and was buried there[8]. Fr Burrup hurried back to inform the others, and shortly after his return he too died of malaria. His is the lone grave at Magomero.

Bishop George Tozer succeeded Bishop Mackenzie, and was appointed to be 'the opposite of Mackenzie.' He decided in 1863 to move the mission to Mt Morambala in Mozambique. This decision was made at the shore of the River Shire in Chikwawa where the remaining missionaries had moved after the death of the bishop and Burrup. At this site two more missionaries died, Dr Dickinson the mission doctor and Fr Scudamore. There were negative perceptions in England of mission engagement against slave raiding and inter-tribal political and military skirmishes.[9] These and malaria led Tozer to take the further decision in 1864 to go to Zanzibar. This led to the resignation of one of the missionaries, Horace Waller. Waller took some of the former captives to Cape Town, where he stopped on his way back to Britain. Bishop Tozer took some of the captives with him, but the rest he left in the care of Chief Kapeni, or to fend for themselves. Those that remained with Chief Kapeni were to become key players in the building of Blantyre Mission.

Christ Church Cathedral in Zanzibar was opened in 1879 on the site of the big slave market as a sign that the missionaries were serious about ridding the area of the slave trade. In Mbweni, five miles away, were St John's Church and a school for the freed slave girls as well as a Freedom Village. Midway between Mbweni and the Cathedral was Kiungani Boys School, which was built to educate the freed slave boys. Kiungani would become an important place of training for missionaries, both teachers and evangelists, and African clergy.

---

[8] In 1961 his remains were moved to Blantyre and interred in the high altar of what is now St Paul's Cathedral. His grave at Chiromo in modern day Mozambique is still marked.

[9] Newell, "'There Were Arguments in Favour of Our Taking Arms': Bishop Mackenzie and the War against the Yao in 1861," *The Society of Malawi Journal*, 45, no. 1, 1992, pp. 15–45.

Growth of the UMCA Mission[10]

Bishop Edward Steere, Tozer's successor at Zanzibar from 1874, intended to return to Malawi. But it was his successor from 1883, Bishop Charles Smythies, who finally led the UMCA back to Malawi via Likoma. The small islands of Likoma and Chizumulu lie about half-way between the north and south ends of the lake, near the eastern [Mozambique] shore. Likoma was seen to be strategic to the planting of the Anglican Church both in Mozambique and Malawi; it became the domain of the church with the bishop as the head. It was a full mission station in the fashion of Mbweni on Zanzibar, with a clinic and later a theological college, St. Andrews. St Peter's Cathedral was begun there in 1903 at Chipyela, the place where witches used to be burnt, as a sign of the superiority of Christianity over traditional beliefs. An imposing building with a design based on Winchester Cathedral, it was consecrated in 1905 but not finished until 1911. The diocese originally covered Nyasaland, Mozambique and part of Tanzania.

Archdeacon Percival Johnson (a.k.a. the Apostle of the Lake) and Charles Janson were the key players in the establishment of the church in these parts. Janson died after a short while but Johnson served for 46 years.[11] The missionaries had a steamer, the *Charles Janson*, assembled at Matope; it sailed up and down the lake supporting missionary activity. It was succeeded in 1902 by the *Chauncy Maples,* which was used for half a century by the missionaries along the lake, docking at lakeshore spots to evangelize the eastern and western lakeshores. It also acted as a theological school for the formation of clergy and as a hospital. Over time it was used, not very successfully, as a commercial venture to help the diocesan finances.

The Malindi mission, at the southern end of the eastern lakeshore in Mangochi district, later became the shipyard for repairs to the *Chauncy Maples,* and provided employment and training for many. St Martin's

---

[10] See Ross and Fiedler, *A Malawi Church History 1860-2020,* pp. 87-91.

[11] Ibid, p. 199.

Hospital at Malindi was the reason for the building of the bridge over the upper Shire River and the creation of the road to the eastern shores of Lake Malawi. St. Martin's remains a major medical facility on that part of the eastern lakeshore.

A clinic at Makanjira, north of Malindi, was and is the other medical facility in the area. Makanjira was one of the villages where Islam had strong roots. The UMCA missionaries tried to convert the people there to Christianity, but with very little success. Makanjira became a symbol of resistance, and a place where Islam influenced not only the practice of faith, but also trade and education. Resistance to the UMCA was resistance to a new culture, English and Western, which posed a threat to the established Islamic religion and system of education. The missionaries had more success in the Mpondas area at the southern tip of the lake near Mangochi. To this day there is a significant Anglican population in this area, and it hosts the cathedral for the Diocese of Upper Shire.

Further north on the central western lakeshore is Nkhotakota, the seat of the Jumbes, and thus a significant hub of Islam. In the precincts of what is now All Saints Cathedral is the fig tree where David Livingstone negotiated the end of slavery with the Jumbe.[12] Another reason for the less complete dominance of Islam there is that Mr Nicoll, the Resident of Nkhotakota, did not favour the prevalence of the Islamic faith and education. He thus invited the UMCA to establish a mission there and take over the education of its children; thus, Nkhotakota became a centre of Anglicanism.[13] Fr Arthur Sim began the mission in 1894, but like so many of the early missionaries he succumbed young to a tropical disease; he died in 1895 and is buried behind All Saints Cathedral. In 1895 Bishop Chauncy Maples (after whom the mission steamer was

---

[12] It is also said that Sir H.H. Johnston bought out the Jumbe. See David Stuart-Mogg, *Mlozi of Central Africa: The End of the Slaver,* Blantyre: Central Africana, 2010, p. 77.

[13] See James Tengatenga, *Church State and Society in Malawi: The Anglican Case*, Zomba: Kachere, 2006, pp. 62, 70.

named) succeeded Bishop Hornby. He was ordained priest at St John's, Mbweni in Zanzibar and had been an archdeacon in the diocese. He was drowned on Lake Malawi on his way back from his consecration as Bishop of Likoma (as the Diocese was named for a while). He is buried in the nave of the cathedral.

Just as the people of Makanjira had feared, some of the Muslim families sent their children to be educated at the mission and "lost" them to Christianity. However, because of the strength of the bonds within families, it became widely accepted over time to have both Islam and Christianity represented within the same family. This, to a great extent, explains the cordial relationship of Muslims and Anglicans in this part of the lakeshore. There has been occasional tension, but for the most part, Islam and Anglicanism have coexisted with mutual respect, and the most difficult disagreements have been between different sects of Islam.

The presence of the UMCA along the lakeshore, in Mozambique and in Tanzania all the way to Zanzibar, explains the place occupied by Anglicans in their comity agreements with the Scottish missions.[14] The loss of Tanzania and Mozambique and subsequent encroachment by the Dutch Reformed, explains why Presbyterians outnumber Anglicans in the area. Mozambique and Tanzania became independent jurisdictions after the Berlin Conference of 1884/5; Mozambique was a Portuguese colony until 1975. Malawi became the British Central Africa Protectorate in 1891, a move that strengthened the position of the Anglicans and Presbyterians.

Chauncy Maples was succeeded as bishop by John Hine in 1896. Gerard Trower, who succeeded him in 1902, sought permission from Canterbury in 1908 to change the name back to the Diocese of Nyasaland. Trower was followed by Cathrew Fisher in 1910, who was in turn succeeded by Arthur Douglas in 1930.

---

[14] These are discussed below.

The Presbyterians

Livingstonia Mission[15]

In 1875, twelve years after the abortion of the UMCA mission by Bishop Tozer, the Free Church of Scotland missionaries arrived at Cape Maclear on Lake Malawi. Their primary focus was the first two of Livingstone's "Three C's", Christianity, Civilization and Commerce. The third was fulfilled through the formation of the commercial African Lakes Company by the Moir brothers from Scotland; it later separated from the mission. The former UMCA missionary Horace Waller was part of the team. He worked with the Livingstonia Mission in an advisory capacity and compiled the two volumes of David Livingstone's last journals.[16]

The first group that came to establish Livingstonia mission was greatly helped by four liberated Africans: Lorenzo Johnston, Thomas Bokwito, Samuel Sambani and Frederick Zarakuti. The Free Church of Scotland's response to the challenge Livingstone had set forth for Africa was to focus on education. Many schools were opened in the Free Church's area of operation in Northern Malawi. The most famous centre was the Overtoun Institution, now the site of the main campus of Livingstonia University. English was used in the classrooms, and the quality of education was high; indeed, it nurtured numerous significant players in early Malawi politics, education and commerce. This is now the area of the Livingstonia Synod of the Church of Central Africa Presbyterian [CCAP].

---

[15] For a detailed history of the Livingstonia mission see John McCracken, *Politics and Christianity in Malawi, 1875-1940: The Impact of the Livingstonia Mission in the Northern Province*, 2nd ed. Zomba: Kachere, 2000. The history is summarized in Ross and Fiedler, *A Malawi Church History 1860-2020*, pp. 38-53.

[16] Horace Waller, *The Last Journal of David Livingstone, in Central Africa from 1865 to his Death, 1866-1868*, vol. 1 & 2, London: John Murray, 1874.

The Dutch Reformed Church[17]

The Central Region, save Nkhotakota, Ntchisi and Kasungu,[18] was the domain of the Dutch Reformed Church, which began its work in Malawi in 1894. The origin of this group was the Dutch Reformed Church in South Africa, which adhered to the idea that a Black person is nothing but "a hewer of wood and a drawer of water," and gave tacit blessing to the policy of apartheid in South Africa. However, in Malawi, the Dutch Reformed behaved like other missionary groups, setting up churches and building schools and hospitals. They too followed the example of Livingstone and the UMCA, opening up Africa to Christianity, Civilization and Commerce. This is now the CCAP, Nkhoma Synod.

Blantyre Mission[19]

The Church of Scotland Mission was set up in 1876 in the south of the country, in the area of Chief Kapeni, with whom some of the freed captives remained in 1863. Some of these former captives became the nucleus of the new mission at Blantyre, named after David Livingstone's birthplace in Scotland. The men who had been freed from slavery helped not only build the church, but also in the evangelization effort. The mission has now become the Blantyre Synod of the CCAP. It was also the beginning of the city of Blantyre. Here the Blantyre Mission built the impressive church of St Michael and All Angels which dates from 1891. Here the Moir brothers of the African Lakes Company set up

---

[17] See Ross and Fiedler, *A Malawi Church History 1860-2020,* pp. 70-77; also, Kamunkhwani's dissertation on the history of Nkhoma Synod, Stellenbosch University, South Africa.

[18] Livingstonia Mission handed over Kasungu to the Dutch Reformed Church in 1929.

[19] See Ross and Fiedler, *A Malawi Church History 1860-2020,* pp. 54-69; also Andrew C. Ross, *Blantyre Mission and The Making of Modern Malawi,* Zomba: Kachere, 1996.

their headquarters at Mandala House, one of the oldest houses in the country and now a historical monument.

The Livingstonia and Blantyre missions united in 1924 to form the Church of Central Africa, Presbyterian [CCAP]. They persuaded the reluctant Dutch Reformed mission to join with them in 1926.[20]

The Roman Catholics

Catholic missionaries first arrived in Malawi in 1889; they tried unsuccessfully to begin a mission in the territory of Muslim Chief Mponda in the lakeshore Mangochi District. The first permanent missions were set up by the Montfort Missionaries near Ntcheu in 1901 and by the White Fathers at Mua in 1902. The Roman Catholics did not participate in the comity agreements, due to the prevalent pre-Vatican II ecclesiology. As a result, Roman Catholicism spread throughout the country. A Malawian province with four dioceses was set up in 1959; by 2019 there were eight dioceses. Catholicism wields a lot of influence in Malawian society and over the Protestant and Muslim populations.[21]

Denominationalism, Comity Agreements and Ecumenism[22]

The nineteenth century comity agreements among the missionaries created spheres of denominational influence, which on the whole mirrored the Berlin Conference's partition of Africa. The comity

---

[20] See Ross and Fiedler, *A Malawi Church History 1860-2020,* pp. 128-132 and 164-178.

[21] More detail about the history of Roman Catholicism in Malawi can be found at www.ecmmw.org/new/about-us/history-of-the-church-in-5 [16.8. 2019]. In the standard Church History (Kenneth R. Ross and Klaus Fiedler, *A Malawi Church History 1860 – 2020*, Mzuzu: Mzuni Press, 2020) read esp. chs. 5, 11, 22, 27, 28.

[22] See also the discussion in Ross and Fiedler, *A Malawi Church History 1860-2020,* pp. 120-128.

agreements were that each denomination's missionaries would occupy a territory of their own and the others would not encroach into it. They were intended to be a way of coping with the denominationalism produced by the Reformation, which presented the unchurched with a divided Christ and created a question: If the missionaries preached the same Jesus Christ, how come they behaved and manifested themselves differently? The differences lay not only in language (e.g., English, Afrikaans, and German) but also in liturgy and church order; differences that confused the converts and other locals. The agreements were also a means of avoiding needless duplication of effort in the early days when resources were scarce. The ecumenical movement had not yet taken root, and the missionaries were bound to the denomination that sent them.

In Malawi there were three spheres of influence which over time, morphed into ethno-political divisions. Unfortunately, the regional lines of disagreement in Malawi are, for the most part, coterminous with the churches' historic comity boundaries. Malawi has turned into an ethno-regional political tinder box as a result. Ethnicity and geographical area went hand in hand; politicization of ethnicity came later. The ethnic divisions in Malawi are an unintended byproduct of the comity agreements.

In addition to the mainline denominations there were also many other church traditions. These ranged from African initiated churches (AICs) to those brought in by "independent" missionaries like Joseph Booth. The AICs were born out of a liberation motif: either one that prized a mix of traditional expressions of faith or a more political one that prized indigenous leadership. The one of note among these is the Providence Industrial Mission of John Chilembwe, a protégé of Joseph Booth.[23]

Pastor John Chilembwe was a champion of the *'Africa for the African'* cry raised by Booth and early Malawian Christians and their connection to the 'Restoration' sentiments of African Americans towards Africa. He had connections with the Black Baptist Mission movement and was

---

[23] See Ross and Fiedler, *A Malawi Church History 1860-2020,* pp. 103-119.

trained and inspired by these descendants of former slaves in the USA. He led an uprising in 1915 against an estate in the Magomero area - shamefully, one owned by a grandson of David Livingstone - where Africans were obliged to work for low wages. It led to the death of a number of white farmers. Chilembwe and his men were soon captured and killed, but John Chilembwe is remembered as "the forerunner and pioneer of the nationalist struggle."[24] He is commemorated on Malawian banknotes and by a national holiday. [25]

Anglicans wanted to be cleared of the activities of Chilembwe and others by claiming that their form of education did not "swell the heads of young people". Archdeacon Glossop giving testimony in 1924 to the Phelps-Stokes Commission on native education in East Africa tried to distance the Anglicans from these events.[26]

Over time growing cooperation developed among the mainline churches in Malawi. Aided by changes after Vatican II, there has been greater unity of purpose and action. Until recently, the Christian Service Committee was the faith-based non-governmental body that brought development to all parts of Malawi. The change from Kamuzuist[27] politics to the new political dispensation was midwifed by the Public Affairs Committee (PAC) formed in 1992, which continues to shape the church's engagement in the public sphere.[28]

---

[24] Kenneth R. Ross, *Malawi and Scotland Together in the Talking Place since 1859,* Mzuzu: Mzuni Press, 2013, p. 81.

[25] See Ross and Fiedler, *A Malawi Church History 1860-2020*, pp. 134-146; also George Shepperson and Thomas Price, *Independent African: John Chilembwe and the Nyasaland Rising of 1915*, Edinburgh: Edinburgh University Press, 1987.

[26] The author's grandfather John T. Tucker was a member of the Phelps-Stokes Commission.

[27] Kamuzu Banda's type of capitalist one party dictatorship deeply rooted in quasi traditional authoritarianism, Machiavellianism and Victorian morality.

[28] This story is told in detail in ch. 5 below.

It is worth recording some Anglicans and their roles in these church bodies. Bishop Peter Nyanja was chair of the Malawi Council of Churches (formed in the late 1920s) when the PAC was formed. Bishop James Tengatenga also chaired the MCC during his time as a diocesan bishop. He had previously served as chair of the MCC's Youth Advisory Council and on its Chaplaincy Committee. Fr Maputwa and Mr Kishindo had stints as General Secretaries of the MCC. Fr Denis Mpassou served as Executive Director of the Christian Service Committee at one point, and also as Executive Director of Chilema Lay Training Centre. Other Anglicans who served in that capacity over the years include Fr (later Bishop) Bernard Malango, Fr George Ndomondo and Fr Kasiya. At the Christian Literature Association in Malawi (CLAIM) Willie Zingani served for a while as Executive Director. Fr Kaswaya and Bishop Tengatenga served terms as chair of PAC while Charles Mapapa served as Executive Director.

The Last UMCA Bishop

Frank Oswald Thorne became Bishop of Nyasaland in 1936 and served until 1961. He served as bishop during momentous times in the history of the world and the British Empire. World War II (1939-1945) was fought and ended. The United Nations came into being in 1945 and the World Council of Churches followed in 1948. In 1952 Queen Elizabeth acceded to the throne of the UK. Thorne's long tenure saw many changes in the church. In 1950, the Anglicans moved the accounts office, the principal administrative hub of the diocese, from Mpondas to Likwenu in order to be closer to the seat of colonial power in Zomba. This later became the diocesan headquarters under Donald Arden.

In the 1950s the diocese was in dire financial straits and difficult decisions had to be made. In 1953 Thorne made the painful decision to sell the *Chauncy Maples,* as the fares did not cover wages and operating expenses. This together with the sale of the printing press caused him a lot of heartache, pain and unpopularity with the Africans. The laity presented their grievances to the Archbishop of York on his visit to Malawi in 1957; but of course, there was nothing he could do. At one of the meetings of white missionaries they resolved to institute austerity measures. They resolved not to bring in food from the UK but to eat whatever was available in the country and to each sacrifice ten percent of their income for the sake of the mission. They did this before they could in clear conscience ask the Africans to do the same (the stipend differential, notwithstanding). In order to help support the church they also instituted self-support (corrupted to *sasapoti* by Malawians) as a way of effecting the 3 selfs concept of Henry Venn.[29] I In many ways the drive was successful over the years, even though the level of giving was not quite sufficient.

African nations and other parts of the Empire were baying for independence. However, the white settler community in the Rhodesias and in Nyasaland wanted to be like the Dominion of South Africa and was eventually granted a Federation of Rhodesia and Nyasaland in 1953. This move was opposed by the African majority and the Scottish CCAP missionaries.[30] In 1960 British Prime Minister Harold Macmillan declared in a speech at Cape Town that "The wind of change is blowing through this continent. Whether we like it or not, this growth of national consciousness is a political fact." This wind of change had reached Central Africa some years before.[31]

Unfortunately, the church was caught in the middle. Thorne chose to tread lightly and refused to support the Africans against the Federation. His reasoning was that since the government of the day was duly constituted, he had a duty to support it even though he did not like it. This did not endear him to the people and he was seen as a supporter of the Federation[32]. The UMCA leadership in London was also colonialist

---

[29] Henry Venn, a 19th century general secretary of CMS, taught that a church was judged to be indigenous when it was self-propagating, self-financing, and self-governing.

[30] Kenneth R. Ross, *Malawi and Scotland, Together in the Talking Place since 1859,* Mzuzu: Mzuni Press, 2013, pp. 136-148.

[31] See Ross and Fiedler, *A Malawi Church History 1860-2020,* pp. 226-240.

[32] Thorne stood in a High Church tradition that urged 'submission to the authorities' on the basis of scriptures such as Romans 13.1-7. See James

in outlook: the General Secretary Gerald Broomfield had little understanding of or sympathy for African nationalism. As if that was not enough grief for the good bishop, the idea of a Province of Central Africa which was to be coterminous with the Federation was being floated. This was not without opposition from the Africans, as the Province was seen as being linked with the Federation. However, the creation of the province (with Botswana included) went ahead in 1955 with Bishop Paget of Harare as the first Archbishop.

Thorne thus became a leader for a generation that had passed and had to make room for the new. In many ways this makes him the last of the UMCA bishops. He retired in 1961, the year the country was granted self-rule. It was a good transition to a different kind of leadership for different times ahead. This was true of the mission society too: the UMCA agreed in 1963 to amalgamate with the Society for the Propagation of the Gospel (SPG) to become the United Society for the Propagation of the Gospel (USPG)from 1965. A rising Likoma boy who was a priest in Tanzania, Josiah Mtekateka, was a representative of the UMCA territories at the event in London marking the merger.

Bishop Frank's successor had to be different. Could he be found among the indigenous clergy? Were Malawian clergy sufficiently trained and prepared to take over leadership?[33] That was not to be as Donald Arden, a British/Australian missionary to Swaziland, was appointed bishop to

---

Tengatenga, "The Good Being the Enemy of the Best: The Politics of Frank Oswald Thorne in Nyasaland and the Federation, 1936-1961," *Religion in Malawi*, no. 6, 1996, pp. 20–29. See also James Tengatenga, *Church, State and Society in Malawi: The Anglican Case*, Zomba: Kachere, 2006, chs. 1 and 3.

[33] For a discussion on this matter see Henry Mbaya, "Resistance to Anglican Missionary Christianity on Likoma Island, Malawi: 1885-196," n.d., 17. and H.H. Mbaya, "The Making of an African Clergy in the Anglican Church in Malawi with Special Focus on the Election of Bishops (1898-1996)," n.d., p. 520. Another discussion of interest here is the dissertation of Jerome T. Moriyama, "The Evolution of an African Ministry in the Work of the Universities' Mission to Central Africa in Tanzania, 1864-1909," University of London, 1984.

succeed him in 1961. This requires that we take a detour in our discussion and take a brief look at theological education.

Theological Training and Priestly Formation

Early training of clergy began at Kiungani Boys School in Zanzibar, which was like a Roman Catholic junior seminary of sorts. Petro Kilekwa,[34] himself a freed slave child, and Leonard Kamungu[35] were among those who went to school there and later became priests in Malawi. Training later moved onto the Tanganyika mainland before floating on the *Chauncy Maples* and later landing at St. Andrews on Likoma. In the 1960s priests were trained in Tanzania. For a brief time, there was some training done at Mpondas. An alumnus of note here is Bishop Dunstan Ainani. Many clergy including Peter Nyanja and Bernard Malango (both later bishops) were trained at the provincial theological college of St. John in Lusaka, Zambia after its move from St Cyprian in Tanzania. At the closure of the provincial college in 1972, Malawian students James Amanze and Emmanuel Karima together with their teacher, Fr Rodney Hunter, moved to the Roman Catholic Kachebere Major Seminary. Anglicans were to remain there until 1978. The last of those trained there was Constantine Kaswaya who was to complete his training at St Peter's Major Seminary in Zomba. In 1978 the Anglicans moved again. This time they joined with the Presbyterians who, in the previous year, had begun a united Theological College at Zomba. Canon George Ndomondo had trained with Presbyterians at Nkhoma. In 1979 Rodney Hunter moved from Kachebere to Zomba Theological College. In 1993 Fr James Tengatenga came to Zomba as lecturer. Another Anglican missionary who taught at Zomba was Fr. Rodney Schofield; the last

---

[34] He served as a priest at Nkope on the lakeshore. One dormitory at Chilema Ecumenical Conference Centre is named after him.

[35] He volunteered to join Bishop Hornby in the establishment of the Church in Zambia and died at Msoro in Eastern Zambia. He was the first missionary from Malawi. The Anglican Theological College in Zomba is named after him. For his life see: John C. Weller, *The Priest from the Lakeside. The Story of Leonard Kamungu and Zambia, 1877 – 1913*.

Malawian Anglican lecturer there was Fr Christopher Mwawa. The Anglicans were to remain at Zomba Theological College until 2005. In 2006 they moved into their own theological college of Leonard Kamungu (also in Zomba) with Canon Alinafe Kalemba as Dean.[36]

In addition to basic priestly formation the Church sent people for further training in different specialties abroad. Some of the religious education advisors and youth workers were sent to Mindolo Ecumenical Centre in Kitwe, Zambia. Others went to the College of the Ascension in Selly Oak, Birmingham, which was popular for religious education and church administration. Others were sent for further training in South Africa, the Solomon Islands, Oxford, UK, or Texas, USA.

Theological Education by Extension (TEE) was established on an ecumenical basis to help with the formation of clergy and the training of laity. Chilema Ecumenical Lay Training Centre was also used for on the job training programmes for priests in the 1970s and 80s. Lay leaders and catechists, Sunday school teachers and women leaders had special courses there as well. Nkhotakota Lay Training Centre in Lake Malawi was mainly used for lay training. Theological education has been a domain of men, especially those training for the priesthood. TEE opened opportunities for women to do theology. The Province of Central Africa and therefore Malawi does not yet ordain women.

Anglican Council in Malawi and 'The Anglican Church in Malawi'

In 1971 the Diocese of Malawi was divided into Lake Malawi and Southern Malawi. Support from USPG, Birmingham and other bilateral bodies continued. The resources coming in through these relationships had to be shared between the two dioceses, and there arose a need for a central office to do so. Plans for an Anglican Council in Malawi were drawn up by Donald Arden in 1971[37] but it was not established

---

[36] Richard Tucker writes further on LKTC and on ACM in ch. 12.

[37] Letter to USPG, 15.2.1971. Accessed by Richard Tucker in USPG archive 20.5.2019.

functionally until 1979. The first officer was a missionary from Birmingham, John Workman.[38] He was the accountant responsible for these resources, seeing to their disbursement as the bishops decided. The first office was in the mission compound at Malosa. In the 1980s it moved to the Lake Malawi HQ in Lilongwe with John Kalande as accountant. He was succeeded by Matthews Kumpolota, who worked for ACM from 1988 to 2003 and visited Birmingham for a consultation meeting in 1998. Mr Kumpolota's title later included that of Administrative Secretary, but he remained primarily an accountant. Cecilia Hasha Dube became the first General Secretary proper with George Willow becoming the accountant, thus separating the two responsibilities and becoming a nascent provincial structure. Ms Dube was succeeded as General Secretary by Canon Christopher Mwawa.

The Central African Federation broke up in 1964, but the Province of Central Africa [PCA] remained as it is at the time of writing, comprising Botswana, Malawi, Zambia and Zimbabwe. The current Archbishop and Primate is Albert Chama, Bishop of Northern Zambia. Malawi has had two bishops as Archbishops of Central Africa: Donald Arden (1971-1980) and Bernard Malango (2002-2008) who began his tenure while Bishop of Northern Zambia. Bishops Peter Nyanja, James Tengatenga and Brighton Malasa have served as Deans of the Province.

Since the 1970s each country in the PCA except Botswana has had an Anglican Council as a way of coordinating the action of its dioceses. Churches in many countries in Africa sought autonomy by becoming provinces (autonomous member churches) of the Anglican Communion. In 1971 the Anglican Consultative Council came up with requirements for the formation of a province, these being that at least four dioceses were required for its formation in addition to the unanimous desire of these dioceses and financial viability. At the time of writing Zimbabwe had five dioceses, with plans for the creation of

---

[38] He came from St Agnes, Moseley and died in Malawi in 1984. Source: Bob Jenkins, *In Touch with the Warm Heart of Africa, 1966-1996,* privately published, n.d. but after 1998.

another, Zambia had five, with plans for the creation of another, and Botswana had one. Malawi had four, with Lake Malawi having resolved in 1995 to divide further after the creation of Northern Malawi (which is yet to be). In 1990 the Episcopal Synod of the CPCA resolved to divide the Province into national provinces. Not much happened in the wake of this resolution until the matter was mooted again in the 2000s. The problems in the Diocese of Harare interfered with progress and led to putting the exercise on the back burner. After the situation in Zimbabwe normalized, the matter was reconsidered in 2011, but no action agreed. Should this go ahead, the ACM will become the provincial structure of the Anglican Church in Malawi. A constitution was drafted and awaits its time of implementation.

Chapter 3

The Church of England in Birmingham to 1966

Before the Diocese

The Diocese of Birmingham was formed only in 1905 – more recently than might have been expected, and more than half a century after a diocese was founded in 1847 in Manchester, its rival and sister city. Christianity in the area goes far further back, of course: Polesworth, Solihull and Yardley have Anglo-Saxon foundations. There were 'minster churches' in the early medieval period at Aston and Coleshill serving large surrounding areas.[1] Birmingham has existed as a town since early medieval times - a charter for a weekly market was granted to Peter de Birmingham in 1166.[2] The adjacent parish church, which became St Martin's in the Bull Ring, is first documented in 1263[3] and by 1676 its parish was the most populous in the area that became the diocese.[4] The town's rapid expansion began in the 18th century with the development of industry and the commerce needed to support it.

With the Reformation, the churches of the area passed to the Church of England. In the 17th century the Church's local monopoly on religion was almost complete, but the following century saw the rise of religious nonconformity in the town. This has been linked to the 18th century cultural transformation known as the Midlands Enlightenment, which put Birmingham at the forefront of worldwide developments in science,

---

[1] Terry Slater, *A Century of Celebrating Christ: The Diocese of Birmingham, 1905-2005,* Chichester, England: Phillimore & Co, 2005. In this chapter referred to simply as 'Slater', pp. 12-14.

[2] wikipedia.org/wiki/History_of_Birmingham#Establishment_and_expansion [18.4.2019].

[3] wikipedia.org/wiki/St Martin's in the Bull Ring [15.4.2019].

[4] Slater, p. 23.

technology, medicine, philosophy and natural history. The Lunar Society of Birmingham's membership included the town's leading thinkers such as Joseph Priestley, Matthew Boulton, James Watt and Erasmus Darwin[5] – now commemorated by a gold-covered statue on Broad Street.

John Wesley, the founder of Methodism, preached many times in Birmingham from the mid-18th century on, but described it as 'this barren soil'. In the 1760s his meetings were attacked by the mob, with stones and dirt being flung at congregations. But as the century went on, a regular Methodist congregation of over 800 was built up in the town. Laws were then in force preventing nonconformists, including Roman Catholics, from playing a full part in society.[6] Tensions between Anglicans and nonconformists resulted in three days of rioting in Birmingham in 1791, during which the home of Joseph Priestley was attacked.[7]

In the late 18th century Birmingham became the centre of a national network of canals that were the main means of carrying goods until the railways superseded them. The canals have long since ceased to carry commercial traffic, but have been reborn as a distinctive leisure feature of the city centre and the region. Birmingham's earlier built-up areas, a product of the industrial revolution of the late 18th-early 19th centuries, became seriously overcrowded and insanitary. By the mid-19th century engineering and metal-working, in particular, had grown to such an extent that the town became known as 'the city of a thousand trades' or 'the workshop of the world'. Its population continued to grow rapidly through the 19th century. New suburbs were added rapidly, and new parishes and churches were established to serve them.[8] The railways arrived in Birmingham in 1837; New Street station opened in 1854, and

---

[5] wikipedia.org/wiki/History_of_Birmingham#Establishment_and_expansion, [18.4.2019].

[6] They were seldom enforced after 1800 and were repealed in 1828.

[7] Slater, pp. 25-27.

[8] Slater, pp. 28-31.

the growth of a network of suburban lines fuelled the city's expansion towards being part of the conurbation of today.

The town finally returned its own members to Parliament after 1832 and was incorporated as a borough in 1838. Spearheaded by a group of influential Nonconformist ministers, the 'Civic Gospel' developed in the 1850s.[9] It influenced Joseph Chamberlain, whose brief mayoral term in 1873-76 was influential in setting out the powers and responsibilities of the town's corporation for its inhabitants' welfare. A Roman Catholic revival in the mid-century saw the opening of St Chad's Cathedral in 1841 and the establishment of the RC Diocese of Birmingham in 1850.[10] The impressive neo-Gothic buildings of St Mary's College on a suburban hilltop at New Oscott house what is now the only RC seminary in England. They were once home to John Henry Newman, recently declared a saint.

All the Christian denominations at this time were facing the loss of working class support.[11] The Church of England ministered faithfully, but "in Birmingham the Church lacked self-confidence."[12] Its effective-ess in the later 19th century was hampered by its slowness to reorganize itself in face of rapid change. Most of the future diocesan area came under Worcester diocese. A diocese for Birmingham was first proposed in 1877, but for a variety of reasons it took almost another 30 years for it to be created. Charles Gore, Bishop of Worcester from 1901-05, worked from 1902 onwards for the creation and funding of the Birmingham bishopric and achieved his goal in 1905.[13]

---

[9] Slater, pp. 33-35.

[10] Elevated to archdiocese status in 1911. en.wikipedia.org/wiki/Roman Catholic_Archdiocese_of_Birmingham [29.4.2019].

[11] Slater, p. 48.

[12] Slater, p. 45.

[13] Slater, p. 50.

The Diocese's Creation and Early Years

Birmingham diocese is densely populated: about 1.5 million people live in an area of only 290 sq. miles [750 km^2]. It is largely urban, covering the City of Birmingham, the built-up area of the Borough of Solihull and part of the Black Country Borough of Sandwell. Its rural fringe includes a modest area of north Warwickshire and a few parishes in Worcestershire.

The 18th century parish church of St Philip, surrounded by a spacious churchyard, was chosen as its cathedral; a statue of Charles Gore stands at its west door. Birmingham city centre is well provided for open spaces, but the cathedral churchyard is one of the few green areas open to the public in the central employment and shopping district. The cathedral has been the setting for many services celebrating the Malawi Partnership. Amongst the notable ones have been the 30th anniversary service in 1996, attended by Donald Arden, former Archbishop of Central Africa, and Jack Biggers, first Bishop of Northern Malawi; the service marking the diocesan centenary in 2005 with the gift of motorbikes for the clergy of Malawi; and the service at Pentecost 2016 marking the Partnership's 50th anniversary.[14]

Gore opted to transfer from Worcester to Birmingham and became its first bishop in 1905. He is described by Slater as "a brilliant theologian, an inspiring teacher and a deeply human man."[15] Under his leadership "Birmingham became an important see very quickly after its formation."[16] Gore at once appointed a commission to enquire into the needs of every parish in the diocese. He was a teacher and guide to his clergy and conducted retreats for his ordination candidates. He was active in

---

[14] See ch. 10 below.

[15] Slater, pp. 53-54. Charles Gore was born in 1853. He was ordained in 1876 and quickly became a leader of the Anglo-Catholic Oxford Movement. He was doctrinally orthodox, but still shocked some by his contribution to the book of essays *Lux Mundi* [1889].

[16] Slater, p. 52.

civic affairs, campaigning against child alcoholism and gambling and for housing reform. He approved of the model housing estate built by the Cadburys at Bournville. He strongly supported the new University of Birmingham, whose Edgbaston campus opened in 1909. He was also active on the national stage, especially in the area of education. In 1911 he became Bishop of Oxford.[17]

Gore's successor was Henry Wakefield, who was bishop 1911-24.[18] The Church of England was at this time riven by disputes between High Church and Low Church parties, particularly over ritual in worship and the use of Roman Catholic services. Wakefield "strove constantly to get the various factions of the Church to work together cooperatively and harmoniously."[19] He was tolerant of Anglo-Catholic and Ritualist practices such as the display of the reserved sacrament in parish churches, "policies which were to cause his successor untold difficulties."[20] Like many other bishops of the time, Wakefield was a staunch advocate of the First World War; he toured the USA and Canada in 1916 to encourage American entry into the conflict.[21] Harborne House was acquired in 1921 as a mansion residence for Bishops of Birmingham, and renamed Bishop's Croft.[22] It has played host to many bishops and other visitors from Malawi in the years since 1966.

The third Bishop of Birmingham, Ernest Barnes, was appointed in 1924 and was to stay for almost 30 years.[23] Barnes was a 'modernist' and

---

[17] Slater, pp. 55-58.

[18] Henry Russell Wakefield was born in 1854 and ordained in 1877. He served in parishes in the London area and in Ramsgate on the Kent coast. Unusually, he was elected as Liberal Mayor of Marylebone, in London.

[19] Slater, p. 60.

[20] Slater, p. 61.

[21] Slater, pp. 61-62.

[22] Slater, p. 66.

[23] Ernest William Barnes was born in 1874. His boyhood was in Birmingham; he was ordained in 1902. His scientific background made him opposed to High

controversial, but much admired in Birmingham. "It was not long before the new bishop came into conflict with the accustomed [high church] practices in many parishes ... he was determined to bring to heel those he considered to be straying from the doctrines of the Church."[24] This proved to be something of a war of attrition, which Barnes only won at the very end of his episcopate. In 1927 a new Prayer Book was published, which would allow some Anglo-Catholic services and practices. Barnes argued against it, not sympathetically but passionately, nationally and in his own diocese. The Prayer Book needed to be approved by Parliament, which ended up rejecting it, to Barnes' great joy.[25]

Understandably, Barnes was not popular with all, but he was always in demand as a preacher and writer. He was active in social affairs, especially the disputes in the coal industry around 1926. He drew attention to social ills and advocated liberal causes. In the 1930s he was early to recognize the dangers of German Nazism. With the start of the Second World War Barnes issued guidance to his clergy.

> "He was determined to ... advise against the nationalistic preaching of the Great War. He wrote: 'Preach as little as possible: pray as much as you can. Before beginning to prepare a sermon, put down your newspaper, turn off the wireless and for at least a quarter of an hour read slowly some passage of the New Testament which reveals the mind of Christ. You are his minister.' The advice found its way into the press and he received grateful letters from all over the country."[26]

Birmingham suffered badly in the air raids of 1940-41, with 2000 of its citizens losing their lives.[27]

Church sacramentalism. He was an ardent pacifist in World War One and became known for his incisive and controversial preaching. Slater, p. 63.

[24] Slater, p. 64.

[25] Slater, pp. 64-65.

[26] Slater, p. 69.

[27] Slater, p. 69.

"The City of Birmingham expanded enormously in physical extent in the 1920s and '30s ... By the end of the 1930s vast municipal housing estates ringed the city on all sides but the west."[28] Churches were provided for these estates, some of them very handsomely designed; many had become too large by the 1960s and some were adapted for multi-purpose use. Diocesan appeals for 'church extension' were launched successfully in 1926 and again in 1935. For the Church, the Second World War was in one respect a blessing in disguise. The inner city area was full of churches, some very big, which were largely losing their congregations, both by the flight to the suburbs and by the decline in churchgoing. Many of these were damaged by bombing and some were not scheduled for rebuilding.[29]

The Post-war Period

Before the war ended in 1945, Birmingham city council began to formulate ambitious plans for slum clearance and new housing estates, with sites reserved for new churches. The diocese determined its needs and the provision and financing of such churches. In 1946 it inaugurated the 'Ten Year Forward Movement', which looked for spiritual renewal and new clergy as well as new buildings all over the developing new suburbs.[30]

Leonard Wilson succeeded Barnes as Bishop of Birmingham in 1953 and remained for 16 years.[31] His theological outlook was similar to that of

---

[28] Slater, p. 123.

[29] Slater, pp. 123-125.

[30] Slater, pp. 127-128.

[31] John Leonard Wilson was born in 1897 into a poor clergy family. He was ordained in 1924 and served in Coventry Cathedral. He worked with CMS in Iran and Egypt before and after his ordination. He served in parishes in the north of England and as Dean of Newcastle. He was made Bishop of Singapore in 1941, just before the Japanese invasion. His family left for Australia but he continued to work as bishop. In 1943 he was interned in prison camp, tortured by the military police for 36 hours, interrogated and starved. He was given

his predecessor, but he was much younger, more human and outgoing. He was also full of energy, exercised within the diocese and more widely.

The second phase of postwar church building was launched in 1956 as the 'Circles without Centres' appeal, aiming to put churches and clergy into communities without one. Half of its huge target of £1.2 million was raised within three years, and on its own terms the appeal was a success. Bishop Wilson was determined that the new churches should be able to seat 400 people so as to accommodate local schools for their annual services.[32] Unfortunately, this was 'Christendom thinking' which assumed that local schools and communities would continue to gather in 'their' parish churches as in time past. After about 1960 it rapidly became clear that this was no longer the case, and within ten years of their opening, most of these churches proved to be larger than needed.

Immigrant communities had long been part of the Birmingham scene. The earliest wave of post-Second World War immigration, which has come to be known as the 'Windrush generation', was from the Caribbean; Asian immigrants soon followed. The white communities of Birmingham and the West Midlands had recently undergone the privations and physical damage of war. Many lived in tight-knit communities and were resentful about having to make space for newcomers.[33] One effect was the growth of racial prejudice, which had some public endorsement. It was in Birmingham in 1968 that a local

---

strength from God with which he ministered to others. He resumed work in Singapore after the liberation, but found he needed to return home to work in the UK. He had a short, unhappy term as Dean of Manchester, 1949-53, during which he clashed with a conservative cathedral chapter. By 1953 he was a national figure, both because his wartime sufferings had given him a great depth of faith which he communicated to others, and because he led the annual televised Festival of Remembrance service.

[32] Slater, p. 128.

[33] A point made by Canon Paul Wilson in correspondence, 20.2.2019.

Conservative MP, Enoch Powell, delivered the infamous, racist 'Rivers of Blood' speech.[34]

Sadly, the churches were not immune to this problem:

> "Earlier generations of missionary priests had done their job well and [the Afro-Caribbean] migrants [young men, soon to be followed by women and children] were solidly Christian: Methodists, Baptists, but mostly Anglican. On Sunday they put on their best clothes and went to their local Anglican parish church to worship God. They were met by puzzlement, curiosity, occasionally a warm welcome, but most frequently by hostility and fear from both congregations and ministers."[35]

In Birmingham as in other British cities, many Black Christians felt rejected by their local churches and were compelled to worship elsewhere. Gradually, Black-led churches were set up, many of them Pentecostal in outlook, and many have grown larger and stronger than the churches that failed to welcome the immigrants. Bishop Wilson responded to the inflow of migrants to Birmingham and Smethwick by appointing a chaplain to them. In due course struggling Anglican churches in inner city areas responded to the changes. Not without heartache, they reinvented themselves from the 1970s on as majority Black congregations.[36] In course of time, deliberate diocesan policy has led to a significant number of the diocese's churches being served by Black clergy from the Caribbean or Africa, or by Asian clergy.

Slater describes Wilson as "not a great theologian, he was a man of the people, partly because he had had to question his faith." His open and questioning approach to faith led him to be an early proponent of

---

[34] www.birminghammail.co.uk/news/midlands-news/enoch-powell-what-rivers-blood-8945556 [14.9.2018]. The speech got Powell dismissed as a shadow Minister.

[35] Slater, p. 200.

[36] Slater tells the story of St James', Aston in *A Century of Celebrating Christ: The Diocese of Birmingham, 1905-2005*, pp. 202-206.

women's ordination. He realized that there was a revolution going on in youth culture in the 1960s, and as a response appointed a 'chaplain to the unattached'. He resigned the see of Birmingham in 1969 at the age of 72.[37] Another notable figure in the diocese in this period was Canon Bryan Green, Rector of St Martin's in the Bull Ring from 1948 to 1969 and known as an evangelist locally and worldwide.

During the fairly short history of the diocese, the parishes had been alive to the mission opportunities on their doorsteps. Work with children and young people was extensive; until the 1960s Sunday schools and uniformed organizations operated on a scale it is hard to imagine 50 years on. Church primary schools were opened in the new suburbs after World War II, though on a rather patchy basis. At the time of writing, the diocese had 49 primary-age schools but just two secondary schools, with plans for two more.

However, when Bishop Wilson arrived in Birmingham in 1953 with wide overseas experience, he found the diocese very inward-looking and lacking understanding of the wider world in which he had spent his ministry. He sought to correct this insularity through an overseas partnership.[38] The initiative of Bishop Wilson and Bishop Donald Arden to set up a partnership between Birmingham and Malawi is described in the following chapter. The thumbnail history of Birmingham and its diocese resumes in chapter 9.

---

[37] Slater, p. 76.

[38] Bob Jenkins, *In Touch with the Warm Heart of Africa, 1966-96*, privately published, n.d. but c.1998, p. 1.

Chapter 4

The Partnership's Beginnings and First Twenty Years, 1961-87

Two Bishops in Search of a Partner

The roots of the Malawi Partnership go back to the early 1950s. Leonard Wilson, in his years as Dean of Manchester, had helped organize a public meeting against the proposed white dominated Central African Federation. The speakers included Dr Hastings Banda and a number of African chiefs from Malawi.[1] Separately, Bishop Wilson's daughter Susan was working as a nurse in St Thomas's Hospital, London, when Dr Banda came to speak. His message was "We want doctors and people out in Malawi, to come and help." She then decided to become a doctor. She and her husband finally reached Malawi about seven years later, and she began work at the Queen Elizabeth Hospital, Blantyre.[2]

The opportunity to break down Birmingham's insularity arose in the 1960s, when "The [Anglican] Communion as a whole began its journey from paternalism to partnership."[3] "In Anglican thinking partnership emerged at the 1963 Third Congress of the Anglican Communion held in Toronto. This congress adopted the highly significant report 'Mutual Responsibility and Interdependence' (MRI) which led to the establishment of the early companion links across the Communion." The idea behind MRI was "to look at needs - for people, finance, skills and infrastructure – across the Communion and to gather and distribute resources to meet those needs. It was a challenge to break out of the

---

[1] Bob Jenkins, *In Touch with the Warm Heart of Africa, 1966-96,* p. 1.

[2] Rev Martin Wilson interviewed by Canon Bob Jenkins, 22.4.1988.

[3] Canon Janice Price, *World Shaped Mission, Exploring new frameworks for the Church of England in world mission,* London: Church House Publishing, 2012, p. 16.

donor/recipient mindset of the colonial era and move into new relationships of equality and mutuality ..."[4] Bishops Wilson and Arden were both at Toronto, where they had a meeting at the suggestion of Bishop Wilson's daughter, Dr Susan Cole-King.[5]

Donald Arden[6] had been consecrated Bishop of Nyasaland in 1961. On arrival he found a diocese in decay, with "hardly a waterproof building in the diocese,"[7] a declining number of UMCA missionaries and a small number of poorly-paid African clergy. The UMCA leadership in London and Malawi still had the paternalistic outlook of early 20th century Anglo-Catholicism and had no plans for devolution to African leadership. By contrast, the missionaries of the Church of Scotland had in 1960 handed over their ecclesiastical responsibilities to the CCAP, which would shortly appoint its first African General Secretary.[8]

"Though Donald Arden was not a Malawian, he was the first of the new breed of bishops to lead the church in Africa as the continent was coming out of colonialism into the newly independent African states. His coming coincided with the granting of self-rule to Malawi leading to its independence and republican status in 1964. This was when

---

[4] Ibid., p. 16.

[5] James Tengatenga, email dated 26.1.2020, reporting a conversation between himself and Dr Cole-King in 1998.

[6] Donald Arden was born in 1916 in Hampshire but grew up in Australia. He trained at Mirfield and was ordained in 1939. He served with the mission society SPG in Southern Africa from 1943 on. In his eight years in the Pretoria area, he served 20 congregations. From 1951-61 he was Director of the Usuthu Mission in the remote and backward kingdom of Swaziland. He was always interested in farming and surprised people by growing excellent pineapples there – they are now the country's main crop. Source: *Donald Arden, 12 April 1916 to 18 July 2014*, obituary leaflet, MACS, UK.

[7] Bishop Donald Arden interviewed by Canon Bob Jenkins, 9.9.1998.

[8] John Stuart, *British Missionaries and the End of Empire*, Grand Rapids: Eerdmans, 2013, pp. 2 and 123.

Nyasaland became Malawi. Thus, the Diocese of Nyasaland became the Diocese of Malawi."[9]

Arden was a man of remarkable vision and energy; he had "twinkling eyes and an infectious smile"[10] and great charisma and persuasiveness. He broke with the UMCA tradition of celibate missionaries by marrying Jane in 1962; they had two sons. Together they set about leading the church into the 20th century worldwide Anglican family. The move of the diocesan HQ from Mpondas near Mangochi to a spacious new site at Malosa began in 1963. Considerable extra resources were needed to develop the Church; it became clear these would not be forthcoming from the expatriate community in Blantyre, which had no interest in changing the cosy *apartheid* of a well-resourced white chaplaincy and an impoverished native church.[11] So from 1963 on, Donald, often accompanied by Jane, travelled overseas with great success to raise funds for the Malawian Church, particularly to the USA.

After Arden spoke to the Convention of the Diocese of Texas in 1963, a partnership was established from 1965. There were a number of exchange visitors from the USA and much mutual support and encouragement.[12] The Texas link was remade with the new Diocese of Lake Malawi from 1971; it was terminated in 1977, following the custom of the Episcopal Church for partnerships to last for six years only. A later link was made between the Diocese of Colorado and the Diocese of Southern Malawi. Its breakdown in 1987 prompted Bishop Aipa of DSM

---

[9] James Tengatenga's words.

[10] *Donald Arden, 12 April 1916 to 18 July 2014*, obituary leaflet, MACS, UK.

[11] "You've no idea the poverty when I came here [1960]. Even the clergy were so tattered; wearing torn trousers, sometimes no shoes, in the city, dirty old white collar around their neck that needed to be thrown away, a suit that had gone purple with age. My heart was terribly moved by it all when I saw it. This is why I couldn't bear to work among Europeans with their relative luxury." Rev John Parslow, interviewed by Canon Bob Jenkins, 19.10.1988.

[12] *Donald Arden, 12 April 1916 to 18 July 2014*, obituary leaflet, MACS, UK.

to comment that the American attitude to a link was like an affair with a young lady, who has a good time for a limited period and then is dropped, whereas Birmingham's attitude was more like a marriage with its ups and downs, but the partners are committed to each other and keep working at it.[13]

Bishop Wilson inclined to a link with Malawi after he visited his daughter Susan there in 1965 and met Arden. For his part, Arden "was keen on links anywhere because we simply hadn't got any effective backing."[14] Under the USPG, mission society attitudes were modernizing, but Malawi needed more resources than a mission society could offer. The two bishops agreed to set up a link. The early years of the link with Birmingham, when few travelers made the slow and expensive journey, were focused on the transfer of resources, especially money, to Malawi: this emphasis has coloured the link up to the present.[15] I have attempted to discover whether any terms of reference were agreed, and concluded after speaking to the two surviving witnesses[16] that there were none.

Bishop Wilson, like his counterpart in Malawi, was a strong and charismatic figure. He set about. Much later, Fr Henry Burgess recorded how he persuaded Birmingham parishes to accept the idea of the partnership and his own first visit to Malawi. His article captures the

---

[13] Quoted in Ven. John Cooper, *Report of the Visit to the Dioceses of Southern Malawi and Lake Malawi by the Archdeacon of Aston on behalf of the Diocesan Council for Mission and Unity, 12th June-26th July 1987*, p. 15. Bishop Aipa's comment was risqué given his own known behaviour towards the opposite sex.

[14] Bishop Donald Arden interviewed by Canon Bob Jenkins, 9.9.1998.

[15] The role of money in the Partnership is discussed in ch. 9 below.

[16] Jane Arden and Bishop Humphrey Taylor, who was at the College of the Ascension preparing to go to Malawi as the Birmingham partnership was being established. Asked about a MoU he commented: 'It would be an uncommon thing. I cannot remember one.' Interview, 12.5.2018.

bishop's brisk, no-nonsense style and reflects his own attitude of warm-hearted paternalism:

> "Years ago, Bishop Donald Arden… was invited by Bishop Wilson to visit Birmingham. The phone rang at [the vicarage] and it was the bishop himself! 'Henry, the Bishop of Malawi is visiting Birmingham. I want you to arrange for him to spend a Sunday at Wylde Green and I want you to let him preach and then meet the congregation. He will stay with you in the church hall until Evensong. Tell the people to be generous and remain all day in church and provide lunch and tea. Evensong could be at 5pm and he will preach again about one of the poorest places on earth. Let me know at the end of the day if the parish would be ready to support him and his people. I hope they will – tell them so.' He came, spent the day, and a hurried vote at the end produced unlimited agreement. Later on, he was sent to one or two other parishes, and finally the 'diocesan conference' [on 21st June 1966] produced universal agreement. That was the start of our relationship, the rest is history.
>
> Soon after I was told a few of the clergy, an Archdeacon and myself, were to be sent there to get acquainted with the situation and people. I tried to back out. The bishop said, 'Henry, you have two curates, one stipendiary – don't argue!' I went and came back absolutely convinced that it would be a duty and privilege to give whatever help possible to such poor but wonderful people. Since then we have helped build schools, hospitals and brought them into a better and more modern world. …."[17]

One existing link was taken up into the diocesan one: St Leonard's, Marston Green was already committed to an SPG project with St Anne's Maternity Hospital at Nkhotakota.[18] There had already been a Birmingham 'pioneer' in Malawi. "In 1960 the Birmingham born priest, the Reverend John Parslow, arrived at the chaplaincy centre in Blantyre

---

[17] Henry Burgess, parish magazine of Emmanuel, Wylde Green, c. 2013.

[18] Bob Jenkins, *In Touch with the Warm Heart of Africa, 1966-96,* c.1998, p. 5.

... A gentle, loving man he had no inherited sense of white supremacy. In the next thirty five years, he exercised his ministry in many parts of Malawi and won the devotion of all classes."[19] A further link was that John Watson, who was appointed Diocesan Secretary by Bishop Wilson, had been a District Officer and Provincial Commissioner in Malawi for 20 years to 1964.

The Link and the Malawian Church under Donald Arden

The link was strengthened by a series of visits in each direction, plus longer periods of service or training. Bishop Donald and Jane Arden paid a launch visit to Birmingham in November 1966 for "two weeks of almost non-stop meetings, visiting schools and colleges in the daytime and spending each evening with a parish or deanery meeting" often numbering 200-300.[20] They were delighted to find "informed enthusiasm ... for the Church in Malawi" and their message was "Your mission and our mission are one."[21] Canon Ronald Gordon, Canon Residentiary of Birmingham Cathedral, filled in for Fr Humphrey Taylor at St Peter's Church, Lilongwe while the latter was in the UK for further training in 1970. George Cole, a vicar in Sutton Coldfield, spent several months of voluntary work at the lay training centre at. Malosa[22] In 1969, Bishop David Porter, Suffragan Bishop of Aston, was a guest of the Diocese of Malawi for 2½ weeks. Dean Msekawanthu then visited Birmingham for 6 months, for some of that time studying at the USPG College of the Ascension in Selly Oak.[23] In 1973 Arden paid an 'in-depth' visit to Birmingham, speaking in every deanery.

---

[19] Ibid., p. 2.

[20] Donald Arden, notes for his memoirs, 16.8.2007.

[21] *Ecclesia*, ed. Donald Arden, February 1967.

[22] Jenkins, *In Touch with the Warm Heart of Africa, 1966-96*, p. 5.

[23] *Ecclesia*, ed. Donald Arden, April 1969.

It was a priority of Arden's to encourage the training and development of clergy and laypeople. Resources were needed to enable the growth of the church; almost half of the first year's grant of £5000 from Birmingham, for instance, went towards diocesan literature work. Other resources came from elsewhere, including the USA and the World Council of Churches.[24] Arden had voiced the need for a training centre for clergy and laity in a diocesan charge in 1962. Chilema Ecumenical Lay Training and Conference Centre at Malosa held its first youth camp and conference in 1965; it was officially opened in 1967. Chilema was a shared dream of Bishop Arden and the General Secretary of CCAP Blantyre Synod, Rev Jonathan Sangaya. Wardens, now known as Executive Directors, have been drawn alternately from both churches. Roman Catholics and Churches of Christ were also on the Chilema board in its early years.[25] Fifty years on, Chilema runs programmes in church leadership development, community living, women's training including home craft and business management, child protection and development including a playgroup named in memory of Rev John Leake, its first warden.

Under Arden the Malosa site came to house a large complex of Anglican institutions, many of them in buildings put up under the direction of Jane Arden, who became an accomplished building director. Alongside the bishop's house and diocesan offices there were Chilema, Malosa Secondary School, St Luke's Hospital and nursing college and the diocesan farm. A visitor in 1972 commented: "This is the most spectacular diocesan HQ for the Anglican Church I have yet seen in Africa."[26]

---

[24] WCC contributed to the cost of the Chilema Ecumenical Centre. Source: Alison Robinson, author's survey, 8.3.2018.

[25] Tengatenga, *Church, State and Society in Malawi: the Anglican Case*, Zomba: Kachere, 2006, p. 90.

[26] Bishop Ian Shevill, USPG Secretary, visit report, February-April 1972. USPG archive TF1275, [20.5.2019].

In 1964 Bishop Arden appointed Josiah Mtekateka as his suffragan and the first African Anglican bishop in Malawi.[27] He was "a giant of a man, both in physical stature and Christian maturity."[28] He had great talents and skills as a pastor, and many people benefited from his wisdom and counsel. His weakness seems to have been in the area of administration. He was given a succession of young white chaplains to help in this area, but the differences in their respective approaches could lead to tensions.[29] The two bishops visited Birmingham together in 1968.[30]

The church was growing organically on the model that has continued to serve it to this day. In each parish, groups of lay Christians are sent out to preach and found little congregations. If these put down roots, they become outstations of the parish. Where possible, the outstation members put up a small church building made with sun-dried or fired bricks. In the past, such buildings in the villages had grass roofs, which let in the wet in the rainy season and harboured bugs. Nowadays churches, like houses, are roofed with iron sheets; congregations usually need help with paying for them. When an outstation reaches a sufficient size and can build a priest's house it can apply to the bishop to have a priest and become a parish in its own right. The rate of growth of the Church is thus determined by the spiritual resources in its parishes and the material resources available to put up buildings and train and pay priests.

---

[27] Josiah Mtekateka was born on Likoma and had worked with the missionaries there, showing natural leadership, honesty and trustworthiness. He was ordained there in 1939 and had served both in Nyasaland and in Tanganyika [as they then were]. Source: Canon Bob Jenkins, interview with Bishop Mtekateka, 6.11.1988.

[28] Jenkins, *In Touch with the Warm Heart of Africa, 1966-96,* p. 6.

[29] Henry Mbaya, *Raising African Bishops in the Anglican Church in Malawi 1924-2000,* uir.unisa.ac.za/bitstream/handle/10500/4483/Mbaya.pdf, 2007, pp. 2018-20, [1.7.2019].

[30] *Donald Arden,* 12 April 1916 to 18 July 2014, obituary leaflet, MACS, UK.

The organic growth of the Anglican Church in Africa in the latter years of the 20th century led to the subdivision of dioceses all over the continent to create new dioceses. Malawi was a large, populous and growing diocese and it became inevitable that it should be divided. In 1971 the Diocese of Southern Malawi was formed to cover the southern region of the country including the main commercial centre of Blantyre and Zomba, then the capital. Donald Arden became bishop of this new diocese, at the same time as he was made Archbishop of Central Africa. DSM was without a cathedral until 1980 when St Paul's, Blantyre was made the cathedral.

Josiah Mtekateka became the first bishop of the Diocese of Lake Malawi, which covered the central and northern regions, including Likoma, and served from 1971 to 1978.[31] The diocese was initially run from Nkhotakota, but President Banda moved the capital to the rapidly expanding city of Lilongwe and the diocesan HQ was transferred there in 1982. Both these dioceses were subdivided in their turn, DLM in 1995 and DSM in 2002.

In common with other Churches, the Anglican Church was exposed to a good deal of official mistrust and harassment in these years. Shortly after independence in 1964, President Banda had moved to consolidate power in his own hands by dismissing several ministers, to be followed by the resignation of others. This 'Cabinet Crisis' prompted an unsuccessful revolt led by one former minister, Henry Chipembere. He was the son of an Anglican Archdeacon and this sufficed, in the paranoid climate of those times, to put the whole Anglican Church under suspicion. Henry Chipembere was helped by Anglican and Scottish CCAP missionaries and was able to leave the country with the help of a Scottish friend. Banda made Malawi a one-party state and in 1971 declared himself Life President.

A USPG visitor commented in 1973: "Expatriates, in the Church or elsewhere, are often needed but seldom wanted, and there are

---

[31] Mtekateka died in 1996 and is buried in the churchyard of St Paul's Cathedral Blantyre.

frequent deportations."[32] Several Anglican missionary clergy were deported down the years. "Fr Ronald Tovey was deported for being outspoken".[33] The Birmingham-trained Fr Humphrey Taylor was from 1967-71 Rector of St Peter's, Lilongwe. The church was founded in 1951 by white settlers and for many years had a more strongly English flavour than other churches. Lilongwe lies on the country's main north-south route. Humphrey and his wife Anne had a constant stream of visitors,[34] with many expatriates, including several visitors from Birmingham. Taylor had a prison ministry, carried on while he was on home leave by his curate, Frank Mkata. On one occasion, unknown to Taylor, he "took a tape recorder into the detention centre to record the singing of the detainees, which was heartbreakingly beautiful."[35] This was reported to the authorities and it sufficed for Taylor and his family to be expelled in 1971. He was able to visit Malawi again in 1984 as General Secretary of USPG.

Fr Jack Biggers, chaplain to Bishop Mtekateka and later to become the first Bishop of Northern Malawi, was deported by President Banda in 1974 for organizing a meeting defending the persecuted Jehovah's Witnesses. CCAP missionaries including Andrew Ross were also expelled or had to leave at short notice.[36] Prominent Malawian clergy suffered too: Rt Rev Patrick Kalilombe was removed from his post as Roman Catholic Bishop of Lilongwe and had to leave the country in 1976 when his way of running his diocese fell foul of the powers-that-be.

---

[32] Canon Michael Hardy, USPG Appointment and Training Secretary, 10.9.1973, USPG archive TF1250 [20.5.2019].

[33] Tengatenga, *Church, State and Society in Malawi: the Anglican Case,* Zomba: Kachere, 2006, p. 98.

[34] They counted 100 bed-nights in the first 6 months of 1971. Interview with Rt Rev Humphrey Taylor, 12.5.2018.

[35] Ann D. Taylor, *Malawi Memories,* UK: The Vale Press, n.d. but after 2001, p. 291.

[36] Kenneth R. Ross, *Malawi and Scotland,* Mzuzu: Mzuni Press, 2013, p. 181.

Ross and Fiedler sum up the position of the churches under the Banda dictatorship thus:

> "In a context where the one-party state sought to close down or heavily restrict all associational life outside the organs of the party itself, church life was the outstanding exception... It is a measure of the strength of the church in Malawian society that the state, even in its most oppressive and totalitarian period, had to respect the integrity of the life of the churches. It was, however, an uneasy relationship built on a tacit agreement that the churches would refrain from any direct criticism of a political nature while the state would not interfere unduly in the life of the churches."[37]

Another expatriate Anglican work lasted for four years from 1970. Three sisters from the Nursing Community of St John the Divine, the nursing order immortalized in the 'Call the Midwife' series on British TV, went to work at St Anne's Maternity Hospital at Nkhotakota. Sister Christine was matron of the hospital and was charged with establishing a midwifery training school. This was demanding work: "The demands of the hospital make it difficult for the sisters to keep their rule ... Pleas of life and death are an unanswerable excuse for missing [daily religious] offices."[38] All three sisters developed gastro-intestinal infections, which in Christine's case troubled her for the rest of her life. However, there were lighter moments: one Christmas the sisters had a gift of umbrellas, and the student midwives danced around the Christmas crib with them![39] The Community moved to a house in a multi-ethnic area of Birmingham in 1975, where Malawian visitors included Bishop Peter Nyanja. At the time of writing DLM was working to rebuild and reopen the midwifery school at Nkhotakota as part of Lake Malawi Anglican University.

---

[37] Ross and Fiedler, *A Malawi Church History 1860-2020*, p. 329.

[38] Miss Nicholl, USPG Personnel Secretary, visit report April-May 1970. Accessed in USPG archives 20.5.2019.

[39] Sister Christine (Hoverd) CSJD, interviewed on 21.2.2017.

Mission Partners – The Last but One Generation of Birmingham Clergy to Serve in Malawi

In the 1970s-80s two missionary couples went to Malawi after serving in Birmingham. In each case the husband was an ordained clergyman and the wife a doctor, and in each case the Partnership played an important role in their getting to Malawi but had little significance once they were there.

Rev Tony Cox had been a curate at St Matthew's, Smethwick, whose vicar, Christopher Hall, was a keen supporter of the link. He met Donald Arden on a visit there and simply asked him for a job in Malawi! He was sent to be a teacher and chaplain at Malosa Secondary School from 1975 on, and then became headmaster from 1980 to 1987. His wife Helen was medical officer at Chancellor College, University of Malawi, in Zomba. Tony summed up their experience on arrival in Malawi in 1975 as "post-colonial sensitivities, lingering expatriate lifestyles and traditional Malawian customs" and Malosa as "something of an island of stability in the midst of a still-sensitive political situation."[40]

Malosa was a mixed age range boarding school, and the only one to be mixed gender. It was one of Tony's missions to raise the status of girls, so that girls could relate to boys as equals with self-confidence and respond to pressures from boys in and out of school. In his first term as head, Tony had to exclude 13 girls for being pregnant; this had dropped to only three by his final year. Girl prefects were given similar roles to boys, and boys had to be prepared to accept their authority. The school began teaching maths to girls separately from boys, with a steep improvement in their exam results.[41]

Tony taught in English; he learned to take the service in Chichewa but unlike his wife, never became proficient in it. He saw himself primarily as a chaplain/teacher of the school and less as a priest of the diocese. However, "unlike some of my colleagues from the USA, I never doubted

---

[40] Paper given to the author on interview, 23.5.2019.

[41] Interview, 23.5.2019.

that my first loyalty was to the diocese in Malawi rather than my diocese or mission agency in the UK."[42] Tony saw occasional visitors from Birmingham, especially Mark Green, Bishop of Aston. Otherwise, the link was "a pretty minor factor." At the time of writing Tony was serving as Chair of MACS [Malawi Association for Christian Support].

Another British priest to serve with the Malawian church at this time was Canon Guy Smith He had served several periods working overseas. Most recently he and his wife Mary had served in a 'Black Country' parish in Lichfield diocese near Birmingham. They were persuaded to go to Malawi in 1979, by USPG and then by the newly appointed Bishop of Lake Malawi, Peter Nyanja. The leadership of the diocese had become African, and "there were only two white priests in our diocese plus a nurse."[43] The family happily settled in Area 18 of Lilongwe, which was regarded as 'a Malawian area', and where the DLM offices were built. Canon Smith worked as training chaplain, travelling a great deal around the diocese. The family stayed for three years, until 1982.

The second clergy couple from Birmingham to serve in Malawi during these years [and slightly later] was Rev Keith and Dr Gill Gale, who were in Lake Malawi diocese from 1981-93. Keith had been curate at St Martin-in-the-Bull-Ring for four years. Both of them had previously worked or studied in Central Africa and were hoping to return there. They met Bishop Nyanja as he visited Birmingham, and he mentioned two possible posts, one for Gill as Medical Officer to Dwangwa Sugar Corporation, the other for Keith as curate in Dwangwa parish, with a ministry to the white senior staff there as well as several black Malawian congregations.[44]

---

[42] Paper given to the author on interview, 23.5.2019.

[43] Mary Smith, widow of Canon Guy, in reply to author's survey of those who had served in Malawi, 26.2.2018.

[44] Rev Keith Gale, reply to author's survey of those who had served in Malawi, 18.3.2018.

Keith tells an anecdote about his wife that sheds light both on the privileged life of the senior staff, most of them Zimbabwean or South African, and their willingness to help when needed.

> "One evening a woman was involved in an accident on the road to the sugar mill. She was hit by a bundle of sugar overhanging the side of a cane lorry. At the clinic Gill realised that her spleen was bleeding into her abdomen. She needed to be operated on at the central hospital in Lilongwe, a 4-5 hour journey by road. Gill knew she would need many units of blood on the way, and put in a call to her 'walking blood bank', volunteers from the senior club. About ten men arrived, all in good spirits, holding their gin and tonics, to each donate a pint of blood. Gill felt the alcohol in the blood would help deaden the lady's pain. So she was sent off in the ambulance in the care of two clinical officers... On reaching Lilongwe she was successfully operated on and in due course returned home."

In 1983 Keith Gale was transferred to Lilongwe to be Rector of St Peter's, where on Sundays he led an English service, with a Malawian voluntary priest leading the Chichewa service as he visited an outstation. Like some other English clergy, he regrets that he "only ever had a rudimentary grasp of Chichewa."[45] He served as Archdeacon of Lilongwe from 1989-93. Dr Gill became director of Malawi against Polio's Lilongwe unit, to be succeeded in 1985 by former Birmingham GP Dr Clive Inman.[46]

John Workman, who served as ACM's accountant 1981-84, should be remembered as another Birmingham missionary in this period.[47]

The era of expatriate leadership in the Anglican Church in Malawi seemed to be drawing to a close. "It is only three years since the departure of the last white expatriate bishop and... the church is in a crucial phase of development under indigenous leadership. With a

---

[45] ibid.

[46] Diocese of Birmingham, *Mirror on Malawi*, October 1986.

[47] See ch. 2 above.

sprinkling of expatriates in hospitals, secondary schools and a theological college the one missionary in pastoral ministry is close to retirement."[48] Tony Cox's experience at Malosa Secondary School would confirm this: when he became headmaster in 1980, 12 of the 26 staff were expatriates [not all of them British], but there were no expatriate staff by 1995.[49]

Rethinking Mission in the Church of England, in Birmingham and in Central Africa

I noted above that "The [Anglican] Communion as a whole began its journey from paternalism to partnership in its mission relations in the 1960s."[50] From the fate of some of the initiatives over the next 20 years it can be concluded that the Church of England found the transition very challenging. A consultative process called Partners in Mission [PIM] emerged from an Anglican Consultative Council meeting in Dublin in 1973.[51] "The purpose of PIM was to engage the churches of the Communion in a process of setting its mission priorities, in which process they would be accompanied by partner churches selected by the host church."[52]

In 1978 Birmingham reluctantly took part in a PIM consultation at Hereford with the five West Midlands dioceses. In 1979 the Province of Central Africa held a similar exercise; this was at a point when it was feared that political tensions might blow the Province apart. Its four

---

[48] Canon Humphrey Taylor, Report of a USPG staff team visit to the Province of Central Africa, April-May 1984. USPG archive TF1470. Taylor must have overlooked Keith Gale, then only in mid-career.

[49] Correspondence with the author, 5.2019.

[50] Janice Price, *World Shaped Mission, Exploring New Frameworks for the Church of England in World Mission,* London: Church House Publishing, 2012, p. 16.

[51] Bob Jenkins, *In Touch with the Warm Heart of Africa, 1966-96,* 1998, p. 6.

[52] Price, *World Shaped Mission, Exploring New Frameworks for the Church of England in World Mission,* London: Church House Publishing, 2012, p. 17.

nations, included Zimbabwe, then under white minority rule as Rhodesia. The external consultants included eight from North America, four from Africa and two from England, including Bishop Mark Green of Aston.[53] For Bishop Mark and the consultants from Uganda and Zaire, in particular, "the 50,000 Anglicans in Malawi were the Church's main resource. What came out chiefly ... was that the greatest need was for spiritual renewal, closely related to evangelism and stewardship." Other work would take on new impetus, with more finance available, if people were set on the path to renewal. As the bishop observed, these comments were equally applicable to Birmingham.[54]

The Church of England took part in the PIM process in 1981.[55] Despite a good debate in General Synod, "the effect of the PIM Consultation ... was marginal."[56]

> "There was as clear a distinction between giving and receiving churches at the end of the process as at the beginning. The giving churches were offered the chance to receive but were unable or unwilling to do so …. The giving church did not value the resources [of the younger churches]."[57]

Alongside the PIM process came another, less ambitious but more successful in implementation, and with a confusingly similar name: Partnership for World Mission [PWM], established in 1978. This was designed to bridge the gap between the central decision making structures of the C of E and the mission agencies, with a view to

---

[53] Jenkins, *In Touch with the Warm Heart of Africa, 1966-96*, c.1998, p. 8.

[54] Bishop Mark Green, *The Church in Malawi, A report [to the Diocese] on his Visit in June 1979*, 8.1979.

[55] The report produced was provocatively entitled *To a Rebellious House*, London: CIO, 1981.

[56] Price, *World Shaped Mission, Exploring New Frameworks for the Church of England in World Mission,* London: Church House Publishing, 2012, p. 17.

[57] Philip Groves, unpublished PhD thesis, quoted in Price, op. cit., p. 17.

strengthening relationships and partnership.[58] PWM has organized an annual world mission conference, regularly attended by the officers responsible for the Birmingham end of the Partnership and on one occasion, in 2014, by a Malawian guest too.

The Malawian Church has been undertaking its own journey from paternalistic relations to partnership and self-sustainability, and this has not yet reached its goal. Arden admitted in a letter to USPG: "I must now confess that we have, in fact, never taken any notice of the breakdown of your grant in our budgeting, and I suspect that many other dioceses would say the same if they were pressed."[59] Such an attitude might be seen as high-handed, but it can be defended as stoutly asserting the right of 'the man on the spot' to know better where the money most needed to be spent than those setting the budget in London. Arden's example of using money for his chosen projects, regardless of the donor's intention, was copied by subsequent bishops who did not all have the same good judgment or scruples.

The massive increase in external resourcing, from Birmingham and many other sources, in Arden's time left the Malawian Church incomparably stronger and better resourced at his retirement as Archbishop in 1981 than it had been 20 years earlier.[60] At the same time it helped create an expectation that external funding would always be found to tackle a problem. A report of a USPG visit in 1985 speaks of the vigour of the church and the Mothers' Union and their potential for growth, but continues:

---

[58] Price, ibid., p. 18.

[59] Letter from Rt Rev Donald Arden to USPG, 2.4.1971 [accessed in archive 21.5.2019].

[60] On his retirement he and Jane moved to London, where they continued to be deeply concerned for the welfare of Malawi and its church. Donald died in 2014 at the age of 98. There is a mitre-shaped stone monument to him in front of the Church of the Ascension at Likwenu, Malosa and some of his ashes are interred there.

"Alongside all that potential, however, one senses a lingering dependence on outside help which stifles even greater potential. Whilst in a materially poor country such as Malawi support from outside will be needed for some time, the climate in which it is sought and given appears to reflect more the relationship of a past era than the era of partnership."[61]

This sense of dependence can still be traced in some quarters in Malawi, and I have to acknowledge that it has both fed, and been fed by, a continuing spirit of paternalism in Birmingham. I would plead only that the needs are very real, and that trying to meet them is easier than exercising the 'tough love' that involves honest face-to-face discussions about resources and priorities.

Hugh Montefiore was Bishop of Birmingham 1978-87.[62] He visited Malawi in 1983 and made a great impact. He had learned to speak some sentences in Chichewa, which caused great excitement. He was impressed with the way the Church ran clinics and hospitals and noted how these practical expressions of love for neighbour brought about conversions. He conducted confirmations in several of the churches and was moved by the worship.[63]

In 1987 the Ven. John Cooper, Archdeacon of Aston, undertook a 6-week visit to Malawi at Birmingham's invitation. On his return a four-page newspaper, complete with photos he had taken, was produced to give the diocese news of Malawi's life and needs. He also wrote a

---

[61] Capes, Moore and Symon, USPG, *Report of a Staff Team Visit to the Province of Central Africa in October 1985,* USPG archive doc. TF1900, para 3.3.4 [20.5.2019].

[62] See ch. 9 below.

[63] Terry Slater, *A Century of Celebrating Christ: the Diocese of Birmingham 1905-2005,* Chichester: Phillimore & Co. 2005, p. 163.

personal report, the most detailed on the link since its inception.[64] The report never quite resolved the tension between the more equal relationship it advocated and the increased transfer of resources it recommended:

> "I hope that we would commit ourselves to an exploration of a deeper and more equal relationship which might contain within it not a diminishing but an increase of material aid in such ways that will enhance and facilitate the work of the Church in Malawi without breeding dependency."[65]

Some of the report's ideas were implemented in the following years: Cooper recommended "that a dialogue is set up between representatives of each diocese to clarify the meaning of the link, the expectations on each side and to clarify its limitations."[66] Regular consultations began at the episcopal visit to Malawi in 1991 and continued at roughly two-yearly intervals for almost 20 years, though they never reached an agreed 'meaning of the link'. Parish donations rose steeply over the following five years to reach almost £40,000 by 1992.

Bishops in Malawi after Donald Arden

Peter Nyanja, Bishop of Lake Malawi, 1978-2005

In 1978, Peter Nyanja succeeded Josiah Mtekateka as the second Bishop of Lake Malawi.[67] He was a striking contrast, both to his predecessor

---

[64] Ven. John Cooper, *Report of the Visit to the Dioceses of Southern Malawi and Lake Malawi by the Archdeacon of Aston on behalf of the Diocesan Council for Mission and Unity, 12th June-26th July 1987.*

[65] Op. cit. p. 21.

[66] Op. cit. p. 16.

[67] Peter Nyanja was born to non-Christian, Nyau-dancing parents in Ntchisi. He became a Christian at teacher training college before 1962 and came to the attention of Donald Arden. He trained for ordination in Tanzania and later in Lusaka. He was ordained in 1971 and became Archdeacon of Nkhotakota in 1977.

and to Bishop Montefiore, who became Bishop of Birmingham the same year. Bishop Hugh was "58 and tall", was converted from Judaism while at school, and had been an outstanding scholar, Vicar of the University Church in Cambridge and Bishop of Kingston-on-Thames. Bishop Peter was "38 and short" and he had been ordained only seven years when appointed [rather than elected] bishop.[68] Shortly after his consecration he accompanied Archbishop Donald to the Lambeth Conference of 1978. They then visited Birmingham for the Partners in Mission consultation attended by all the West Midlands Diocesan Bishops.[69]

Unlike his tall, dynamic predecessor, Bishop Peter was more introvert, a soft-spoken, cautious, reserved man, with less years of ordained experience.[70] It is not surprising that it took time for him to grow into his role. Rev Keith Gale described his relationship with Nyanja as "cordial, but distant". He confessed the bishop could get annoyed by a clash of cultures, e.g., between European and African attitudes to time when leading services.[71] Bishop Alinafe Kalemba, who was confirmed by Nyanja in 1981, described how it was easy for African converts to 'imitate the missionaries' without having an internal spiritual change. He suggested that Peter had been like that at the start – just a good administrator carrying out his office. However, he had an experience of spiritual renewal in the 1990s and grew to be a spiritual father to the diocese. All aspects of life were related to the gospel and evangelism was given a bigger role.[72]

Nyanja oversaw the move of the diocesan HQ from Nkhotakota to Lilongwe in 1982, and did valuable inter-church work as chair of various Christian bodies. However, in the political turbulence of the early 1990s

---

[68] Ed. Donald Arden, *Mpingo Newsletter*, August 1978.

[69] Unsigned obituary, 2005, possibly by Canon Bob Jenkins.

[70] H.H. Mbaya, *Raising Bishops in the Anglican Church in Malawi, 1924-2000*, p. 20.

[71] Rev Keith Gale, Response to survey sent by author, 7.3.2018.

[72] Interview with Rt Rev Alinafe Kalemba, 18.6.2018.

he was felt to be 'out of his depth.'[73] Twenty-seven years is a long time to be bishop, particularly for someone of Bishop Peter's cautious disposition, and it has been suggested that by the end of his time the development of the diocese was held back.[74] For Birmingham, he was "a wonderful host, who took great care over his visitors" and "loved and cared for his clergy and people."[75]

Dunstan Ainani, Bishop of Southern Malawi 1981-87

Dunstan Ainani came from a Muslim and subsequently military background. He came late into the ministry, in the 1960s, and had been a catechist for years. Working very closely with Arden, Ainani spearheaded the indigenization programme for church music that was based in Chilema. He composed some indigenous hymns, which he popularized in his ministry as a priest. Ainani has been described as "very evangelical in his style of churchmanship" and close to Arden in his vision for the church. His style contrasted with that of Bishops Mtekateka, Nyanja and others who had been brought up in the strict UMCA tradition. He was not very highly educated, but a prudent priest who seemed to create and make use of available opportunities. He has been described both as appearing "dictatorial" and as a big father-like figure, respected but of whom others were in awe.[76]

A story is told of Bishop Ainani: On a trip to England, he was visiting Birmingham and decided to call on Bishop Montefiore without prior notice or appointment, assuming that as a brother bishop he would make himself free to see him. The staff member answering the door at Bishop's Croft asked this African gentleman claiming to be a bishop of

---

[73] See ch. 5 below.

[74] Very Rev Baird Mponda, 15.6.2018.

[75] Unsigned obituary, 2005, possibly by Canon Bob Jenkins.

[76] H.H. Mbaya, *Raising Bishops in the Anglican Church in Malawi, 1924-2000*, pp 21-22; Tony Cox, interview 23.5.2019.

Malawi whether he had an appointment. The bishop said no, and felt insulted to be turned away. Another cultural misunderstanding![77]

---

[77] Rev. Dr. Christopher Race, interview, 20.3.2018.

Chapter 5

The Malawian Church in Times of Stress, 1987-94

The Malawian Church at the Silver Jubilee

The years from 1987 to 1994 were times of great stress, but from 1992 onward times of great promise for Malawi.

A vicious civil war in Mozambique lasted from 1975-92. Malawian troops became involved when RENAMO insurgents based themselves in Malawi and attacked the key rail line from Blantyre to the Mozambican ports.[1] In 1988 the frail Malawian economy was stretched by an influx of some one million refugees. They were not placed in fenced encampments but welcomed and given food and hospitality by local Malawians. The refugees were given land to farm where possible, which increased the pressure on cultivable land.[2] In 1989 natural disasters, including cyclones, earth tremors and floods affected many parts of Malawi, especially around the lake. A special appeal was issued in Birmingham enabling extra gifts of money to be sent.[3]

Bishop Mark Santer became Bishop of Birmingham in 1987[4]; Nathaniel Aipa was consecrated as Bishop of Southern Malawi the same year. It was decided that the silver jubilee of the link in 1991 should be marked by Bishop Mark making an official visit to Malawi. He went as head of a ten strong 'diocesan family group' which included his wife Henriette, a clinical psychologist; Janice Miller, who represented the Mothers' Union; and Susan Johnson, a Reader from Aston parish church whose

---

[1]   Wikipedia "Mozambique Civil War" [26.3.2018].

[2]   Rt Rev James Tengatenga, in correspondence, 6.6.2018.

[3]   Jenkins, *In Touch with the Warm Heart of Africa,* pp. 10-11.

[4]   See ch. 9 below.

early upbringing in rural Jamaica gave her a natural empathy and understanding of the life of rural Malawians.[5]

By this point the country was in a parlous state and the rule of law was breaking down. The group visited the historic sites of the Malawian Anglican church – the shrine in Magomero to Bishop Charles Mackenzie and St Peter's Cathedral on Likoma Island. They witnessed St Anne's Hospital, Nkhotakota, struggling to offer healthcare in face of extreme poverty and lack of medical resources. They made a visit, later described by Bishop Mark as "a heartbreaking experience,"[6] to a camp of Mozambican refugees in Nkhata Bay:

> "Within weeks of the camp being formed, the church was being built – just poles holding up a rough-thatched roof, a beaten mud floor, the font at one end, altar at the other. At first the only wall was behind the altar; on it were painted the cross and simple relief designs, coloured by ochres and white clay … a place of … worship for the living church which has materially nothing.
>
> "When Bishops Peter Nyanja and Mark Santer visited the camp, they were welcomed by the whole community; people of all ages lining the roadway. The hundreds of orphans smiled, waved and knelt for a blessing; adults reached out to touch hands with the bishops and their party. In the church amid singing, prayers and joyful welcome, the people with nothing gave gifts to Bishop Mark – a clay teapot cup and saucer, a small plate, all crudely hand-fashioned, fired in the embers of an open cooking hearth; and two woven basket bowls. 'Pray for our safe return,' they asked. 'Pray for our lost ones, and let us pray for you.'"[7]

---

[5] Interview with Rt Rev Mark Santer, 23.1.2017 and correspondence with Bishop Mark, 24.1.2019.

[6] Interview with Rt Rev Mark Santer, 23.1.2017.

[7] *Celebrating 25 Years of Companionship*, Birmingham Diocesan Synod, 2.3.1992.

The faithful gave generous gifts even out of their often acute poverty.[8] The visit left Bishop Mark with a deeper understanding of Malawi and a firm commitment to its future welfare.

Bishop Mark spent time with the two Anglican bishops, Peter Nyanja and Nathaniel Aipa.[9] Aipa was charming and charismatic, but could be manipulative rather than pastoral towards clergy and lay leaders.[10]. Events proved that he lacked the steadiness and integrity required. Like others, he was reluctant to protest in the face of abuses. In 1990 he reportedly said "I myself am responsible for the Christians in my diocese". This was taken to mean that he was not prepared to put his flock at risk by being prophetic.[11]

One has to feel great sympathy for the two bishops. Their theological formation had been in the UMCA tradition which included 'respect for the proper authorities' [Romans 13] and 'keeping one's distance from politics where possible.'[12] Neither bishop proved to be adequately resourced personally or theologically to deal with the challenges that faced the churches, not least those soon to come on the political front. It became clear that both were struggling; Bishop Mark acted as mentor and brother bishop to them, Aipa in particular.[13] Tengatenga paints "a

---

[8] Ibid.

[9] Benson Nathaniel Aipa grew up in the Malindi area and was strongly influenced by prominent African clergy such as Habil Chipembere. He worked for a few years as a teacher before ordination. He was sent to St John's College, Lusaka, in 1964 for further theological training, and trained at the College of the Ascension in 1984. He became warden of the training centre at Chilema, then Archdeacon and Vicar General. Source: H.H. Mbaya, *Raising Bishops in the Anglican Church in Malawi, 1924-2000,* p. 23.

[10] Canon John Cooper, interview, 12.7.2019.

[11] James Tengatenga, *Church, State and Society in Malawi: the Anglican Case*, Zomba: Kachere, 2006, p. 144.

[12] See ibid. chs. 3 and 4.

[13] Interview with Rev Dr Christopher Race, 15.3.2018.

picture of an assimilated Church which was so muzzled that it capitulated to everything that the state dictated."[14] But putting one's head above the parapet had often proved to be a dangerous course in Banda's Malawi.

The Catholic Bishops Light the Fuse

In early 1992 Malawi faced a perfect storm of problems and misfortunes:

The AIDS epidemic was raging, taking out members of the community as productive young adults and leaving hundreds of thousands of orphans;

A severe drought had reduced crop yields, resulting in widespread hunger which became worse as the year went on;

The repayment of international debts acquired in the early years of independence was crippling the country's economy;

The dictatorship of President Hastings 'Kamuzu' Banda was in its 28th year, with its attendant evils of corruption, an economy captive to the state, arbitrary detention, state violence, a tainted justice system and a climate of fear. The 'Life President' was elderly and isolated. The much hated Minister of State, John Tembo, was the power behind the throne and there were fears that he would succeed Banda.

Yet 2½ years later, the whole political climate had changed, and the Banda era had come to a peaceful end. Considerable credit for this must go to the effective ecumenical action of some of the main churches in Malawi – Roman Catholic, CCAP and Anglican – and their closest associates overseas – the RC Church in England, Church of Scotland and Diocese of Birmingham.[15]

---

[14] Tengatenga, *Church, State and Society in Malawi: the Anglican Case*, p. 147.

[15] A full account and analysis of this period can be found in Tengatenga, *Church, State and Society in Malawi: the Anglican Case,* pp. 147-89. See also Ross and Fiedler, *A Malawi Church History 1860-2020,* pp. 347-361 and

The fuse was lit when the Roman Catholic bishops produced a Lenten Pastoral Letter to be read in all churches on 8 March 1992. This applied Catholic social teaching to the sad state of the country and laid some of the blame on the government:

> "In our society we are aware of a growing gap between the rich and the poor with regard to expectations, living standards and development... We appeal for a more just and equal distribution of the nation's wealth... Bribery and nepotism are growing in political, economic and social life."

The letter went on to bemoan falling standards in education and unequal access to it: "Access to education should not depend on whom the candidate knows or how much money he possesses". It stressed the importance of a church-state partnership in education in which "the government has a duty to respect the rights and legitimate aspirations of the Churches" [note the plural]. The letter noted shortcomings and inequalities in the health system and discussed the AIDS crisis. Turning to participation in public life, the letter pointedly said that "No one person can claim to have a monopoly of truth and wisdom" and spoke of "a climate of mistrust and fear". It continued "We cannot ignore or turn a blind eye to our people's experience of unfairness and injustice".[16]

Why was the Pastoral Letter produced at this moment? One can point to the changing world political climate. The Western powers had seen Banda as a useful ally in the Cold War which was being waged in Africa too; with the end of communism there was no further reason to support him.[17] Eastern European nations had freed themselves from dictatorship; a Polish Pope who was close to these changes had visited

---

Kenneth R. Ross, *Gospel Ferment in Malawi: Theological Essays,* Blantyre: Mambo-Kachere, 1995, pp. 9-29.

[16] The full text of the Bishops' Pastoral Letter can be found in Kenneth R. Ross (ed), *Christianity in Malawi: A Source Book,* Gweru: Mambo-Kachere, 1996, pp. 203-216, or Mzuzu: Mzuni Press, 2020, pp. 258-272.

[17] Tengatenga, *Church, State and Society in Malawi: the Anglican Case,* p. 147.

Malawi in 1989 and no doubt stirred up the courage of the bishops. These events should be set in a wider African context: "Catholic bishops' pastoral letters have often been catalysts for ecumenical action, as was the case in Malawi where political protest on the part of the dominant Protestant [including Anglican] churches was virtually unknown after independence in 1964. Opposition to one-party rule by the Catholic bishops began early in the 1980s, however, and reached a climax in 1992 with the publication of the Lenten Pastoral Letter, *Living our Faith.*"[18] External links are as important to the Catholic Church as to the Anglican Church in Malawi, and arguably work more effectively: "AMECEA [the Episcopal group for East African Churches] must take a good deal of the credit for the Malawi bishops' pastoral letter in 1992, and it then kept encouraging the bishops when they lost their nerve somewhat due to the furore it provoked."[19]

The Pastoral Letter's implied criticism of the President was obvious and the effect was immediate. Death threats were issued against the Catholic Bishops. Mgr. John Roche, the priest said to be the principal drafter of the Pastoral Letter,[20] was arrested as he preached in Mzuzu on Good Friday and deported. The President attempted to divide and rule the churches, but without success. To quote Tengatenga:

> "Something was happening here that the churches realized could not be done by one church alone. They had caught on to the idea that Dr Banda relied on isolating "trouble makers" and they were not going to give him that pleasure again. It became incumbent upon the church leaders to gather together and formulate strategy."[21]

---

[18] Nigel de Gruchy, *Christianity and Democracy,* Cambridge: Cambridge UP, 1995, p. 184. Words in square brackets added by author.

[19] Paul Gifford, *African Christianity: Its Public Role,* London: Hurst and Co, 1998, p. 310. Also quoted in Tengatenga, p. 148.

[20] Rt Rev Mark Santer, in correspondence, 24.1.2019.

[21] Tengatenga, *Church, State and Society in Malawi: the Anglican Case,* p. 151.

The Church of Scotland publicly disowned the president, who had been nominally an elder of the Kirk for 50 years, but had never become an active member of the CCAP.[22]

International Church Support

Church leaders in Birmingham were quick off the mark. Within ten days of the Pastoral Letter, the joint presidents of the Birmingham Council of Christian Churches, including Bishop Santer, issued a statement supporting the Catholic bishops and their letter. "An attack on one bishop or pastor of the Church of God is an attack upon all."[23] This was followed up in June by a joint public letter of support addressed to the leaders of all Christian Churches in Malawi.

Rev Christopher Race, a Birmingham clergyman who had been brought up in Central Africa, became the 'eyes and ears' of the bishop. He made about six visits to Malawi during 1992. On the first of these in March he took a letter of support for the Anglican bishops from the Archbishop of Canterbury.[24] He travelled with the Papal Legate; their car was stoned. He was able to have secret meetings with opposition politicians Aleke Banda and Orton Chirwa, who was shortly to die in prison under suspicious circumstances. He also met Dr Hetherwick Ntaba, then Minister of Health, for long discussions.[25]

This was a very public contest: "The issue is devolving into a contest for credibility, in which the Catholic Bishops, and the wider Christian Church are at the present time the more believed. However, if the Party is to regain its control and monopoly over Malawi, there is no doubt that the

---

[22] Kenneth R. Ross, *Malawi and Scotland,* Mzuzu: Mzuni Press, 2013, pp. 190-191.

[23] Statement by the Joint Presidents of the Birmingham Council of Christian Churches: Malawi, 17.3.1992.

[24] Most Rev George Carey to the Bishops of Lake Malawi and Southern Malawi, 19.3.1992.

[25] Interview with Rev Dr Christopher Race, 15.3.2018.

witness of the Church must be broken."[26] The government cut all phone lines to the Bishops and the Catholic White Fathers. However, the Fathers' previous phone number had been allocated to a brothel! So daily bulletins were sent out by fax from the brothel.[27]

Protests broke out at the university and Zomba Theological College. Events moved rapidly on the economic front too.

> "In May… a new salary scale for government employees granted 80% increases at the top and 25% or less at the bottom. The cotton mill at Blantyre followed suit and provoked the first strike in Malawi's history. It ended in looting of government shops, the police opening fire and left at least 38 dead. The Paris Donors Club decided to suspend long-term aid to Malawi, virtually ensuring bankruptcy for a country reeling from the worst drought in living memory which was wiping out its only other source of foreign exchange, agricultural exports."[28]

July brought a week's official visit by representatives of the Council of Churches for Britain and Ireland (CCBI), drawn from the RC Church, the Church of Scotland and the Church of England, the latter represented by Bishop Mark. They had two aims: to demonstrate to the government of Malawi that what was going on there was known about in the wider church; and, by coming together as representatives of the three Churches, to show that they could not be played off against one another. They took care not to see the President or any government representatives, not wishing to be seen to be taking over the proper role of the local churches.[29] They issued a report highly critical of the state of Malawi, stating that human rights were widely violated; the government monopolized the means of public communication; the electoral system was manipulated; Christian hospitals were being

---

[26] Rev Christopher Race, Confidential Report on Malawi Visit, 24-29.3.1992.

[27] Interview with Rev Dr Christopher Race, 15.3.2018. Another version of the story locates the fax machine in a garage.

[28] Donald Arden, *Malawi Comes of Age, Nkhani Zaulere*, January 1993.

[29] Rt Rev Mark Santer, in correspondence, 24.1.2019.

starved of funds; and there was a threat of widespread famine. However, "under the pressure of great national events, the leaders of three historic Christian traditions have been finding themselves to be sisters and brothers in Christ in quite a new way. Indeed, during our visit we rejoiced to see this happening before our eyes."[30]

The Anglican bishops took their full part in public affairs. The Christian Council of Malawi chaired by Bishop Nyanja produced an open letter to the government in August 1992 calling on human rights grounds for a properly monitored referendum on a multi-party system and reminding government "that the Church has the mandate to speak on behalf of those on the margin of our society."[31]

Two days later came the formation of the Public Affairs Committee [PAC], made up of the Malawi Council of Churches, the Roman Catholic Episcopal Conference, the Muslim Association, the Chamber of Commerce and the Law Society. For the first time, every part of Malawian civil society joined forces to demand democratic change, initially a referendum on the system of government.

Birmingham Diocesan Synod had debated a Malawi motion annually since the Partnership's foundation. In November 1992 the synod pledged its solidarity with the Malawian church in prayer and practical support, its backing for the PAC and its hopes for a good political outcome.

Referendum and Multi-party Elections

Events moved rapidly. In response to the sustained and high-profile campaign both inside and outside Malawi, the government agreed to hold a referendum on a multi-party system, though they insisted at first on separate ballot boxes for votes for a multi-party or a single-party system!

---

[30] Statement by Representatives of CCBI, 26.7.1992.

[31] Christian Council of Malawi, *Open Letter to the Government of Malawi*, 26.8.1992.

Church leaders badly needed a 'safe space' to discern their way forward free from informers or interference. It was agreed to invite PAC representatives to a conference at Swanwick, Derbyshire, which took place in February 1993. Birmingham played a major role in bringing this about: Bishop Mark obtained funds from C of E central sources to cover delegates' travel costs[32] and two Birmingham clergy, Christopher Race and David Newsome, were on the organizing team. The Malawi government got wind of the conference, tried hard to get an invitation but was rebuffed by CCBI. It then resorted to the hopeless expedient of posting security men at the nearest station at Alfreton![33]

The conference produced proposals for 'Education for Participatory Democracy' – something unknown to Malawians – and for monitors to check that the referendum should be free, fair and democratic. Amongst the working documents were ones on 'Lobbying and Action with International Bodies' and for an International Visitors' Programme; it was clear that Malawi needed to be kept in the public eye.[34] Emmanuel Chinkwita, PAC's acting Chairman, considered that "The Pastoral Letter was really a catalyst, but the pivotal event in the process of change was the Swanwick meeting where the strategy was formed which guided the PAC in the National Referendum and the General Election."[35]

This was an ecumenical work. "The putting into action of that political organization and mobilization call was carried out and, in some cases, led by Anglican clergy, who made up most of the district coordinators ... [In the Central Region, the Catholic priest and I] recruited, mobilized and

---

[32] Letter from Rt Rev Mark Santer to R. Last, Church House Westminster, 4.2.1993.

[33] Interview with Rt Rev Mark Santer, 23.1.2017.

[34] Swanwick Conference document, 18.2.1993.

[35] Quoted in Kenneth R. Ross, *Malawi and Scotland,* p. 194.

coordinated the work of PAC and civic education in the region. Very dangerous work in those days."[36]

Early in 1993 the Catholic Bishops issued another Pastoral Letter. They stated: "What people are seeking is genuine democracy in which the leaders are servants of the people who elected them and not their masters, in which leaders are answerable and accountable for their actions to those they lead, a true government of the people; not a government by or for the privileged few." They adduced a careful list of advantages and disadvantages of the single-party and multi-party systems, from which it was perfectly clear that they favoured the latter.[37] The CCAP Blantyre Synod also issued a full statement.[38] Nothing corresponding was produced by the Anglican bishops; in Bishop Aipa's case, simply an open letter urging the faithful to vote wisely and to abstain from violence.[39]

The promised referendum was held on 14 June 1993. Despite government pressure, the muzzling and arrest of opposition leaders, and harassment, intimidation and violence by paramilitaries and the police,[40] the outcome was clear: almost two-to-one in favour of a multi-party system. Ecumenical observers from the UK included Revs Christopher Race and Tony Cox. The referendum result led to a general election in May 1994 at which Banda was succeeded as President by the leader of the United Democratic Front, Bakili Muluzi, a Muslim. The era

---

[36] Rt Rev James Tengatenga, correspondence, 6.6.2018.

[37] "Choosing our Future: Pastoral Letter to the Catholic Faithful", 2.2.1993, quoted in Ross and Fiedler, *A Malawi Church History, 1860-2020,* p. 357.

[38] Statement on the role of the Church in the Transformation of Malawi in the Context of Justice and Peace, Blantyre Synod CCAP, January 22-23 1993. Both documents are reproduced in Kenneth R. Ross, *Christianity in Malawi: a Source Book,* Gweru: Mambo-Kachere, 1996, pp. 218-35.

[39] Letter to clergy and faithful of the Diocese of Southern Malawi, 30.4.1993.

[40] Noted by a delegation from CCBI including Rt Rev Humphrey Taylor, visiting 27.4 to 2.5.1993.

of multi-party democracy had arrived. All subsequent changes of President have been peaceful: either after elections judged free and fair, or in one case, on the death of the incumbent.

How does one assess the churches' role in bringing the Banda dictatorship to an end? It is generally agreed to have been highly significant; I would suggest it was a case study in African churches working ecumenically with effective support from their overseas partners. Does such close co-operation continue, 25 years on? "I would say that even though it [ecumenical engagement in political/social action] is not as pronounced, there are still vestiges of it at work in the Public Affairs Committee..."[41] The Malawian churches seem to have slipped back from co-operation to competition mode as churches grow and multiply and new churches are built, often in close proximity to each other. In the UK too ecumenism is no longer the force that it was in the years after the 1987 Swanwick Conference.

Human Rights and Development

The struggle for democracy went on in tandem with the drive for human rights in Malawi, External helpers included Amnesty International and the British law societies. "A delegation of the law societies from Wales, Scotland and England at the invitation of the Malawi Law Society in September 1992 were able to meet with political prisoners, judges, magistrates and government officials, producing a powerful and distressing report on the status of human rights."[42] Their delegation made possible the first meeting in eight years between Vera and Orton Chirwa [prominent political prisoners, married but held separately] three weeks before his death."[43] The lawyers' report was followed up

---

[41] Rt Rev James Tengatenga, in correspondence, 6.6.2018.

[42] 'Human Rights in Malawi', Report of a Joint Delegation, 17-27.9.1992.

[43] Malawi Report presented to General Assembly of Church of Scotland, May 1993.

by another visit in October 1993 and a report on 'Constitutional Change in Malawi'.[44]

After the Swanwick conference in February 1993, a Malawi Human Rights Network was set up and met in London for 18 months. This included Malawian politicians in exile, the legal profession in England and Scotland, the TUC, the Church of Scotland, the Roman Catholic White Fathers, and the Diocese of Birmingham, represented by Revs Newsome and Race.[45] Newsome recalls an episode at a Human Rights Network meeting in London:

> "A representative of UDF [the party whose candidate became president in 1994] at one point said in exasperation 'Why don't the churches step aside now and let the politicians, you know, take over?' - at which point I exploded and said that the church's responsibility is to be the moral voice and I think it is essential that they are constantly nagging the political parties as they come to formulate a constitution, that proper safeguards for human rights are built in and that we don't have hostages for fortune in the future."[46]

Intensive activity to help the transition to democracy went on with international support, both in Malawi and elsewhere. An Amnesty International meeting at the House of Commons in May 1993 was addressed by Vera Chirwa and also by Christopher Race.[47]

After the Presidential election a meeting of the PAC with Ecumenical Partners was held in September 1994 with encouragement from the WCC. David Newsome, who attended, reported that "an advantage over the previous PAC/CCBI conference at Swanwick… was that the

---

[44] Report of a Delegation of the Council of the Bar in England and the Scottish Faculty of Advocates, 7-17.10. 1993.

[45] Minutes of Malawi Human Rights [Information] Network [MHRN], March 1993-94, loaned by Rev David Newsome.

[46] Bob Jenkins, interview with Rev David Newsome, 24.6.1993.

[47] Programme and attendance list circulated with minutes of MHRN meeting on 23.2.1994.

majority of partners came from other parts of Africa and were able to speak directly from their own non-European context."[48] Issues emerging included the resurgence of regionalism, which President Banda had attempted to resolve by making Chichewa the national language and suppressing the rest.

The development of Malawi had been woefully neglected during the Banda years and there was much ground to make up. A Malawi Development Group, chaired by Bishop Arden and with strong church representation, was set up in February 1995 to bring together the work of groups working on the political agenda, human rights issues and church matters. Its large membership included Bishop Mark Santer and David Newsome. The Group's concerns covered a wide range of issues around education, health and women's rights, including the plight of AIDS widows who might have their property seized by their husband's family.[49] The National Initiative for Civic Education in Malawi was set up in 1998.

One early decision of the Muluzi government in September 1994 was to abolish fees for primary education and make it free. Consequently, enrolment jumped from 1.8mn in 1993 to 3.2mn. This led to severe shortages of classrooms and teachers' houses. 15,000 untrained teachers were employed to reduce the burden. The size of classes jumped, and many are still unacceptably large: 100 pupils and more is common.

The Church's Struggle to Adjust to New Times

The turbulent times in Malawi did not prevent a programme of extended clergy visits to Birmingham being arranged with financial support from USPG.[50] Canon George Ndomondo, Director of Chilema, visited during 1992 and the Very Rev Constantine Kaswaya., Dean of

---

[48] Record by Rev David Newsome, n.d.

[49] Records of Malawi Development Group meetings, 17.2.1995, 8.4.1995, 4.7.1995, 17.10.95, 14.5.1996, Donald Arden, loaned by Rev David Newsome.

[50] Letter from G Grace, USPG, to Bishop Aipa, DSM, 13.11.1992.

Blantyre, was in Birmingham for 6 months in 1993, mostly attached to the city centre church of St Martin's in the Bull Ring.[51]

Rapidly changing times were exposing the weaknesses of the Malawian church's leadership. Race observed the conflict between the nation's traditional leaders and its entrepreneurs, with peasants and unskilled labourers caught between them. "In many ways, the situation within the Churches, and particularly the Anglican dioceses, is a mirror of these three secular groups. Our bishops are traditionalists, mostly responding with traditional reactions; our leading and functional laity are becoming highly frustrated; our parishes beginning to reflect the isolation which lack of leadership skills produces; highly competent clergy and laity are either being discouraged or dismissed."[52]

The value of consultations between Malawi and Birmingham became obvious, and the first such visit took place in June 1993. The visiting group of clergy – John Cooper, Christopher Race and David Newsome – produced a report of "considerable frankness", which was highly critical of the state of the church in Malawi, under five heads:

(1) Episcopal isolation and over-centralized decision making, leading to uncertainty, friction and low morale;

(2) The low standard of education of the clergy, with unhappiness expressed at the ecumenical training at Zomba Theological College, and older clergy overstretched and under-trained;

(3) Rapidly changing needs and expectations in ministry, with neither diocese having "the resources to respond effectively to any of these challenges";

(4) A criticism aimed at the Anglican Communion as a whole: withdrawal of expatriate support since independence, in contrast to the external support given to the RC and CCAP in Malawi. "Anglican institutions are decrepit, neglected and disowned by the wider Anglican body,

---

[51] Constantine Kaswaya, report, *My six months in the Diocese of Birmingham*, 28.2.1993-27.8.1993.

[52] Rev Christopher Race, Confidential report, *Malawi: an Update*, 11.5.1992.

specifically the Church of England. Without the support that has come from the Diocese of Birmingham the situation would have become an open scandal";[53]

(5) An unrealistic and fragile financial base, a problem dating back to colonial times but made worse by the drought and the national economic crisis, and severely affecting the church's provision of schools and hospitals. Clergy stipends were desperately low and conditions of service and pension provision were poor. Salaries of lay workers were low, even by Malawian standards.

In the light of these challenges, most of them reflecting longstanding problems, three priorities were identified:

(1) Education and encouragement of clergy and lay workers

(2) The maintenance of significant financial support in the short term

(3) The development of proper income-producing schemes under local and effective management in the long-term.[54]

The third of these has been dismissed as well-intentioned but unrealistic;[55] it has proved the hardest to achieve during the years since then.

---

[53] Report of the Birmingham visiting group, October 1993.

[54] Ibid.

[55] 'exotic' - Klaus Fiedler, in correspondence, 9.2018; cf. Rt Rev Christopher Boyle, 6.2018

Chapter 6

New Era, New Challenges, New Dioceses, 1994-2002

The Churches' Role in the Struggle against HIV/AIDS

The years of stagnation under Banda and malnutrition aggravated by successive droughts contributed to many public health problems. Among the most distressing of these was poor maternal and child health.[1] HIV/AIDS was the most serious, however. During roughly the period 1985-2005, the AIDS pandemic had a devastating effect on the Malawian economy, society and family life. It has been suggested that the loss of agricultural productivity due to AIDS was one factor in the nationwide famine in 2002.[2] The Anglican Church was not generally in the forefront of the struggle against HIV/AIDS; and Birmingham's contribution was largely indirect, through support for the work of the dioceses. But the story needs to be told at length.

Bishop Tengatenga reports that the churches had been teaching about AIDS and were the primary care givers since the beginning of the pandemic, well before the government programmes got into gear. When the government and the NGOs got more engaged the churches became side-lined. He was involved since the late 1980s, as was the Christian Health Association of Malawi. With 40% of health care in Malawi being provided by the churches most of the burden fell on the church. At one point during the height of the crisis it carried 60% of the burden.[3]

---

[1] Discussed in ch. 10 below in connection with the Birmingham Children's Hospital/ Queen Elizabeth Central Hospital, Blantyre link.

[2] www.avert.org/hiv-aids-malawi.htm, quoted in Wikipedia article on HIV/AIDS in Malawi, [21.5.2018]. For the church's response to the famine, see ch. 7.

[3] Correspondence with Rt Rev James Tengatenga, 6.2018.

Stephen Mayes, then Vicar of Water Orton in Birmingham, made an exchange visit to St Paul's Cathedral, Blantyre in 1993. He found the heavy incidence of AIDS contrasted with its denial in society and church alike. He commented:

> The endless funerals. Three or four a week for the whole time I was there... I suspect a lot of them were AIDS deaths. Quite a few of them were young people... The description of the illness was very vague. Not been well for a long time, wasting away, losing weight, having sickness... but there was never any mention of AIDS.

He recalled seeing posters about AIDS and taking precautions, but the churches' activity seemed very low-key.[4]

Fr Eston Pembamoyo recalls:

> "My brother died of AIDS in 1995, as I was training for ordination at Zomba Theological College. He was followed by my sister-in-law in 1996, leaving us with their four children to bring up. As Deacon at Liwonde from 1996 I mounted posters in the church about tackling HIV/AIDS. In 1998 I was attacked by some members of the congregation for breaking the rules about what could go up in a church, but I was defended by newly consecrated Bishop James Tengatenga."[5]

Tengatenga set about tackling the problem on becoming Bishop of Southern Malawi in 1998. Rev Dr Susan Cole-King, Bishop Wilson's daughter, had spent 10-15 years as a doctor in Malawi and had acquired a thorough understanding of development issues.[6] She was invited by Bishop James to visit the Diocese to stimulate a response to the pastoral, theological and social challenges of HIV/AIDS in the context of Christian spirituality, and she made two lengthy visits in 2000.[7] With her

---

[4] Rev Stephen Mayes, interview with Canon Bob Jenkins, 1.6.1998.

[5] In conversation, 4.7.2018.

[6] Interview by Canon Bob Jenkins with Rev Martin Wilson, Dr Cole-King's brother, 22.4.1988.

[7] Rev Dr Anne Bayley, Report of Diocese of Southern Malawi HIV/AIDS Visit July/August 2001.

help the diocese started Family Life Workshops for clergy and church leaders; they were also run successfully in the Northern diocese. The aim was to change attitudes and get the church to see that AIDS was a priority for the whole church, not just its health services or schools. The response was encouraging, but many priests were still reluctant.

In January 2001, shortly before her untimely death, Dr Cole-King wrote a passionate paper entitled 'The Body of Christ has AIDS'.[8] The scale of the problem in Malawi, as in neighbouring Zambia and Zimbabwe, was frightening: almost 1/3 of the adult population in some areas was reckoned to be HIV-positive. The most urgent problem faced by the churches was the rapidly increasing number of orphans, looked after mostly by relatives, often grandparents. With per capita annual income in 1999 of less than $200, Malawi was [and remains] one of the poorest countries in the world, and the situation was deteriorating. Poor nutrition and lack of access to education and information contributed to the spread of AIDS. Hospitals were unsanitary and needles often had to be reused. Lack of work opportunities led men to migrate and become open to casual sexual contacts.

Cultural factors also led to the spread of AIDS. "African society tends to be hierarchical and patriarchal and the low status of women means that girls are taught to do what men want and not to refuse men if they ask for sexual favours." This meant that rape was common and largely unrecognized, and sexual abuse was also rife. Other cultural beliefs and practices unhelpful for the spread of AIDS were reinforced through the *chinamwali* initiation rituals. These included a one-sided emphasis on a woman's body as an instrument for pleasing her husband, the belief that men needed and were entitled to more than one partner, and the practice of teenage brides being married to older sexually experienced men.[9] Sexualized images in Western media and the spread of

---

[8] *The Body of Christ has Aids [sic]: The Role of the Church in the Aids Epidemic in Sub-Saharan Africa,* Report to Diocese of Southern Malawi, 2001.

[9] Molly Longwe, *Growing Up. A Chewa Girls' Initiation*, Zomba: Kachere, 2006.

pornography also had a negative influence. There was resistance to the use of condoms; they were long disapproved of by the Anglican Church and still are by the RC.

Dr Cole-King commended the health care services provided by churches, but commented: "Apart from the care services run by Church health facilities, the response from the churches institutionally has been characterized by a deafening silence – at least until very recently" but admitted this was largely true in Britain as well. One cause of the problem: "As in other African countries, the Church has regarded AIDS as a health problem to be dealt with by the health services, and not something the whole church needs to get involved with as integral to its ministry."

For Dr Cole-King, the first task for the Church in Africa was "to build on and develop the resources of Christian compassion within the worshipping communities, to reduce stigma and denial, and make the church a safe place for people to admit to being HIV positive or having AIDS…" The deep-rooted assumption that sin and suffering were related had to be challenged. Maintaining hope and solidarity were challenges: "To say 'The Body of Christ has AIDS' is more than saying that the Church has AIDS. The Christ who takes on our flesh and shares our suffering, the Christ who identifies with the hungry, the sick and the prisoner, is surely to be encountered in the person living with AIDS."[10]

A few years later, Bishop Tengatenga was to use the same title and some of the same imagery as he gave homilies at diocesan conferences. From an Anglo-Catholic perspective the consecrated bread, as the body of Christ, was regarded as sacred and treated with the greatest care. "So, it should be with the body of Christ that is the person with HIV/AIDS

---

[10] All quotations above: The Body of Christ has Aids [sic]: The Role of the Church in the Aids Epidemic in Sub-Saharan Africa, Report to Diocese of Southern Malawi, 2001.

... If this is our concept of the Body of Christ then in the face of HIV/AIDS, care is only natural and stigma is unnatural."[11]

Bishop Christopher Boyle described HIV/AIDS as "invisible" on his arrival in Northern Malawi in 2001. He made it one of his top priorities to tackle it; breaking the silence was key. It was found that knowing about one's HIV status brought behaviour change. Backed by the Diocesan Synod he gave his diocese four resolutions to live by:

To speak the truth

To act only out of love

To overcome the fatigue of denial and stigma

To begin to live in hope.[12]

Bishop Santer visited Malawi after his retirement from Birmingham in 2002. On Likoma Island where the incidence of HIV/AIDS was high, he and Bishop Boyle helped promote the government-run VCT [Voluntary Counselling and Testing] programme - a fine example of church and government working closely together. [13] Bishop Boyle used a true story about a visit to Likoma to encourage HIV testing.

"A married couple, both positive, both ill, asked for his prayers. Of course, he agreed to pray, but said 'first I went to talk with you: please go to be tested for HIV.' He reported a long pause before the husband said 'Bishop, if we test positive, it is a death sentence.' Bishop Christopher repeated his plea ... another long silence. Then the man said 'Bishop, we cannot go' but his wife said 'Bishop, we **will** go!' Worried about this marital disagreement, the Bishop tried once more, and to show his respect for the couple as clearly as possible, he knelt down in front of them, saying: 'Chonde, chonde, chonde [Chewa for 'please']; go

---

[11] Email from James Tengatenga to Glen Williams, Strategies for Hope, 21.5.2014.

[12] The Friends of Bishop Christopher Newsletter no. 5, October 2002; also in interview, 30.5.2018.

[13] Interview, 30.5.2018 and correspondence, 4.10.2018.

and be tested!' ... That couple did go for testing. Both are now receiving ARV; they are in good health..."[14]

Anti-retroviral [ARV] treatment, which enables sufferers to live with HIV without developing AIDS, was available expensively in the developed world from about 1996. However, it was not until 2004, after many millions of deaths across Africa, that a cheaper, generic version could be used in Malawi.

After Dr Cole-King's death, Bishops Tengatenga and Boyle invited Rev Dr Anne Bayley to act as consultant and partner in the fight against AIDS. Like Dr Cole-King, she was an ordained English woman doctor with extensive working experience in Africa. A surgeon, her work in Zambia in the early 1980s had been seminal in the identification of the AIDS virus. Dr Bayley made visits to all four dioceses, annually from 2001 to 52010. From 2005 on, she worked alongside Matilda Chiutula, the National AIDS Co-ordinator at ACM. With local teams she set up workshops covering every area of behaviour that could affect the incidence of HIV/AIDS or successful living with HIV: married love and family life, hygiene and conserving water. Given that the effectiveness of ARV was dependent on proper nutrition, they gave high priority to more and better food. Birmingham financially supported Dr Bayley's trips in 2004 and 2008 but were otherwise little involved in the struggle against HIV/AIDS.[15]

A UK charity, supported by a large coalition of health and development charities and churches in Africa, including DSM, developed the *Called to Care* toolkit, "a set of practical, action-oriented handbooks on issues related to HIV and AIDS for churches and communities in sub-Saharan

---

[14] Reported by Rev Dr Anne Bayley, DNM, visit report 17.7. to 7.8.2006.

[15] At least, in the view of Dr Bayley: her email to Bishop James Tengatenga, 21.6.2007.

Africa."[16] Dr Bayley co-authored two of the series. 'Time to Talk'[17] with Bishop Tengatenga, was based on the family life workshops they had led in DSM, which tried to overcome the cultural difficulty of talking about love and sex within marriage. 'More and Better Food: Farming, climate change, health and the AIDS epidemic', co-written with a Malawian environmental educator, Mugove Walter Nyika, promoted the principles of permaculture and sustainable agriculture.[18] Its content was tested at workshops in DUS in 2009-10 led by priests from DUS.

Diocese of Northern Malawi created, 1995; Diocese of Southern Malawi

In 1995 the Diocese of Lake Malawi was split and the Diocese of Northern Malawi created, with St Peter's, Likoma as its cathedral.[19] All Saints, Nkhotakota became the cathedral for Lake Malawi. The splitting of the Diocese of Southern Malawi followed in 2002.

The Diocese of Southern Malawi became embroiled in a leadership crisis in the mid-1990s. There were complaints of financial irregularities involving Bishop Aipa, and the Mothers' Union worker. To be fair, such issues were not new: Birmingham had expressed concerns about the unclear size and location of diocesan funds in 1987, before Bishop Aipa's appointment.[20] Parishes in DSM were complaining about lack of transparency and accountability in the diocesan finances by 1994 and some were refusing to send diocesan quotas. During 1995 a Board of

---

[16] *Parenting: a Journey of Love* Oxford: Strategies for Hope Trust, 2011, Preface, About the Called to Care toolkit.

[17] Anne Bayley and James Tengatenga, *Time to Talk, A guide to family life in the age of AIDS,* Oxford, UK: Strategies for Hope Trust, 2006.

[18] Anne Bayley and Mugove Walter Nyika, *More and Better Food: Farming, climate change, health and the AIDS epidemic,* Oxford, UK: Strategies for Hope Trust, 2011.

[19] The first years of the diocese are described in ch. 7.

[20] Confidential note appended to Archdeacon of Aston's Report on Visit to Malawi, June-July 1987.

Enquiry looked into allegations that substantial funds sent to the bishop and the MU worker between 1992 and 1995 by a Lutheran church in Germany had been misappropriated for their personal use.[21] The Board found the bishop and the MU worker guilty, censured him and recommended to the Archbishop that he be asked to resign.[22] Further allegations of sexual immorality on the bishop's part came to light, prompting a petition from all but one of the diocesan clergy asking him to step down.[23]

The diocese had been "virtually without a bishop since December 1994;"[24] Bishop Aipa finally resigned in August 1996. Canon David Lee quickly put out a circular to supporting churches in Birmingham to say that he had met with the Board of Enquiry and could reassure churches that monies sent had been correctly routed through the diocesan accounts and their funds had arrived safely and been correctly used.[25] In 1997 Dr James Amanze, who taught Religious Studies at the University of Botswana, was elected as the new bishop but withdrew his acceptance.[26] James Tengatenga was then elected bishop in early 1998, shortly before the death of Bishop Aipa. But Bishop Aipa's portrait still hangs on the wall of the dining hall at Chilema!

James Tengatenga's life before becoming a bishop was unusually cosmopolitan for a Malawian.[27] He was no stranger to Birmingham: in

---

[21] Correspondence between Matthew Chinthiti, Chairman, Diocesan Board of Finance/ Board of Enquiry, and Rev (Mrs) Almuth Voll, Usingen, Germany.

[22] Minutes of Diocesan Standing Committee, 16.12.1995.

[23] Petition from DSM clergy to Bishop Aipa, 5.8.1996.

[24] *Nkhani Zaulere,* ed. Bishop Donald Arden, May 1997.

[25] Canon David Lee, *The Resignation of Bishop Nathaniel Aipa of the Diocese of Southern Malawi*, n.d. but shortly after 30.8.1996.

[26] Canon David Lee, news release, 29.9.1997.

[27] James Tengatenga was born in 1958 in Zimbabwe but came from the Ngoni culture of Ntcheu, Malawi. He studied at Zomba Theological College and received his Diploma in 1982. He went straight to the Theological Seminary of

1989-90 he had spent nine months studying community work at the College of the Ascension, Selly Oak. He reported that he found church members 'vague' about the Malawi link. He was attached to the parish of St Giles, Rowley Regis, where several families invited him for meals. His presence gave them something tangible about Malawi to relate to and he felt he had "given Birmingham a taste of Malawi". His wife Josie and two young children joined him for three months and were given a warm reception.[28]

The news of Tengatenga's election was received with enthusiasm in Birmingham. "I find it difficult to say how delighted I am to hear this. Nobody knows better than you what demands this post will make upon your spiritual, moral and physical strength."[29] Birmingham was represented at Bishop James' consecration by John Austin, Bishop of Aston, and David Lee. They took a silver pectoral cross [a bishop's cross worn on the chest on a chain] as a sign of the link with Malawi,[30] Birmingham's gift to other bishops on their consecration too.

In his enthronement sermon Bishop James sought to draw a line under the recent past in the diocese: "The proclamation of the gospel requires us to be people of integrity who not only preach the gospel but live it… We have for too long relaxed and our morality both personally and with regards to social responsibility has left a lot to be desired."[31] He looked

---

the Southwest in Texas and did another three years' study. In 1984 he married Joselyn [Josie]; they have three children. Ordained in 1985, he worked for eight years as a parish minister in Lilongwe, largely at St Mary's, Biwi, and as youth worker. From 1993 to 1998 he taught theology at Zomba Theological College, then at Chancellor College in Zomba, the oldest university in Malawi. Source: *James Tengatenga, the Road to Lordship*, 1998: Bishop's Consecration Committee, Blantyre.

[28] Tengatenga, interview with Canon Bob Jenkins, 23.7.1990.

[29] Rt Rev Mark Santer, letter to Rev James Tengatenga, 25.2.1998.

[30] Rt Rev Mark Santer, letter to Rev James Tengatenga, 24.3.1998.

[31] Rt Rev James Tengatenga, Charge at Enthronement, 10.5.1998.

at the Anglican Church in Malawi in the light of Henry Venn's three *selfs* and judged it to be self-governing (he was the third Bishop of Southern Malawi since the missionaries), not as self-sustaining as it could and should be, and lazy about being self-propagating, which he put down to the 'comity agreements' of the past.[32]

Bishop James announced the public, prophetic aspect of his work and firmly closed the door on any return to the churches' role in the Banda era in the part of his charge addressed 'To our Politicians with Love':

> We will support the government when it does good but we will not hold our peace when it does wrong. It is our calling in Christ to mirror the will of God to the world and especially to this our mother land. We will not sit quietly when injustice and the gravy train get the better of our politicians whatever their political shade or persuasion. Never again will we obey the state when it tells us that the church's role is to pray and bless the status quo.

He called for a new partnership between clergy and laity that would transcend buck-passing or power seeking, and called for a fresh commitment: "The clergy are called not to poverty but to ministry and so are the laity."[33]

The diocese inherited by Bishop James was by African standards not large in extent, but it was densely populated. The growth of the church and the creation of new parishes had continued during the convulsions of the Aipa affair – a salutary reminder where the real work of the diocese was going on! So, after four years, with the approval of the Province, Bishop James resolved to split the diocese.

Redefining the Partnership and Broadening the Scope

Consultation visits from Birmingham to Malawi had begun in 1993 and continued biennially through the 1990s and 2000s, most of them taking place in Malawi. The Birmingham team in 1994 included Archdeacon

---

[32] See ch. 2 above, pp. 32 and 35.

[33] Rt Rev James Tengatenga, Charge at Enthronement, 10.5.1998.

John Cooper, who had many years' experience, and Joanna Hunt and Rev David Lee, both newcomers to Malawi but former CMS missionaries in Africa. Both would be looking after the Link into the new millennium and David Lee as Director of Mission was a frequent visitor until 2003. The Malawian team was led by Bishops Nyanja and Aipa.

With the stabilizing of the political situation, the consultations from 1994 onward "inevitably had to address the practical and pedestrian specifics of the link."[34] These included the pursuit of transparency and accountability in the use of funds, and the need to make the Malawian church more self-sustaining through income generating projects [IGPs].

Partnership projects at this time included:

Providing lorries to dioceses for transporting goods and clergy;

Buying residential properties in Lilongwe for rental - a reliable source of income for the Anglican Council in Malawi [ACM];

A Project Development Officer from the UK, asked for by ACM to help with grant applications and bring in more funding from overseas. Geoffrey Stone, an accountant, was appointed jointly by Birmingham, USPG and ACM in 1996.[35] In the event, his work was more in the area of accounts and financial management. He was reporting on visits to dioceses and institutions in Malawi during 1997;

Malawian church music: the Director of Music at St Martin's in the Bull Ring and his family went to Malawi in 1995 to record and research Malawian church music. The result was the audio tape *'Tiyimbe!'* and an accompanying booklet of music, some of which found its way into the repertoire of churches in Birmingham;

Youth exchanges – see the next section;

---

[34] Ven. John Cooper, Report of the Consultation Visit, 31 July-12 August 1994, 21.9.1994.

[35] David Lee, Anglican Consultation in Malawi, 17.8.96, draft record, n.d.

Theological training: the Bishop Josiah Trust was set up to provide small grants for Malawian church leaders to train within Africa. Lay training was recognized as a need but little was agreed.

An 'Agreed Statement' on the Link produced in 1996 gives a good idea of perceived priorities at the time. This recognized that "When the link began, the monetary benefits for the Church in Malawi were the principal expression of the link. In recent years, the link has developed a more holistic understanding of … our relationship in Christ …" The link activities were identified as: prayer for one another; exchange visits in both directions at diocesan, ACM and parish levels, including clergy and laity, old and young; and financial support. Oddly, there was no mention of project support. Parishes were encouraged to "explore specific links with particular activities at the grassroots level", an anticipation of the parish link programme set up from 2000 on. The final category was training and education, envisaging training courses for Malawians in Birmingham and Malawi and longer stays to work in one another's country.[36]

In May 1998 the centre of Birmingham saw one of its biggest demonstrations ever. Some 70,000 people[37] from the UK and worldwide joined hands to form a human chain around the G8 Summit due to take place there. Organized by the Jubilee 2000 movement and drawing inspiration from Biblical ideas of debt remission, this was the most public demonstration yet calling for the G8 Nations to 'break the chains of debt'.[38] These chains had been forged over the years since the oil crisis of 1973, when large quantities of funds were looking for borrowers. Many millions of dollars were lent to developing nations, some for vanity projects, regardless of whether the borrowing nations

---

[36] Birmingham-Malawi Link – proposed Agreed Statement describing the Link between the Anglican Church in Birmingham and Malawi, n.d. but after August 1996.

[37] Including the author and about 20 members of my church in Sutton Coldfield.

[38] Jubilee 2000 Coalition, 26.5.1998.

had any prospect of being able to repay. A petition was handed to Clare Short, a Birmingham MP and Secretary of State for International Development.

Just before the demonstration Bishop Santer had written to the World Bank asking for the inclusion of Malawi on the Highly Indebted Poor Countries [HIPC] list, which would lead to some debt remission. He expressed support for the Jubilee 2000 campaign and added: "As one who lives and ministers in the West, I am convinced that we have a moral and spiritual responsibility towards countries whose economic history and sometimes their own economic mismanagement have led them to their present grave situation." The reply showed that the World Bank was looking carefully at Malawi's inclusion on the HIPC list, which came about shortly afterwards.[39] The results of the campaign on the political front came gradually. The G8 Summit in Gleneagles, Scotland in 2005 was the high-water mark of the multi-pronged campaign to 'Make Poverty History'.

In 2000 Bishop Santer visited Malawi leading a group of ten from Birmingham, the first such group visit since 1991 and his 'farewell visit' to Malawi. The group included four people who had worked in Africa for a number of years and five for whom it was a first taste of Africa, including Mary Edwards, Diocesan Director of Education, and Erica Parker, the MU representative. The two week visit included the three dioceses and the British High Commission. Birmingham played an advocacy role with the UK Department for International Development [DfID]. DfID's focus in education in Malawi since 1994 had been on the lower years of primary school. Birmingham argued for a corresponding expansion of secondary education, and a meeting was arranged early in 2001 with Clare Short, MP. There is no evidence that government policy was changed, but the seriousness of the effort, set alongside the approach in 1998 to the World Bank, says much about the depth of commitment to the Link in Birmingham and by Bishop Mark.

---

[39] Letter from Rt Rev M. Santer to J.D. Wolfensohn, President, The World. Bank, 15.4.1998; reply from A. von Trotsenburg, The World Bank, 12.5.1998.

Youth Exchanges

The first party of young people from Birmingham had gone to Malawi in 1981 under the leadership of Julie Wills, the diocesan youth officer;[40] they helped build a priest's house. A regular programme of youth exchanges began in 1996, and their results fully justify the careful and time-consuming preparation that went into them in Birmingham and Malawi. In August 1996 a group went to Northern Diocese and Lake Diocese. The group of 12, largely young women, was led by Joanna Hunt and Paula Hollingsworth. Paula, who had spent two years in Uganda with CMS, saw it as her role to "make people think." She reflected on the group's more intense experience of nature and their new insights into scripture. "The programme is planned by people in Malawi, because it's their country, they know what they want to show us ... Very often, as a visitor to Africa, you're quite out of control but that makes you realize how important in Britain the issue of autonomy and control is. We always control, we make decisions and that doesn't happen to you in Africa."[41] Comments from the group included: "Churches were always full to bursting, worship was lively and impassioned" and "The overwhelming generosity and kindness is a lasting memory."[42]

Group members raised a considerable sum towards the cost of a return visit from the same two dioceses; a sponsored visit to every church in the diocese raised £7000. A group of 12 led by the DLM Youth Coordinator Fr Francis Kaulanda supported by Henry Mankhokwe from DNM came to Birmingham for three weeks over Easter 1998 and was hosted by 16 different parishes. So "several thousand people, if you include those who were in the churches where they were on Sundays, would have been part of their visit." Two comments from the visitors were: "We have learnt to appreciate our gifts because we have seen them appreciated here" and "I have learnt that we are the body of

---

[40] Jenkins, *In Touch with the Warm Heart of Africa, 1966-96*, c.1998, p. 9.

[41] Rev Paula Hollingsworth, interview with Bob Jenkins, 25.9.1998.

[42] Jo Hunt, *Birmingham-Malawi Youth Exchange*, n.d.

Christ despite all our differences."[43] Twenty years on, then-Bishop Francis recalled minor cultural misunderstandings. An English soup and bread meal was a surprise to the young people: "When is the real meal?" Giving cards as gifts was new to the Malawians. Francis himself needed clothes instead! A family allowed him to choose from their large surplus stock.[44] Rev Stephen Mayes, who co-hosted the visit, described it as "a wonderful time – totally exhausting" and commented on the amazing singing of this group who had not met each other before: "… one would have thought they were a fully-trained, well-rehearsed choir, they had an enormous repertoire of songs which they just switched on at the drop of a hat."[45]

Visits to and from Southern Malawi were arranged once stable leadership there was restored. In August 1999 a group of 13 from Birmingham visited for a month, seeing all five archdeaconries. The group included Rachel Jepson, later a lay member of General Synod for Birmingham. In April 2001 a highly successful return visit took place, led by the DSM Youth Chaplain, Fr Eston Pembamoyo, and co-led by Oscar Mponda and Irene Msini. The Birmingham organizers were Rev Stephen Mayes and Jo Hunt. All the visitors were in their 20s or 30s and most were already working. After four days' orientation they stayed about a week with volunteer hosts in parishes in the south and north of the diocese. As in 1998, the visit included a trip to London; in this case, also a very chilly seaside visit to Hunstanton in Norfolk. Particularly memorable for the Birmingham hosts was a Malawian meal at St Paul's, Balsall Heath prepared and served by the visitors to about 40 'guests'.

With Fr Eston's help I have been able to trace the influence of the visit on some group members' lives and careers. Mercy Likonje returned to the UK; she is married to a Scot and living in Scotland. Peter Makawa planned to become a car mechanic, but his lively personality and musical gifts led him to raise his ambitions. One of his host churches was

---

[43] Ibid.

[44] Rt Rev Francis Kaulanda, interview, 14.6.2018.

[45] Rev Stephen Mayes, interview with Bob Jenkins, 1.6.1998.

St Columba's, Sutton Coldfield, where I was vicar. Church members helped fund Peter through a course at the college of journalism, and at the time of writing he was a successful broadcaster based in Mzuzu.[46]

A further young people's group from Southern Malawi led by Josie Tengatenga visited Birmingham in 2003. A different form of youth exchange was the 2005 visit to Birmingham of Ndirande Anglican Voices, a choir largely of young adult members of St John's Church in Ndirande, a shanty town suburb of Blantyre.[47]

---

[46] Conversation with Fr Eston Pembamoyo, 07.2018, and author's personal records.

[47] The story of the trip is in ch. 10.

Chapter 7

Bishop Christopher Boyle and the beginnings of the Diocese of Northern Malawi

Picture the scene: a visitor from Birmingham and the Bishop of Northern Malawi are drinking a sundowner gin and tonic together - a moment of relaxation after a demanding day visiting parishes and outstations over dirt roads, dusty in the dry season and muddy in the rains. The bishop, Englishman Christopher Boyle, has just said Evening Prayer with his visitor.[1] Such a post-colonial style of ministry should by rights not have worked in the 21st century – but it did!

Jackson Biggers, First Bishop, 1995-2000

The Diocese of Northern Malawi [DNM] was formed out of Lake Diocese in 1995. It covers the country's Northern Province, with the rapidly growing town of Mzuzu as its capital, and some of the most remote and impoverished rural areas in the country. It includes the historic centre of Malawian Anglicanism on Likoma Island.

Unusually for an African diocese at the turn of the 21st century, the first two bishops elected were white. The first was Jackson Biggers, who served 1995-2000. Fr Biggers was an American Episcopalian who had served in Malawi from 1965-69 as priest of St Peter's Church Lilongwe and then as chaplain to Bishop Mtekateka. He was in Malawi again from 1971-74; serving as Archdeacon of Lilongwe he organized the building of the suburban church of St Mary's, Biwi. He was expelled in 1974 as *persona non grata* for organizing a meeting defending the persecuted Jehovah's Witnesses. For 18 years before his consecration, he had been Rector of the high Anglo-Catholic Church of the Redeemer in Biloxi,

---

[1] Canons Peter Howell-Jones [interview, 16.8.2018] and Paul Wilson both have fond memories of such moments.

Mississippi.[2] Biggers was a staunch Catholic Anglican who preserved something of the UMCA outlook on ministry of earlier times. He regarded Likoma Island as the spiritual heart of the diocese[3] and began repairs to St Peter's Cathedral. He was a strong traditionalist and known as a stickler for 'doing liturgy right' in a way that, for some, could quench the Spirit.

> "Very little thought had been given to funding a diocese; there was no diocesan office or diocesan secretary; the clergy body was quite elderly. Bishop Jack had to launch it from scratch."[4] "There was almost no infrastructure; it took six months to get a telephone."[5]

Biggers was aware of his anomalous position as a white bishop leading an African diocese, but asked himself: "What could I do, in that unusual situation which a Malawian might not be able to do? Find funds abroad."[6] This he did very effectively, but with the result that the diocese came to be seen as an entity run by foreigners, with all the finance for its operation coming from outside.[7] With the low level of local incomes, Northern Diocese has remained financially dependent for all of its existence so far. In such a case, dependency syndrome is a constant danger, and it has been said that Bishop Biggers built it in from the outset.[8] He set up a companion link with the traditionalist Anglo-Catholic diocese of Fort Worth, Texas, which led to a flow of money and influence from that quarter and visits in both directions. The bishop

---

[2] A Brief Biography of the Bishop Elect, 4.6.1995; interview with Rt Rev Christopher Boyle, 30.5.2018; http://www.nmalawianglican.org/organization/dhistory.html/Brief History of Bishop Emeritus, [16.8.2019].

[3] Visit report by Canon David Lee, 1996.

[4] Interview with Rt Rev Christopher Boyle, 30.5.2018.

[5] Rt Rev Jack Biggers, correspondence with author, 18.7.2018.

[6] ibid.

[7] Conversation with Rt Rev Alinafe Kalemba, 18.6.2018.

[8] Ibid.

commented that the Diocese of Fort Worth "despite turmoil and divisions on the broader scale has remained a wonderful partner."[9]

In 1997 the bishop was "planning to build a modest HQ in the grounds of St Mark's Church at Mzuzu – bishop's house, meeting rooms, guesthouse and office."[10] These were built with the help of a Festina loan of £25,000 from USPG, to be repaid over ten years at £2500 a year. Birmingham agreed to pay this annually and deduct it from the money given to DNM by Birmingham.[11] The diocese purchased its first boat, the *Gabriel,* with help from Birmingham and Fort Worth.[12] During the interregnum after Biggers' departure, Bob Jenkins, just retired from a Birmingham parish, performed the last of his many great services to the Malawi Partnership by going to Mzuzu as Acting Diocesan Secretary.

Christopher Boyle: Earlier Life and Ministry, Election as Bishop

One of Birmingham's great gifts to the Malawi Partnership was the priest who became the second Bishop of Northern Malawi and counts as Birmingham's last missionary to Malawi. Christopher Boyle was born in Birmingham in 1951 and was drawn through music into the life of the church at St Gabriel, Weoley Castle. Under the influence of "seeing the gospel lived" in the life of the then vicar, Martyn Collins, he "began a journey towards ordination – it felt a very quick one. Once the decision was made, every door seemed flung open."[13] He read theology at Kings College London and prepared for ordination at St Augustine's Canterbury. He served as curate at Emmanuel, Wylde Green with Canon Henry Burgess.

---

[9] Rt Rev Jack Biggers, correspondence with author, 18.7.2018.

[10] *Nkhani Zaulere,* ed. Rt Rev Donald. Arden, May 1997.

[11] Letter from Canon David Lee to Rt Rev Jack Biggers, 30.7.2000.

[12] Rt Rev Jack Biggers, *Notes from Northern Malawi,* Fall 1997.

[13] Interview with Rt Rev Christopher Boyle, 30.5.2018.

"I was aware of the Malawi/Birmingham Link from day one of my ordination in 1976. I prayed on the first evening of every month for the church in Malawi and the Birmingham Link. Canon Henry Burgess ... had an acute, enduring awareness and commitment to the church overseas. He had been instrumental in founding the Friends of Malawi. It was in Wylde Green Church that I first met and spoke with Archbishop Donald Arden in the late 1970s ... My own awareness, knowledge and commitment were strengthened greatly from the 1980s when I went to be Bishop Hugh Montefiore's chaplain [1980-83]. The visits of Bishop Hugh and Bishop Mark Green, when he was Bishop of Aston, to Malawi were significant and I had involvement in their preparation. I had previously heard Bishop Laurence Brown talk eloquently and passionately about his visit to Malawi. Sustained and committed leadership from the Bishops energized and gave visibility to the Link."[14]

Christopher became Rector of the busy parish of St Mary and St Margaret, Castle Bromwich in 1983. For two months in July-August 1988 he was Acting Dean of St Paul's Cathedral, Blantyre. The experience was "life-changing, life-enriching, life-giving ... invigorating, refocusing. It was very refreshing to be just a priest, pastor and compassionate listener."[15] An interview at the time captures the impact:

"One ought to talk about the people first. Their sense of warmth, their sense of gaiety – I've never seen people that seemed to smile so spontaneously ... smile first, speak first, forgive first ..." He commented on the church: "The vitality of the place, the vitality of the faith. Even if they lack some of the finesse ... in terms of organization ... the music, which I found electrifying, all sung unaccompanied in the Chichewa Mass."[16]

Every aspect of Christopher's ministry since ordination seemed to have helped make him 'ready, willing and able' when invited to be a candidate for bishop in Malawi. As a bachelor, like his predecessor, he

---

[14] Written answer to survey sent by the author, 17.4.2018.

[15] Interview with Rt Rev Christopher Boyle, 30.5.2018.

[16] Fr Christopher Boyle interviewed by Canon Bob Jenkins, 12.9.1988.

was ready to take on the hardships and inconveniences of leading a new diocese. "It seemed that following rapid attempts at Africanization from the 1960s to 1990s a deficit of leadership emerged: lack of education, a 'brain-drain' from Malawi and deaths through HIV/AIDS. Hence it seemed [in 2000 there was] a need to import leadership."[17]

DNM was then the country's smallest and poorest diocese, comprising just 14 parishes. It was clear that the new bishop would need a support package. He was recognized by USPG as a missionary bishop and 'The Friends of Bishop Christopher' was formed to enable well-wishers in Birmingham to contribute regularly towards his stipend. The bishop produced a series of Newsletters for supporters every few months during his time as bishop, and his candour in sharing joys, sorrows and challenges makes them a precious resource. He was consecrated in April 2001, with Birmingham represented by John Austin, Bishop of Aston and Bishop Montefiore as preacher. He returned to the United College of the Ascension in Birmingham to prepare himself for his task, before being enthroned in August.[18]

This chapter covers Bishop Christopher's ministry in some detail. But in many areas experience in DNM would be typical of that in Malawi as a whole during this decade. These include: the HIV/AIDS pandemic; the famine of 2002; the church's provision for health and education; and issues around poverty, hunger and disease.

Famine Relief, 2002

Within a few months of Bishop Christopher's arrival, an urgent priority beckoned: famine. Priests came to him complaining of hunger. In February 2002, Fr Fanuel Magangani [later to succeed Christopher as bishop] asked him to go to the Karonga district, in the north, after

---

[17] Written answer to survey sent by the author, 17.4.2018.

[18] Rt Rev Christopher Boyle, Newsletter to The Friends of the Diocese of Northern Malawi, 2001.

flooding there had destroyed the crops. He visited a Teacher Development Centre in Chilumba:

"The place was crammed with local leadership, traditional leaders. One man said: 'Bishop, the people in my village have not eaten for three weeks. What are you going to do?' I promised to leave no stone unturned to get food for the community. I decided to release some stipend money to buy maize and fuel for the diocesan blue lorry to go to Karonga with food for the villagers."[19]

For the next six months the diocese mounted a sustained, systematic relief campaign. The Bishop had daily meetings with the diocesan relief team.

The underlying causes of the famine included widespread soil erosion, "declining soil fertility and restricted access to agricultural inputs during the 1990s; deepening poverty which eradicated asset buffers that the poor could exchange for food to bridge food gaps; the erosion of social capital and informal support systems in poor communities; the demographic and economic consequences of HIV/AIDS; and the relative neglect of the smallholder agriculture sector."[20]

But there were also trigger factors: a combination of bad luck and inadequate policies. After two years of good harvest, localized floods reduced the 2000/01 maize harvest and left a shortfall which reached 600,000 tonnes. However, there was "misplaced complacency. Donors failed to react to signals of an impending food crisis, [and] the Strategic Grain Reserve [SGR] was sold … The decision to sell the SGR followed advice from the IMF to reduce the level of buffer stocks from 165,000 to 60,000 tonnes. Instead, almost all of the reserve was sold, much of it on local markets, against IMF advice to export it …" There were also

---

[19] Interview with Rt Rev Christopher Boyle, 30.5.2018.

[20] *Death by Starvation in Malawi: the link between macro-economic and structural policies and the agricultural disaster in Malawi*, 13.6.02; and *State of Disaster: Causes, Consequences and Policy Lessons from Malawi*; both Action Aid, London, Lilongwe, and Washington DC, June 2002.

"suspicions of corrupt practice around the SGR sale."[21] In the face of a 'blame game' between the Malawi Government and the IMF and vacillation on the part of the big donors, it fell to churches and NGOs to bridge the gap. Alongside Birmingham, other donors including the Diocese of Fort Worth responded promptly and generously.

It quickly became apparent that this was a national [indeed, an African regional] emergency. After denying a famine, the government belatedly declared a State of National Disaster on 6 March 2002. On 17 March Bishop Christopher was called by the BBC journalist Ed Stourton and spoke on the Radio 4 Sunday programme about the crisis. He and his fellow bishops turned to Birmingham. With the help of Arun Arora, Diocesan Communications Officer, a Malawi Famine Appeal entitled 'A £5IVER FOR LIFE' was launched on 20 March. This was initially to be an Easter appeal lasting until Pentecost, but was later extended to October: see the famine appeal notice printed on the page after next. The Birmingham Evening Mail agreed to run a joint campaign with the Diocese of Birmingham. Bishop Christopher appealed for urgent relief rather than recriminations: "*'For God's sake help us to save these people,'* implores the Rt Rev Christopher Boyle.[22] Under the headline "Every penny will buy food for the dying" David Lee assured donors that "We're using relationships that we've built up over 35 years, so we know the individuals who will be handling the money and the administration."[23]

Lee arranged for reporter Laura Marsh and photographer Loretta Brennan to visit Malawi at the end of March to see the relief effort at work. They were taken to Mtunthama in Kasungu (DLM) and accompanied Bishop Boyle on maize distribution trips to villages in DNM. The result was a series of heartrending pictures and headlines: "EASTER 2002 Despair in the eyes of a child"[24] "YOU'VE GIVEN US HOPE.

---

[21] Ibid.

[22] *Birmingham Evening Mail*, 21.3.2002.

[23] *Birmingham Evening Mail*, 22.3.2002.

[24] *Birmingham Evening Mail*, 30.3.2002.

Our arrival in the tiny outpost village of Mgoza signaled hope at last for 200 starving families in Africa's forgotten famine"[25] "Selling sex to survive"[26] "Hungry pupils miss out on school"[27] "Families too weak to bury victims."[28] Bishop Santer added: "Our 20,000 reasons to be hopeful", describing the first £20,000 raised as a sign of Easter hope.[29]

The appeal was a spectacular success and "attracted more support than anyone envisaged … between March and July … the dioceses in Malawi have not been able to use the funds at the rate at which we have received them, and so … we took the decision to transfer funds at the rate at which the church in Malawi can use them …"[30] Tranches of £5000 each were sent to dioceses as they were ready. By the end of October, the total raised exceeded £200,000; of this about two thirds came from parishes and one third from the Evening Mail/ public appeal.

David Lee visited Malawi in September 2002 and wrote a report on the famine and appeal.[31] He noted that the big players were involved by then. The UN World Food Programme [WFP] was building up its supply of food for distribution, in the light of evidence that hunger would continue to get worse until the 2003 harvest. A Disasters Emergency Committee Southern Africa Crisis Appeal had been set up. The UK government had contributed £25m. The churches may be said to have proved their effectiveness: their relief contribution, including Birmingham's, was modest but significant. "Although not relief agencies with the skills they bring, the churches are using their local knowledge to help people in the short term, whilst the major relief agencies draw

---

[25] Ibid, p. 2.

[26] Ibid, p. 3.

[27] Ibid.

[28] Ibid, 2.4.2002.

[29] Ibid, 1.4.2002, p. 11.

[30] Canon David Lee, *Making a Difference: The Malawi Famine and the Birmingham Appeal,* 30.9.2002, p. 2.

[31] Ibid.

A £5IVER FOR LIFE
Diocese of Birmingham
Malawi Famine Appeal

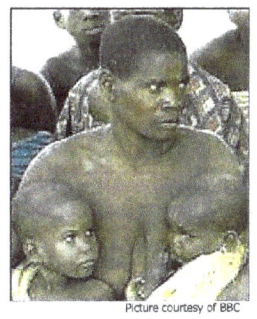

Picture courtesy of BBC

"People in some villages are crying - they haven't eaten for 21 days. Everywhere the response is the same. There is no food".

On the 6th March 2002, the President of Malawi declared a national disaster following the worst famine to have hit the country in over 50 years.

Food is available, but only at inflated prices, beyond the means of most people. The Aid Agencies are putting measures in place to help Malawi, but meanwhile, people are dying of hunger.

£5 will buy a child food for a month. Please give a fiver this Easter….
and save a life

E-mail from Bishop Christopher Boyle, Diocese of Northern Malawi (11 March 2002)
"The number affected is 70% of the population. Many people are feeding on wild roots which make them sick and some die. The food is critically short and lives are threatened, particularly the vulnerable: the very young, the elderly and the sick".

E-mail from Bishop Peter Nyanja, Diocese of Lake Malawi (12 March 2002):
"Please treat this as a matter of emergency. Things are getting out of hand everyday in this country. There is no food. The latest reports from parishes are that the number of people dying is at an increase."

Interview with Bishop James Tengatenga, Diocese of Southern Malawi (14th March 2002)
"I learned of a mother in Kasungu with no food left who tried to sell her children for £5 to whoever could look after them. Yet, £20 will feed a family of 4 for a month".

All funds will be spent in Malawi to help local people.
Please make Cheques and Gift Aid payable to :
"Malawi Famine Appeal"
175, Harborne Park Road, Harborne, Birmingham B17 0BH

up plans and begin their relief work. I am very glad to say that in every part of the country I met people who have been helped by the Birmingham Appeal, and some who would not be alive today without it."[32]

Southern Diocese had been split during the year, and each of the four dioceses tackled the problems differently.

> "The Diocese of Northern Malawi has created a Relief Committee chaired by the Bishop which carefully researches the need in an area, working with parish committees which include local leaders, whether church goers or not. The Diocese has drawn £35,000, and used all of it and also extra funding from other sources [including the British government]. The Diocese has adopted a twin track approach to the problem. Relief is provided by the free distribution of maize in 50Kg sacks. 200,000 Kg of maize has been given out, accompanied by 9000Kg of vitamin-enriched flour [Likuni phala] for mothers and children. Relief has been given to 5 prisons and those caring for orphans."[33]

In Lake Diocese, Bishop Nyanja witnessed the dissolution of social ties:

> "loss of life in many areas of the country, broken homes whereby husbands have left home leaving their wives and children or vice versa. Children have been damped [sic] at the door of the church ... Many cases of theft which has led to loss of limbs or entire life." The thefts included sugar cane and maize from the bishop's own garden. He also appealed to outsiders not to come up with good advice: "... your immediate reaction is to hurry in making some suggestions for us in both long or short term. Kindly, do not pick a blame on us when some of your suggestions can not apply to the situation we are facing. Experience is the best teacher."[34]

---

[32] Canon David Lee, *Making a Difference: The Malawi Famine and the Birmingham Appeal,* 30.9.2002, p. 5.

[33] Ibid.

[34] Rt Rev Peter Nyanja, *Malawi's Food Crisis 2002,* Open Letter to 'Sisters and Brothers in the Lord', 6.9.2002.

The diocese was setting up feeding centres in every archdeaconry and had drawn £20,000 for the purchase of maize.

Upper Shire was without a bishop but had an energetic administration. David Lee visited "a remote region of central Malawi [where] two things struck [him]: the people there were predominantly Muslim, and the distribution was arranged by the District Commissioner and the local MP. Both the commitment to the needy, of whatever faith, and ... the cooperation with the local administration are encouraging glimpses of the future."[35] The diocese had drawn £25,000 for famine relief and planned further substantial deliveries in the autumn of 2002. The newly-formed Diocese of Southern Malawi [based in Blantyre] had just received a first grant of £5000 and "used it to purchase 500 starter packs and 100 bags of vitamin-enriched flour."[36]

Lee was concerned to ensure that funds were being properly used and accounted for, and was reassured to find that accounting was incomplete and there was no sign of misuse of funds. His visit left him with "three abiding impressions. First, the sobering recognition of the vast scale and complexity of the situation, which will require years to achieve significant change. A fresh admiration for those who are working very hard to make a difference. [And] thankfulness and joy when meeting people who have been helped – and are here today, in better shape, to tell their stories."[37]

The 2002 famine relief campaign was in my view one of the Partnership's finest hours. Malawi's rain-fed agriculture makes it increasingly vulnerable to the effects of extreme weather driven by climate change. Poor harvests in other years, including 2005 and 2014, have led to hunger and other appeals for help. However, the country has never again been quite as unprepared as in 2002.

---

[35] Canon David Lee, *Making a Difference: The Malawi Famine and the Birmingham Appeal,* 30.9.2002, pp. 6-7.

[36] Ibid, p. 7.

[37] Ibid, pp. 7-8.

Bishop Christopher's Priorities

Bishop Christopher identified four priority areas on his arrival: how he tackled them can be traced from reports in his Newsletters.

HIV/AIDS

See chapter 6 above for a discussion of the struggle against AIDS in DNM and the other dioceses.

Education in schools

An educated population is healthier, has smaller families, is more economically productive, and takes a better part in the democratic process. Christopher prioritized education by appointing education secretaries, despite the diocese's small size and meagre resources: Elizabeth Crossley, an Englishwoman supported by USPG, until 2004, and Willy Musukwa from 2005. "Diocesan work in education is vital to Malawi and its future. The education system is creaking under the pressure of numbers, lack of resources, and seeking to deliver the curriculum with many untrained teachers who are themselves just out of high school." The secondary school certificate [MCSE] pass rate in 2005 was a miserable 18%. "The Diocese has an important role in helping to maintain standards; ensuring high professional and personal expectations of the staff; and providing realistic and sustainable in-service training."[38] The first of the teachers' skills share visits from Birmingham in 2006[39] majored on DNM and was prompted by this felt need.

More was needed: teaching posts in rural Malawi were and are unpopular, and the Bishop tried to pay financial incentives. New schools were opened, including two day secondary schools in Karonga District. Schools in rural Malawi often start with simple classrooms made of mud and sticks with grass roofs. When the Bishop visited a parish they would show him what they were doing and schools were

---

[38] The Friends of Bishop Christopher Newsletter no. 4, April 2002.

[39] See chapter 10.

helped to develop. Among these was the primary school at Msomba, near Chintheche, on the lake shore. Under Bishops Christopher and Fanuel this hosted many visitors from Birmingham who were treated to memorable open-air assemblies with dancing and drama. The kitchen project for giving breakfast to children there was supported by Liz and Jim Carr and their church in Boldmere. Msomba was chosen as the location for the classroom block funded by Birmingham for the Partnership's 50th anniversary in 2016. It was a priority to train school committees and PTAs in their role, so they were involved and contributed. Willy Musukwa much appreciated that before he left, the Bishop and he visited every church involved with a school in the diocese, even those that could be reached only on foot.[40]

Parish Visitations

Parishes in Malawi are large, covering extensive rural areas and with anything up to 20 outstations led by visiting catechists. Numbers preparing for confirmation are also large – over 100 is quite common – unlike the situation in the UK where parishes and candidate numbers are far smaller. This means that confirmation visits, usually combined with talks with local church leaders, are an essential part of a bishop's ministry as well as a key moment in the life of a parish. On occasion Christopher extended these visits for up to 10 days, also meeting leaders of other churches, traditional leaders, and NGO and government officials. Thus, he became more aware of gifts and weaknesses in church and community. In January 2003 he reported:

> "Last month on Likoma Island, while I was spending 10 days there, we had a hugely challenging time. I was visiting the Cathedral with a team of two priests and the Diocesan Youth Officer in order to take an in depth look at the life and ministry of the Cathedral. It was a good opportunity to spend time with people in their villages and hear of their

---

[40] Interview with Willy Musukwa, 21.6.2018.

concerns and needs. I visited every village and every institution served by the Cathedral."[41]

The challenges arose from the sudden deaths on the island of both a young clergy wife and her mother, a sad but not uncommon event at a time when the population was weakened by hunger and HIV/AIDS. The parishes were encouraged by visits and Christopher was nourished, even when the travel was "brain scrambling and gut wrenching."[42] This account captures the characteristic Malawian balance of High Church solemnity and exuberance:

"The vitality and vibrancy of the Church in Malawi is marvelous, as I saw in… St Joseph's, Chintheche, where we had a diocesan youth event. Over 200 young people came together for a solemn pontifical mass – all with drums, dancing and Alleluias to the right and to the left."[43]

The bishop also visited seven prisons in the north where he wanted to get chaplains, taking in soap, mangoes, blankets and learning materials.

Building up Clergy Numbers

The clergy body on Christopher's arrival needed rejuvenating, and his newsletters mention ordinations of priests and deacons year by year. He stated on departure that "For me theological education and training to equip clergy laypeople and future church leaders has been a priority … If we are to enable the Church … to be the body of Christ we need well motivated, well trained and well- disciplined clergy"[44] - who had a regular stipend, proper training and decent housing.

In the light of the traumatic experience of famine in 2002, a fifth priority was added - **food security.** The Bishop obtained grants from the British High Commission and [US] Episcopal Relief & Development, and in autumn 2002 he purchased two hectares of land off the Mzuzu - Nkhata

---

[41] The Friends of Bishop Christopher Newsletter no. 6, January 2003.

[42] Ibid.

[43] Ibid.

[44] The Friends of Bishop Christopher, Farewell Newsletter, October 2009.

Bay road for an innovative 'demonstration garden.' The vision was to help people develop their farming skills by modelling better farming techniques including creating strong ridges across the contour strengthened with a deep rooted grass to control soil erosion, using compost and agro-forestry to improve soil fertility naturally and practicing crop rotation and diversity. "We cannot continue simply to give people handouts. They need to be able to feed themselves and, by means of the model garden, to be shown how exhausted and depleted soil can be reclaimed with good farming practices."[45]

The garden became a kind of lay training centre: the Bishop reported that: "Chiwowa Chisala, the demonstration garden … came into its own this year [2004]. A dedicated staff … have worked diligently throughout the year ensuring that groups of 16 people from all 20 parishes in the diocese, from all denominations and none, attended a week's course at the garden that included improved techniques for farming, nutrition and hygiene, and HIV/AIDS."[46] The garden welcomed many visitors from Birmingham including Bishops John Sentamu and David Urquhart and Andrew Watson, as Bishop of Aston; it features in the 50th anniversary DVD 'Matilda's Malawi'. Regrettably it has now closed due to withdrawal of external funding.

Another diocesan priority area which emerged was **Projects**.

"The Project Office [oversaw] the building of roads, bridges, churches, clergy houses; school blocks including a science lab, library and head teacher's office, house and admin block at Tirola; pit latrines, boreholes – the latter transforming the lives of women whose job it was to fetch water … extensive building work at Chiwowa Chisala … and the provision of safe, reliable transport on road and lake."[47] "These were typically

---

[45] The Friends of Bishop Christopher Newsletter no. 5, October 2002.

[46] The Friends of Bishop Christopher Newsletters nos. 11, February 2005 and 12, June 2005.

[47] Rt Rev Christopher Boyle, correspondence, 19.9.2018.

financed from outside, with a 25% contribution from the local community, usually in the form of sand and fired bricks."[48]

Openness to the World

Short term visitors from overseas have long been a feature of the life of the Malawian Church. In the Partnership's early years these were largely bishops and priests; lay visitor numbers increased with easier air travel and after 1994, an improved security situation. Visitors from Birmingham multiplied during Christopher's time.

> "From the start I was receiving regular visits from a host of contacts in Birmingham. These were of great value. Bishops Hugh [Montefiore], John Austin, Sentamu plus party, David, the Rev Dr Anne Bayley. It seemed from May 2002 there was not a month without visitors. They gave Birmingham a window into our lives and gave us in Malawi a window into the life of Birmingham and the wider church of which we are a part.

> "This grew, developed and was life changing. Importantly it helped to complete for us the picture of Christ. Those who came had their lives changed … Malawi and Malawians were enabled to extend the gifts of hospitality and generosity for which they are renowned – the 'Warm Heart of Africa.' It is born out of *'ubuntu'* and offered the experience of it."[49]

Many have commented on the transformative effect of visiting Malawi, and I would confirm this for myself. My initial personal visit on a Sabbatical in 2007 led to a deep commitment to Malawi that continues to this day. Claire Campbell-Smith visited DNM for seven weeks in 2006 to research an MA dissertation on 'Partnership as a Paradigm of Mission in Northern Malawi'. During this time a group from a Birmingham parish

---

[48] Interview with Rt Rev Christopher Boyle, 30.5.2018.

[49] Rt Rev Christopher Boyle, reply to survey from author, April 2018. Ubuntu is described as 'I am because you are' – a person is a person through other persons. See: What is Ubuntu? Reverend Mpho Tutu, YouTube [24.7.2018].

visited the diocese in July and a teachers' skills share team led workshops there in August.[50]

Discussing the effect of visits from overseas in terms of giving and receiving, Campbell-Smith reported:

> "Several Birmingham participants emphasized giving in human resource, through programmes like Skills Share or clergy lecturing at Malawi's theological college... In Malawi, several participants referred to insights and skills received which in turn, benefit the church.
>
> "Many Birmingham participants referred to prayer, while more than one felt the most important thing Birmingham gives is solidarity and affirmation, so that the Malawian church knows that 'outside the muddle and struggle of keeping going, there's somebody there who's really *for* us'."[51]

Those in Northern Malawi strongly emphasized giving in relational and spiritual terms. Respondents stressed the power of prayer and the value of the friendship, fellowship, encouragement, understanding and challenge brought by visitors to Malawi or taken on exchange visits to Birmingham, together with an embodied awareness of the wider church.

> "A frequent emphasis was that Malawians' joy in worship encourages and strengthens people from Birmingham. Their faith and resilience in the midst of desperate circumstances and their sense of community give people a new perspective, helping them to 'grow in faith'. For those who visit Malawi, seeing such poverty can be life-changing, challenging their norms and values. Malawi thus gives Birmingham the opportunity to serve, to 'meet some of the needs of the world'. As giving is a gospel imperative, 'We are making

---

[50] Claire Campbell-Smith, 'Partnership as a Paradigm of Mission in Northern Malawi', unpublished University of Manchester MA dissertation, 2007, p. 76. The teachers' skills share programme is described in ch. 10.

[51] Ibid., p. 42

them better Christians. By giving us something, they are being blessed'. This turns a one-way flow of resources into a two-way exchange.

"This was echoed by Birmingham participants who emphasized that, by visiting Malawi or encountering visitors from there, people are touched and challenged spiritually by 'the enthusiasm, the generosity, and the self-evidence of the spiritual and of God', are encouraged by contact with a church in which so many are still active, and receive real insights into the challenges people and the Church face in a different culture, plus an appreciation of their common humanity. More than one person referred to Birmingham receiving the opportunity to give, and also the gift of friendship which... cuts through any material inequality."[52]

Less visits are now being made in each direction. Bishop Alinafe Kalemba confirmed that Bishop Christopher wanted the Malawian church to be connected to the worldwide church. He helped Alinafe, as Dean of LKTC, to attend meetings abroad, funding his attendance at conferences in South Africa and Canterbury.[53]

Bishop Christopher as Colleague and as Person

Christopher balanced a natural caution with openness to ideas from colleagues in Birmingham or Malawi. He valued his staff colleagues highly and was much appreciated in return. He devoted one complete issue of the Newsletter to describing them and their activities in loving detail.[54] Bernard Mainga was recruited as Diocesan Secretary in 2005. He commented: "Working with Bishop Boyle was fantastic. No regrets. He was strategic, able to see issues in advance. He mentored me, made me who I am today. He'd encourage me to make a decision. Then if it

---

[52] Ibid, pp. 42-43.

[53] Rt Rev Alinafe Kalemba, interview, 18.6.2018.

[54] The Friends of Bishop Christopher Newsletter no. 9, April 2004.

was wrong, to learn from my mistakes."[55] Bernard was endlessly helpful in arranging visits and hospitality for many visitors from Birmingham including myself. Willy Musukwa was appointed Education Secretary, also in 2005: "It was very good working for Chris Boyle. He assisted me; I went to him for advice. When I made a good suggestion, he accepted it. One of the best people I have worked for."[56] Bishop Kalemba described Christopher as "a man of prayer, a man of meditation. He was a very good colleague, a spiritual father. You could go to him chaotic, but leave with a sense of peace and come back energized and inspired."[57]

Language and culture are deeply linked.

> "Missionary interest … in the vernaculars of societies beyond the West touched on the affected cultures in a very profound way. In most of these cultures, language is the intimate, articulate expression of culture, and so close are the two that language can be said to be commensurate with culture, which it suffuses and embodies … Societies that have been less broken up by technological change have a more integrated, holistic view of life, and language as complete cultural experience fits naturally into this worldview."[58]

The Bishop led all his services in Chichewa but preached only in English using an interpreter. I asked Willy and Bernard whether this was a drawback. "It was not a drawback that he never learned Chichewa. President Banda only spoke in English!"[59] "Speaking the language would have been an advantage. Roman Catholic priests undergo language training; this was not possible for Christopher."[60] The Bishop

---

[55] Bernard Mainga, interview, 22.6.2018.

[56] Willy Musukwa, interview, 21.6.2018.

[57] Rt Rev Alinafe Kalemba, interview, 18.6.2018.

[58] Lamin Sanneh, *Translating the Message: The Missionary Impact on Culture,* Maryknoll, NY: Orbis, 2nd ed., 2009, p. 3.

[59] Willy Musukwa, interview, 21.6.2018.

[60] Bernard Mainga, interview, 22.6.2018.

commented that: "I had lessons in Chichewa before I went and continued almost weekly during my whole time as bishop … While I was never fluent in Chichewa, I got to understand speeches after services … despite all the issues, not being able to speak the language was a drawback." He also pointed out that the diocese spent time and money translating the Anglican Eucharist into Chitumbuka, the most widely spoken local language in the Northern Region.[61]

Those in Birmingham were colleagues too:

> "[The partnership] had a significant effect on my ministry particularly through the support of David Lee, Peter Howell-Jones, Sally Hayden nee Bossingham … and the [Task Group] in general, all of whom were committed participants in the Link. With partners I was able to discuss issues, share concerns, shape my own thinking, and test our theories, policies and 'direction of travel.' Each side was a conduit and interpreter to the other, to ensure each was fully heard and respected – every voice mattered. It was a means for receipt of funds and emotional support."[62]

Christopher stepped down as Bishop of Northern Malawi in 2009 and returned to the UK to become Assistant Bishop in the Diocese of Leicester. That July he addressed Birmingham Diocesan Synod about his work in Malawi; the response fell only a little short of a standing ovation.[63]

Christopher reflected in a final newsletter:

> "Malawi has taught me more about what belonging means …. My time in Malawi has been a[n] experience where I have been retrained and remade. I have been stripped of all the things that we usually rely on in the West. Instead, I have been part of a culture that is not driven by 'intellectualizing' or problem solving or achieving but where 'being' is more important than 'having' or 'doing'. Poverty is a great leveller. I

---

[61] Rt Rev Christopher Boyle, in correspondence, 4.10.2018.

[62] Written answer to survey sent by the author, 17.4.2018.

[63] Minutes of Birmingham Diocesan Synod, 15.07.2009, DS.127.02, and author's recollection.

found a spirit of generosity among people with so little, and a huge sense of gratitude. Wherever I went, I received generous gifts and a warm welcome.

"I didn't go to Malawi with a prescribed agenda but to engage. I saw wonderful growth in myself. My prayer life has deepened and I have discovered fresh insights on listening and prayer. I was challenged to practice virtues I had previously felt were in short supply. I do believe I am now more patient. Northern Malawi will always remain in my heart."[64]

---

[64] The Friends of Bishop Christopher, Farewell Newsletter, October 2009.

Dr Susan Cole-King and Bishop Leonard Wilson in about 1960

L: Bishops Josiah Mtekateka and
Donald Arden.   R: Donald and Jane Arden in about 1980

Bishop Hugh Montefiore exchanging gifts with Malawian hosts in 1983

Bishops Peter Nyanja and Mark Santer on the visit to DLM in 1991

A Birmingham lorry is presented to DLM in the 1990s. Bishop Peter Nyanja is at centre, Archdeacon John Cooper and Canon David Lee to left and right of him.

Youth exchange 1999: Rachel Jepson tries her hand at brickmaking

Famine relief in 2002 in the Mzimba area of DNM. Sacks of maize and beans are distributed from the diocesan lorry to villagers, mostly women. Some of them have had to walk many miles without food or water.

Birmingham visitors in 2003. From left: Matthews Kumpolota, ACM, Canon Peter Howell-Jones, Michele Gilmore, Archbishop Bernard Malango, Bishop of Birmingham John Sentamu and his wife Margaret

Ndirande Anglican Voices sing and dance on their visit to Birmingham in 2005. Bishop Sentamu may be seen at back on right.

A motorbike for Malawi at Birmingham Cathedral, 2005. Bishop Sentamu [centre] is seen with Malawian Bishops Christopher, Bernard and James

The demonstration garden set up by Bishop Christopher Boyle in DNM

Mothers' Union members from South Lunzu parish, DSM, wear their uniforms with pride

Bishop David Urquhart accepts a gift from Agnes Mkoko. Looking on are Simon and Margaret Morgan, Mission Encounter group members who made return trips to serve the church in Malawi

Bishop Andrew Watson speaks to children at Msomba, DNM, in 2010

Franklin Mkamwera, deputy head of Msomba primary school, with Jackie Brocklebank and Judith Grubb in 2014

Liz and Jim Carr with Fr Francis Takilima and headteacher Chrispin Dakilira visiting Liwaladzi School, DLM, in 2011

A rural classroom with children using chairs and tables sent by container from Birmingham

A container loaded in Birmingham with the team: Jan, Judith, Laetitia, Brian, Richard and Julian

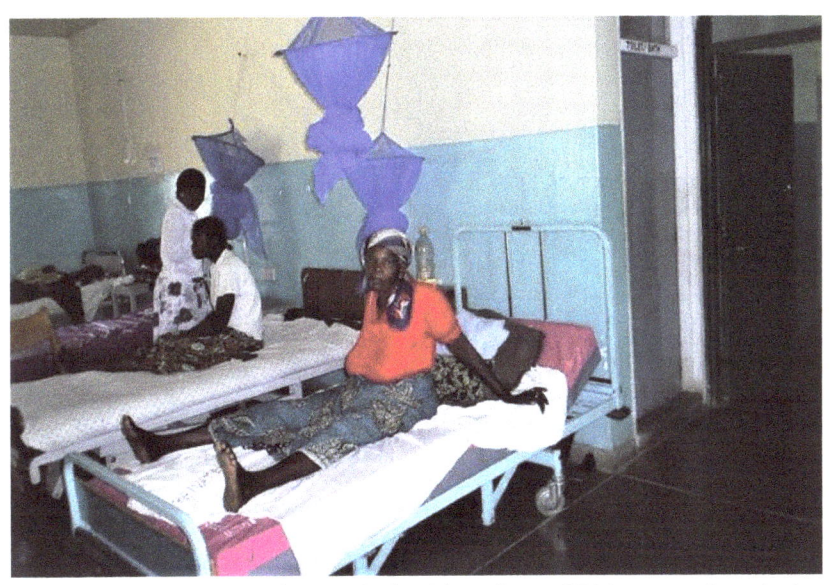

A patient at St Anne's Hospital, Nkhotakota, DLM, uses a hospital bed sent by container from Birmingham

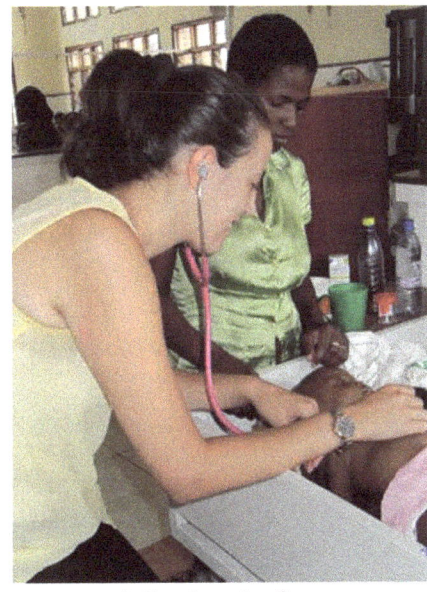

L: Dr Mandy Goldstein, BCH, with Agnes and Charity, the first two nurses to come to train there. R: Dr Sofia Omar, BCH, on the ward in QECH 2012

Matilda Chirwa at her home village of Mtunthama in 2014 with Bishop David. Birmingham's 50th anniversary video was based on her life

Bishop Alinafe Kalemba visiting Quinton Primary School in 2015

Malawian bishops' visit to Birmingham in 2016. From left: Bishops Maurice Sinclair, Brighton Malasa, Francis Kaulanda, David Urquhart, Fanuel Magangani and Alinafe Kalemba

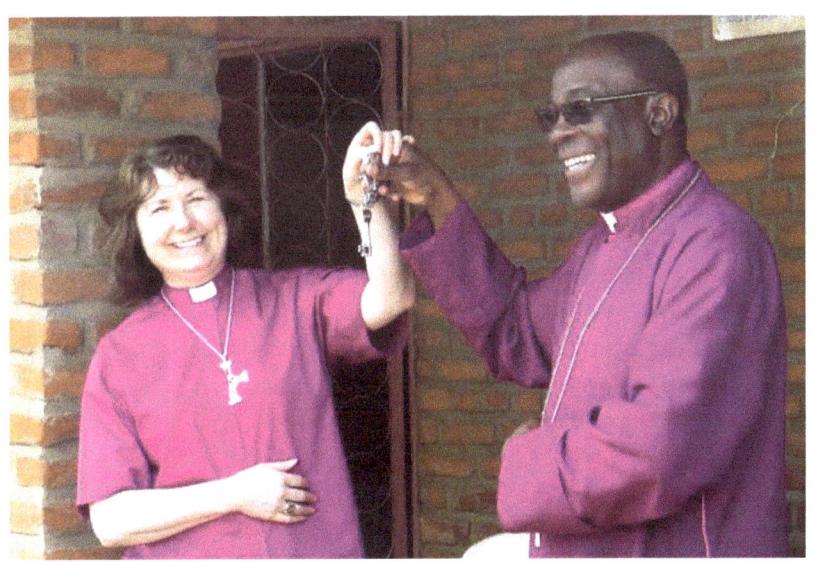

Dedication of the 50th anniversary classroom block at Ntchisi, DLM, 2017. Bishops Anne Hollinghurst, Aston, and Francis Kaulanda

Chapter 8

Women in Partnership

The Mothers' Union

Malawi has traditionally been a matriarchal society, particularly among the Chewa tribes of the central and southern regions, with roles in leadership and ritual reserved for women or girls: "When the Dutch Reformed Church came to Dowa District [in central Malawi] in 1892 the Chewa were a matriarchal society: a man lived with his wife's people and played a marginal role. He did not even own his own children or property." The coming of the Christian Church, especially in its Roman Catholic and Anglican forms with an exclusively male priesthood, shifted Malawian society in a patriarchal direction.[1] But in the 21st century, women are in a majority in the churches – as they are in the UK.

Belonging is of the essence of being for Malawians, indeed for Africans more generally.[2] Membership of the Mothers' [MU] is seen as a 'badge of belonging' for committed Anglican women. Unlike British MU members, those in Malawi have a uniform which they wear with pride. This acts as a leveller in society: it is striking to see a woman very senior in, say, commerce or the central bank don her blue and white MU uniform and be seen as the equal of every other member. Leadership in the MU is a channel for women with leadership or organizational skills. In many Malawian parishes, the MU is led by the priest's wife. This is not just out of respect for her position: many wives have had training in community development alongside their husbands in college. By extension, bishops' wives often play a prominent role in the diocesan

---

[1] Samson Kambalu, *The Jive Talker,* London: Jonathan Cape, 2008, p. 7. I am also grateful to Fr Eston Pembamoyo for this insight.

[2] See the discussion of 'ubuntu' in ch. 7 above.

MU. The St Agnes Guild functions as the junior wing of the MU in Malawi.

The MU's in Birmingham and Malawi had regular contact including prayer partnerships in the years before 2000. Janice Miller represented the MU on the group that went out with Bishop Santer in 1991. However, contact grew into active co-operation after Christopher Boyle was appointed Bishop of Northern Malawi in 2000. A diocesan link with Birmingham was quickly established and recognized by MU headquarters at Mary Sumner House, London. Alongside the centrally organized 'Wave of Prayer' for each other there has been much person-to-person contact and prayer. MU Presidents in Birmingham are expected to be involved in the Partnership; under the Terms of Reference of the Malawi Task Group proposed in 2018 the serving Diocesan President would be a member *ex-officio*. For a brief period in 2014-15 Claire Laland and her two successor presidents were all on the group. At the time of writing, the current president and two former presidents were once again group members.

Membership of the MU in the UK is open to men too, and one Bishop of Birmingham was inveigled into joining in 2005 when a Malawian group visited for the Birmingham diocesan centenary. Claire Laland tells the story:

> "At a party gifts were being given by Bishop Sentamu to the Malawian guests and in true African style Agnes [Mkoko] received her gift on her knees. I jokingly said 'Don't expect the Mothers' Union in Birmingham to follow this custom, Bishop'. Whereupon Bishop Sentamu replied, 'That's the problem, Claire. If you went down on your knees, I would join tomorrow'. I quickly went on my knees to much laughter and the next day sent him a form for diocesan membership. The following day it was announced he was to be the next Archbishop of York, but he assured me he would find space in his diary for me to enroll him and his wife, Margaret, before they left Birmingham. I eventually enrolled them

at their last service before leaving the diocese... I was on crutches having just come out of hospital after a knee replacement."[3]

The MU is one of the lead agencies for the Church and Community Mobilisation Process [CCMP], which has been changing the face of church-linked community development this century. It is described as "a complete transformational, community-based process which uses facilitator-led Bible studies to work with church groups to encourage them to initiate economic, social and physical transformation within their communities."[4] One such MU programme supported by the Birmingham MU is the Literacy and Financial Education Programme [LFEP].[5] This began in Northern Malawi in 2000 as the Literacy and Development Project and was then expanded across the whole country and to other African nations. Through facilitated Bible study and discussion participants begin to:

Tackle local issues such as domestic violence and harmful traditional practices

Raise awareness of health issues and participate in local HIV/AIDS awareness initiatives

Set up income generating projects and small businesses

Promote knowledge of women's rights, including democratic and inheritance rights.

The programme focuses on building knowledge and skills in business development and forming community savings groups. As a result, women are now gaining financial independence, have more autonomy to manage their lives and are becoming household decision-makers as

---

[3] Canon Claire Laland, Birmingham MU Diocesan President 2001-06, correspondence with author, 31.7.2018.

[4] www.mothersunionlichfield.org.uk/wp-content/uploads/2015/church-and-community-mobilisation-process, [2.10.2018].

[5] Canon Jackie Brocklebank, Birmingham MU Diocesan President 2013-18, in reply to survey from author, 02.2018.

well as community leaders. A huge achievement is that attitudes towards women gradually change as they are given education and value through the groups. Both genders discuss together the positive contributions of women, and realize how much more women can do than raise a family and run a home. As women contribute to the family income as a result of learning they enjoy greater equality in their married relationships, and personal faith has also increased.[6]

In 2014 a group including the Diocesan President, Jackie Brocklebank, and two other trustees visited Karonga District, 4 hours' drive north of Mzuzu, with the MU worker Bester Thindwa. They visited four groups deep in the bush, meeting the trainers and members with a view to seeing in practice both permaculture and the credit and savings groups set up under the LFEP in action.[7] One group member later commented:

> "It's really difficult not to be seen as useful just for what we can provide, especially as we can see the need is great. But just giving cash is not an answer as it does not provide self-worth or a sense of achievement. I thought the initiatives of setting up small credit unions, providing an outreach worker for support, sending a pig or a goat, really work."[8]

Since 2008 MU members and other well-wishers have used the Malawi containers which have been sent at least annually as the conduit for many gifts, used but in good serviceable condition.[9] Over much of the past two decades MU members have been a significant group of visitors to Malawi, alongside bishops and clergy and teachers. MU members have been prominent among lay visitors to Birmingham from Malawi.

---

[6] www.mothersunion.org/projects/literacy-and-financial-education[3.8.2018]. See also www.cofebirmingham.com/Malawi/Mothers-Union [2.8.2018].

[7] Canon Jackie Brocklebank, correspondence with author, 30.9.2018.

[8] Judith Grubb, reply to survey from author, 03.2018.

[9] See ch. 10 below for more about the containers.

Hospitality

Hospitality in both directions has been a key aspect of the Partnership. It is of course not the preserve of women, let alone of MU members. Hospitality was a notable characteristic of the early Christian community: "Do not forget to entertain strangers, for by so doing some people have entertained angels without knowing it."[10]

Janice Price speaks of hospitality as an aspect of mission:

> "Hospitality is an attitude of the heart which is about openness to the other. Here it goes beyond the image of hospitality as welcoming those who are already known and loved to the welcome of the stranger ... As Pohl says, 'Jesus, who was dependent on the hospitality of others during much of his earthly sojourn, also served as the gracious host in his words and in his actions.' Hospitality, as a practice first of the heart and only then of the table, is participative and practical. It is about a generous acknowledgement and meeting of common humanity as well as meeting the needs of humanity, emotional, spiritual and physical, with generosity. As such it mirrors the activity of God towards creation.
>
> The practice of hospitality can be difficult and demanding. Guest and host have different ways of living and being together. Complex cultural conventions shape such encounters which include the way property is treated, meals are taken and gifts are exchanged. Women often bear the burden of hospitality which can become a burden as well as a joy."[11]

Within a long-term partnership, strangers can be vouched for and welcomed, not just as brothers and sisters in Christ but as those already known and loved. The opportunity to give hospitality is transformative and becomes a blessing to giver and receiver. Liz and Jim Carr testified:

> "The other significant draw [to supporting the Partnership] was the visit of Ndirande Anglican Voices in '05 – two of the young men in the choir

---

[10] Hebrews 13.2. See also Romans 12.13; Titus 1.8; 1 Peter 4.5.

[11] Janice Price, *World-Shaped Mission,* London: Church House Publishing, 2012, p. 24.

stayed with us and we've remained in touch to this day ... We've always tried to offer appropriate hospitality and to make guests feel relaxed and at home. We feel we manage to give genuine friendship, mutual understanding – and lots of laughter! Of course, we receive the same in return – Malawians are great guests!"[12]

Jackie Brocklebank shares her experience from December 2014:

"Bishop Francis [Kaulanda] and Nellie spent Christmas with us. They visited Castle Bromwich for a carol service when here and they saw snow! We had a lovely family Christmas with them and some frank discussions about lots of things. We gave them English food but Bishop Francis brought his own supply of *nsima* which Nellie and I cooked up for everyone ... Bishop Francis and Nellie are amazing Christians – very easy to talk to and pray with. They sang us a song in our living room which I shall never forget. It was good to share some of the time with all the family especially as our son Ralph had been teaching in Malawi."[13]

Like so many others, I can testify that a visit to Malawi is transformative to all who experience it. In the course of many visits, I have enjoyed the hospitality of countless meals in Malawian homes. The host or hostess has first poured warm water from a jug over my hands and offered me a towel. This little ritual reflects politeness, concern for hygiene and love, and indeed, it recalls Jesus' humble gesture of washing his disciples' feet.

"[My visit] certainly did [change me]. It opened my eyes to the terrible poverty that is in countries like Malawi and I realized how fragile life is with the poverty and diseases like AIDS killing so many people in this beautiful country. It also made me passionate about trying to fund raise and support this country and keeping it high profile in our churches."[14]

---

[12] Liz and Jim Carr, reply to survey from author, 26.3.2018.

[13] Canon Jackie Brocklebank in reply to survey from author, 2.2018.

[14] Gill Edwards, who took part in the first teachers' skills share trip in 2006, in reply to survey from author, 18.3.2018.

The impressions of Malawian visitors to the UK can be equally powerful, as shown in the reports of the youth exchanges.[15] Baird Mponda made a first visit to the UK in 2014 as Dean of All Saints Cathedral, Nkhotakota:

> "I am so much moved with the treasure the church has in terms of the history and how that history is preserved, inspired with the Christian life, the profound faith, not just numerical following but spiritual. Church buildings are not full on Sunday as is the case in Africa but there is a great deal of spiritual commitment, you would easily see that in the faces of Christians. They are also serious about the Malawi Birmingham Link which gives so much for the church in Malawi."[16]

Baird also expressed his shock at the extreme contrast between the resources available to schools in Malawi and the UK, and to priests in the two nations.

Notable Anglican Women

Margaret Marango Banda

Many notable women have been involved in the Malawi Birmingham Partnership. I have chosen to profile three, two in Malawi and one in Birmingham.

Margaret Marango Banda was born in 1926 in a CCAP mission hospital in Northern Malawi and was the grand-daughter of a Free Church of Scotland minister. She became an Anglican in 1947. She worked for the Malawi Broadcasting Corporation from 1965 to 1986 and trained in speech and radio production. In 1981 she was nominated to stand as an MP, but President Banda [no relation] refused to allow it, then and again in 1987. She was appointed regional Chair of the Association for the Advancement of Women in Malawi (CCAM in Chichewa) in 1987. She was then also MU Provincial President for Central Africa, and in that capacity was invited to the Lambeth Conference in 1988. She was asked

---

[15] Ch .6 above.

[16] www.cofebirmingham.com/documents/view/dean-nkhotakota-cathedral-visits-uk, 4.12.2014 [5.8.2018].

to be at a three-week seminar of CCAM at the same time, but she knew where her priorities lay: "My God first, then my family and lastly any other thing". On the morning she was due to leave for England she was arrested and detained without charge for almost 2½ years. She suffered with poor health, and "in detention my health deteriorated so much that it is now bad. I am always in and out of hospitals, but by God's own will I am alive."[17]

While she was in detention, she and a friend, jailed with her, sang hymns in Chitumbuka, not the guards' language. Archbishop Runcie visited Malawi during this time and sought information from the President about Mrs Banda in prison. It is not clear whether he was allowed to actually visit her, but his inquiries alerted the regime that she was known about abroad. She was released in 1992; she met and greatly impressed Bishop Santer on his visit. She came to the UK for the Swanwick Conference in 1993, and was taken to meet Archbishop Runcie, who was then living in retirement in St Albans.[18]

> "During the Malawi elections in 1994 the people in my constituency elected me as their representative in Parliament for the first term in the New Malawi. I am the only woman MP from northern Malawi... It is a joy to serve the people well, both spiritually and politically, if one is a believing Christian... I serve both rural and urban people and I am managing well despite my poor health."

Reflecting on her various leadership roles, she said: "Today I am a lay leader, a Reader and MU ex-officio adviser. I have been trained as a deaconess but as yet there is no ordination of women priests in Malawi. I have a strong hope that one day we will have women priests..."[19]

---

[17] Interview in *Anglican World,* Michaelmas, 1995.

[18] Interview with Rt Rev Mark Santer, 23.1.2017.

[19] Interview in *Anglican World,* Michaelmas 1995.

Agnes Mkoko[20]

Agnes Mkoko was born in 1952 in Malindi to Anglican parents. Her father was a teacher/catechist and she grew up with Bible studies in the home. She was married young to George, and caught up with secondary schooling by correspondence. George died aged 49 when their last-born was only 6. She has seven children and has cared for five orphans – "But I thank God, Richard, for what he has done for me."

Agnes started work in 1980 as full-time St Agnes Guild coordinator with the Diocese of Southern Malawi. She worked with the MU from 1988 and became one of the MU Provincial Trainers in the Province of Central Africa. She has gained many qualifications including a Women's Leadership Course which she took in 1992-93 at the College of the Ascension, Birmingham, and a Diploma in Theology through TEEM [Theological Education by Extension Malawi]. Agnes pays tribute to the friendship of the Ardens: "Jane Arden assisted me a lot - whenever we were in the UK we were in their hands. After the death of my husband in 1994 when I wasn't sure about the future, Donald found me: 'You are like a firefighter, Agnes. You must not run away with the extinguisher.'" She has served on many church boards and councils including the All Africa Council of Churches and the WCC in Geneva.

After DSM was split in 2002, Agnes became part of the staff of Diocese of Upper Shire. In 2010 she was 'retired' after 20 plus years' service at short notice by the incoming bishop, who cited the ACM conditions of service. However, under MU global rules she need not retire until 60. "I knelt down and thanked God for the privilege of serving him all these years, and I asked him: what next?" So, she moved to Blantyre in 2010 and served as Diocesan [Women's and Men's] Guilds Co-ordinator for DSM for a couple of years from 2015. She says: "I have made many friends in Birmingham and other parts of UK too numerous to mention. Eileen Eggington, Project Officer of MACS, is a great friend too. The UK is like my second home."

---

[20] This section is based on an interview with Agnes on 18.6.2018.

Agnes was part of the group chosen to come from Malawi to Birmingham in 2005 for the diocesan centenary. She stayed with Claire Laland and the two have become close friends. Agnes wrote some prayers for the MU book 'Be with me' edited by Claire. Claire has regularly asked her for Malawi prayer items for Praying Together, Birmingham's quarterly prayer booklet. Agnes has regularly received gifts sent on the Birmingham containers, particularly for the needs of children: school and nursery furniture, children's clothing, illustrated books and school bags. Some of these have gone to the nursery run by Agnes in her home parish of South Lunzu. Others have gone to the community project she runs in a remote rural area near Mwanza, which has been visited by many friends from Birmingham.

Claire Laland[21]

Claire was born in Chiswick, London in 1936 and so grew up during the war years when air raids were frequent. She was married in 1960 to Carl who was a Parsee of the Zoroastrian faith, and came to Birmingham in 1970 as a mother of 5 children under 9 years of age. Carl died in 1996. She became involved in the Media Awareness Project [MAP], a national ecumenical project hosted by Mothers' Union and funded by the Jerusalem Trust. She edited the MAP Bulletin for 15 or so years from 1988, interviewing various Christians and other public figures with responsibilities in the media. On becoming Archdeacon of Aston, John Barton asked her to join the Diocesan Communications Committee, on which she served for some 20 years.

After serving the MU in parish and deanery, Claire became Vice-President and then Media Chairman for Birmingham Diocese. She became Diocesan President in January 2001, and joined the Malawi Task Group that year. She stayed in office until 2006 and was made one of the first lay canons in 2005. In discussion of who should be invited from Malawi to celebrate the diocesan centenary in 2005, Claire pointed out that all the names were clergy and male. Since the Mothers'

---

[21] Section based on a note prepared by Canon Claire Laland.

Union played such a large part the in church life in Malawi, surely a MU member should be invited. Archbishop Bernard Malango, Bishop of Upper Shire, was consulted and suggested the invitation go to Agnes Mkoko.

In 2014 Claire and Margaret Fulford, another former MU Diocesan President, travelled in Malawi, guided by Agnes Mkoko.

> "We visited one small village where Agnes has been working. She has set up a nursery class and taught the members how to knit and irrigation ... The members also showed us clay ovens they were making to sell. These ovens use less fuel and produce less smoke so making the cooking process healthier."[22]

They met MU members and found out more about the projects they were involved in. Their work impressed the visitors wherever they went: craft work, educational work, feeding schemes etc. The support the MU in Malawi received from Birmingham was much appreciated, not only in gifts of goods and money but in prayer support throughout the year.[23]

The Ordination of Women

The ordination of women to the priesthood in England dates from 1994, and had its reverberations in Malawi. Fr Rodney Hunter, a tutor at Zomba Theological College, wrote an open letter in 1993 to the Bishop of Lake Malawi opposing the ordination of women as priests on the grounds of loyalty to the UMCA's Anglo-Catholic conception of the Church, and concern that such a move would distance it from the Roman Catholics. He feared pressure for change, foreseeing that "Our partners in Birmingham will soon be visiting us with women priests who, if only out of politeness, will be invited to preach. Malawians visiting England will be won over, and support for women's ordination will be made to appear as a sign of a progressive attitude..." He declared that

---

[22] Claire Laland, Trip to Malawi in 2014 by Margaret Fulford and Claire Laland, 25.7.2018.

[23] Ibid.

"I am sure the view which I have expressed is closer to the mind of the Malawi Church than any voice from Birmingham or USPG."[24]

The Mothers' Union, by contrast, issued a statement in 1994 supporting the ordination of women by reference to scripture, both OT and NT, and on cultural grounds, including that "in African tradition, women were regarded as the very keepers of life." They continued: "We (MU) see priests as servants of the people – a role most church leaders tend to ignore today, because they want people to treat them with all the respect befitting leaders."[25]

Women priests in England have not yet been followed by women priests or deacons in Malawi. In anticipation that they would, Josie Tengatenga, wife of the bishop, trained at Zomba Theological College with the programme for priests. She was employed as training chaplain in DSM [when the diocese was based in Malosa], then as youth coordinator in DSM [in Blantyre]. The DSM synod resolved in 2013 to approve the ordination of women and proposed the issue to the Synod of the Province of Central Africa.[26] When the issue was discussed there in 2013, the motion to stick with a male-only priesthood was moved by Bishop Magangani on three grounds: the church was not yet ready for change; change would lead to division; and Biblical arguments. The synod voted to retain the *status quo*. But the diversity of views among bishops, priests and lay Christians in Malawi on the theological and practical aspects of women's ordination needs to be borne in mind.

Birmingham has always made clear its view that this is a decision for the local church. Various women priests, including Paula Hollingsworth in 1996 and Emma Sykes in 2013 and 2017, have visited Malawi down the years. They have exercised a pastoral, preaching and teaching ministry; they have not performed the priestly functions of presiding at Holy Communion, giving the blessing or pronouncing forgiveness of sins. Emma performed a baptism in 2013 at the invitation of the parish priest.

---

[24] Letter reproduced in Kenneth R. Ross, *Christianity in Malawi,* pp. 109-14.

[25] Reproduced in Kenneth R. Ross, *Christianity in Malawi,* pp. 109-14.

[26] Resolutions of the Seventh Synod of the Diocese of Southern Malawi, 2013.

The first visit of a woman bishop, Anne Hollinghurst, Bishop of Aston, took place in 2017.

Chapter 9

The Birmingham End of the Partnership, 1966-2016

During the half century we are looking at, the local economy, society and ethnic makeup of Birmingham and the wider West Midlands area were undergoing rapid changes, which profoundly affected the churches, schools and other institutions of the diocese.

The City and the Area

In 1966 the West Midlands was a heavily industrialized area. The strong engineering tradition that had earned Birmingham the name of 'city of a thousand trades' was largely intact. The motor industry was particularly prominent, in the form of both component makers and large assembly plants. The area was also heavily polluted, and poor air and water quality, together with unhealthy work places, were factors in the shortening of many lives. A violent shakeout of British industrial capacity occurred around the early 1980s and hit the West Midlands especially hard, leading to the region having the highest rate of adult unemployment in the country by 1985.[1] A prominent local instance was the large car assembly plant in Longbridge in south west Birmingham, which was successively part of Austin, BMC, British Leyland, BL and finally Rover. This struggled from the 1970s onwards; Bishop Hugh Montefiore got involved in trying to reconcile the warring parties in a damaging series of strikes in the 1980s.[2] The company progressively reduced its labour force and the Longbridge works eventually closed in 2005. The region still has a significant motor industry, with two large Jaguar Land Rover assembly plants in the diocese.

---

[1] Terry Slater, *A Century of Celebrating Christ: The Diocese of Birmingham, 1905-2005,* Chichester: Phillimore & Co, 2005, p. 192.

[2] Ibid, p. 84.

The Church of England recognized the speed of change and decay in English cities in the 1980s: "The recent dramatic reduction and redistribution of employment in the manufacturing industries around which so many of our great cities were built, and the decentralization of the new and growing industries to smaller towns and even rural areas, have speeded the process of decay in parts of once-flourishing industrial cities to an unprecedented degree."[3] Concern about the consequences of these changes led the Archbishop of Canterbury to set up the Commission which produced the report *Faith in the City* in 1985. This found that the industrial closures of the 1980s were causing social breakdown and distress locally, especially in inner-city and outer-fringe local authority housing estates. Neglected housing, little local employment and poor schools were leading to despair, criminality and drug abuse, and these problems have proved very hard to shift. The 1985 report was followed locally by *Faith in the City of Birmingham* [1988], which revealed the level of hurt in the Black and Asian communities in the city, documented the wide range of social action projects being undertaken by the church and gave recommendations to government, city and church.[4]

After the depression of the 1980s Birmingham set about reinventing itself as a centre for exhibitions, conferences and culture. The National Exhibition Centre in Solihull had already opened in 1976: Symphony Hall in Birmingham and the adjacent International Convention Centre both opened in 1991. The Bull Ring shopping centre and New Street station both had major upgrades in the early 21st century. The city centre has felt vibrant and prosperous and attracted large numbers of visitors – at least, until the growth of online shopping and Covid-19 combined to put a chilling effect on all city centres.

---

[3] *Faith in the City, A Call for Action by Church and Nation*, The Report of the Archbishop of Canterbury's Commission on Urban Priority Areas, London: Church House Publishing, 1985, p. xiii.

[4] Slater, *A Century of Celebrating Christ: The Diocese of Birmingham, 1905-2005*, pp. 192-194.

The early phases of immigration into the city were described in chapter 3. An increasingly racially and religiously mixed population, coupled with the economic distress of the 1980s, led to tensions which boiled over in the so-called 'Handsworth riots' of 1985. "Growing numbers of Black and Asian British youth were being severely disadvantaged by the multiple deprivations of poor housing, inadequate education and lack of employment opportunities. The consequence was a growing 'gang' culture of crime and drugs …"[5] One tragic incident of warfare between Black gangs was the accidental shooting dead of two Black teenage girls at New Year 2003, shortly after the arrival of Bishop Sentamu; this led to his launching an initiative to combat guns, gangs and knives.

A parallel wave of immigration to Birmingham was from Asia, especially Pakistan, India and Afghanistan. Several wards in deprived areas in the east of the city became solidly Muslim, including some areas served by church schools. Educational changes handed more power to school governors, and in 2014 an alleged campaign attempting to impose an Islamist agenda on local schools was uncovered and dubbed 'Trojan Horse'. The reputation of education in the city suffered in the ensuing row.[6] Church schools in east Birmingham have always striven to reconcile national requirements, Christian standards and Muslim sensibilities, and they were given a clean bill of health.

Birmingham has become an ethnically 'super-diverse' city, with communities drawn from almost 200 nations; but those from African nations, particularly from Malawi, remain quite small.

The Diocese, its Bishops and Church Life

In 1969, Bishop Laurence Brown[7] succeeded Leonard Wilson. He was a popular and much-loved bishop, a pastor and administrator rather than

---

[5] Slater, ibid, p. 207.

[6] www.theguardian.com/world/2017/sep/01/trojan-horse-the-real-story-behind-the-fake-islamic-plot-to-take-over-schools, [15.10.2018].

[7] Laurence Brown had a background in parish ministry and church administration and a lifelong commitment to the Boy Scout movement. He had

a great theologian.[8] He and his wife visited Malawi for three weeks in 1971, attending the inauguration of the Diocese of Lake Malawi in Nkhotakota and the enthronement of Bishop Josiah Mtekateka as its first bishop on Likoma.[9] He made a further visit in 1975, shortly before he retired in 1977.

His successor, Hugh Montefiore, was a man of great intellectual distinction who developed a high national profile.[10] As Bishop of Birmingham from 1978-87 he saw it as "the first priority of my episcopate to take a lead ... in sharing the Good News about God with the people of this city."[11] He visited Malawi in 1983 and made a great impact.[12] He was a man of enormous energy, who increasingly was as active outside Birmingham as he was in it, notably in the House of Lords, where the most senior bishops sit by right. Slater sums him up as "a

---

been Suffragan Bishop of Warrington before he was 'translated' [transferred] to Birmingham in 1969.

[8] Terry Slater, *A Century of Celebrating Christ: The Diocese of Birmingham, 1905-2005,* pp. 77-79.

[9] *Ecclesia,* edited by Bishop Donald Arden, September 1971.

[10] Hugh Montefiore was born in 1920 into a prominent Jewish family. He became a Christian at 16 after seeing a vision of Christ. He joined the army in World War Two, saw service in the Far East and was ordained in 1949. He worked in Cambridge from 1951 to 1970, first as tutor at the theological college Westcott House, then as Fellow and Dean of Caius College, and from 1963 on as vicar of the university church of Great St Mary's. During this time, he began to get a reputation as an early environmental prophet. He warned that human exploitation of the planet was threatening its future, but commented that "Religion, far from being outmoded, provides the only hope of man's deliverance." He was Area Bishop of Kingston, in south London, from 1970-78. Sources: Terry Slater, *A Century of Celebrating Christ: The Diocese of Birmingham, 1905-2005,* pp. 80-82; *Church Times,* 26.4.2019.

[11] Sermon on installation, 4.3.1978, quoted in Slater, op. cit., p. 83.

[12] See ch. 4 above.

great teacher ... as well as a prophet, a wise administrator, and a pastor who gave himself freely to others."[13]

Mark Santer served as 7th Bishop of Birmingham from 1987 to 2002.[14] He was a man of great theological depth and remarkably well-read. He served from 1983 to 1998 as Co-Chair of ARCIC, the Anglican-Roman Catholic International Commission. The priorities for his ministry in Birmingham were: "the unity of the Church; the value and dignity of human beings created in the divine image; and for justice that reflects the mercy of God."[15] He was fully involved in public affairs and not afraid to be controversial. He was publicly scornful of Birmingham City Council's proposal to rebrand Christmas as 'Winterval'. He made official diocesan visits to Malawi in 1991[16] and 2000[17] as well as other visits during the turbulent years 1992-93.

Bishop Mark's successor John Sentamu was very different in background and character; he became the Church of England's first African-born bishop.[18] Bishop Sentamu became Bishop of Birmingham

---

[13] Ibid., p. 85.

[14] Mark Santer was born in 1936. He was ordained in 1963 and his early years of ministry were devoted to theological teaching and ordination training. He was a tutor at Cuddesdon College, Oxford, and then, like his predecessor, spent some years in Cambridge: he was Fellow and Dean of Clare College, then principal of the theological college Westcott House. He was Area Bishop of Kensington (London) from 1981-87.

[15] Terry Slater, *A Century of Celebrating Christ: The Diocese of Birmingham, 1905-2005,* pp. 88-96. Quote is from p. 92.

[16] See ch. 5 above.

[17] See ch. 6 above.

[18] John Tucker Mugabi Sentamu was born in 1949 in Uganda to parents who were both teachers. His upbringing was Christian and British-influenced. He studied law and aged 25 found himself being made a judge just as Idi Amin's reign of violence began. His judicial activities soon put his life at risk, and he and his wife escaped to England in 1974. He read theology at Cambridge and trained for ordination. He worked as a prison chaplain, became curate of a

in 2002, but after little more than three years in office, was appointed Archbishop of York in 2005. He had an infectious enthusiasm, unbounded energy and a very persuasive manner. Children and young people were at the heart of his ministry in the diocese. He made one visit to Malawi in 2003 with his wife and diocesan staff. With Canon Peter Howell-Jones he began planning for the reimagining of the Malawi Partnership; some parts of it only came into being after his departure.

David Urquhart has been Bishop of Birmingham from 2006.[19] He is a good judge of colleagues and an expert networker. He launched 'Transforming Church' to enable the diocese to minister more effectively in the changing mission context, of which he was keenly aware. He has worked successfully with representatives of several political parties on Birmingham City Council in an effort to fight poverty and social exclusion. Bishop David has had a host of responsibilities outside the diocese, including serving as the Archbishop of Canterbury's Envoy to China and as a member of the Banking Standards Board. As 'Convenor of the Lords Spiritual' he has coordinated the work of the 26 Church of England bishops in the House of Lords. He has been lead bishop on business and economic policy and taken a close interest in

---

parish and then priest in charge of a large parish in the Brixton area of south London. In 1996 he was made Area Bishop of Stepney (London).

[19] David Andrew Urquhart was born in 1952, comes from an old Scottish family and was brought up in the Highlands of Scotland. He was educated at the English public school of Rugby. His Christian faith became well established during a gap year after school in Idi Amin's Uganda. He took a degree at business school and worked in the oil industry as an executive with BP. He then trained for ministry at Wycliffe Hall, Oxford and was ordained in 1984. He ministered in the Yorkshire town of Hull and was vicar of a large city centre church in Coventry for 8 years from 1992-2000. He was Suffragan Bishop of Birkenhead in Liverpool Diocese from 2000-2006. www.cofebirmingham.com/about-us/who-we-are/bishop-of-birmingham [9.1.2019].

local government and foreign affairs. Bishop David is due to retire in October 2022.[20]

The visible decline in church participation in the 1960s led the churches of Birmingham to realize the need to organize high-profile evangelistic events together. A succession of events included the visits of the American Arthur Blessitt in 1971-72 and the Englishman David Watson in 1981. The biggest of all was Mission England in 1984, which saw Billy Graham preach at a week of rallies which attracted crowds from all over the Midlands to Villa Park football stadium. Archbishop Desmond Tutu came to speak at a week-long mission in 1989.[21] The diocese marked its centenary in 2005 by inviting the evangelist J John to speak over the course of a fortnight on the Ten Commandments under the title 'Just 10'.

In the 1970s and 1980s the 'charismatic renewal' was a force for the revitalizing of UK church life in the historic denominations, notably in the areas of music, prayer and fellowship. Birmingham was included in this movement: the diocese had an active Renewal Group and parish life in several places was profoundly affected. The 1990s was the nationally designated 'Decade of Evangelism'; many of the events organized were outdoors, including a televised 'Songs of Praise' celebration in Victoria Square in the city centre in 1995.[22] The millennium was marked by the gift from the diocese to the city of a 'Flame of Hope' atop a large globe in Centenary Square; the flame was lit at New Year 2000 and kept burning for several years.[23]

---

[20] www.cofebirmingham.com/news/2015/05/18/bishop-birmingham-appoint ed-new-convenor-lords-spiritual [9.1.2019].

[21] Terry Slater, *A Century of Celebrating Christ: The Diocese of Birmingham, 1905-2005*, pp. 171-180.

[22] The Jubilee 2000 'Drop the Debt' rally in 1998 is described in chapter 6.

[23] Terry Slater, *A Century of Celebrating Christ: The Diocese of Birmingham, 1905-2005*, pp. 181-190.

But these 50 years, especially the earlier ones, were a period of general decline in churchgoing and church activity in the UK that affected all the historic Christian Churches. "It is not exaggerated to conclude that between 1960 and 1985 the Church of England as a going concern was effectively reduced to not much more than half its previous size."[24] Churchgoing in the Church of England declined steeply from 3.5% of the population in 1968 to 2.5% in 1985, then a little more slowly, reaching 1.3% in 2016.[25] The decline among children was more pronounced than for adults. Birmingham is a largely urban, industrial or ex-industrial, multi-ethnic diocese where Anglican churchgoing has always been lower locally than nationally, but the trends are similar. Corresponding figures for Birmingham are: 1968, 2.1% of population; 1985, 1.5%; 1996, 1.3%; 2006, 1.1% and 2016, 0.8% of population.[26]

Asked about the decline, Bishop David commented that we need to look at the impact of the Christian Church, not just the numbers attending, and added: "Because of faith we keep active and witnessing in a society where there is little faith."[27] Against the gloomy background of these trends, support for the Malawi Partnership, as expressed in monetary giving and other ways, has continued strong, at least until recent years.

The Role of Money

> "Giving money is both a great gift and a potential hazard in linking ... The challenges of linking between a materially well-resourced diocese in

---

[24] Adrian Hastings, *A History of English Christianity, 1920-1985*, London: Collins/Fount Paperbacks, 1987, p. 602.

[25] Churchgoing is measured by Usual Sunday Attendance, all age, the best measure available for the period since 1968 but not collected before then. Source: Church of England Participation Summary, 1960-2016 in 2016 Statistics for Mission, www.churchofengland.org/more/policy-and-thinking/ research-and-statistics.

[26] I am indebted to Dr Ken Eames of C of E Research and Statistics, London, for supplying these figures.

[27] Interview with Bishop David Urquhart, 18.7.2019.

England and a materially less well-resourced diocese are many. Some Links do not involve giving financially and Links should not be defined by financial transaction. Other Links see the giving of money as an important part of expressing concern for and solidarity with those with whom they are linked and an expression of their own thankfulness to God for his generosity. To what extent will these material differences distort the understanding of giving and receiving? How does the English partner guard against old colonial patterns of power and control? What is the place of money in partnerships and how does it enable all parties to participate in God's mission?"[28]

The questions raised by Janice Price are very pertinent to the Malawi Partnership, which links a materially well-resourced diocese with the Church in one of Africa's poorest countries. The issues are well recognized, but my sense is that there has been little candid discussion of them between the parties, at least in recent years.[29]

From the time the Malawi link was set up in 1966 there was a heavy stress on monetary giving. The Birmingham diocesan conference that approved the link agreed to send £5000 per year to help the Diocese of Malawi.[30] This was an ambitious target that was met or almost met in each of the next 10 years. Over the 15 years to 1980, Birmingham's giving to Malawi was running at the remarkably high rate of 6.7% of diocesan Common Fund. The money was used for clergy housing and pensions and for projects such as building new churches, including St Mary's, Biwi in Lilongwe.[31] By the mid-1970s soaring inflation in the UK was eating away at the real value of giving. However, higher targets

---

[28] Janice Price, *World-Shaped Mission,* London: Church House Publishing, 2012, p. 33.

[29] There is a useful discussion of the role of money in Brian Wakelin, *Money – Master or Servant in Church to Church Partnerships?* Cambridge: Grove Books, 2017. Wakelin stresses the need for 'transparent accountability'.

[30] Terry Slater, *A Century of Celebrating Christ: The Diocese of Birmingham, 1905-2005,* p. 162.

[31] Bob Jenkins, *In Touch with the Warm Heart of Africa, 1966-1996,* p. 5.

were set and generally reached: giving from parishes to the Malawi General Fund reached £20,000 for the first time in 1985. For many years PCCs were expected to give and reminders were issued.

As the dioceses progressively increased from one to four, the costs of administration increased, and the bulk of the Birmingham money went to the dioceses as grants toward their costs, with some also going to ACM. In 1995 Paul Wilson, Diocesan Director of Finance, moved to make Malawi finance more effective and bring it into line with UK charity legislation. He arranged the setting up of the Diocese of Birmingham Malawi Fund under custodianship of the Diocesan Trustees, with the members of the Coordinating Committee as managers.[32]

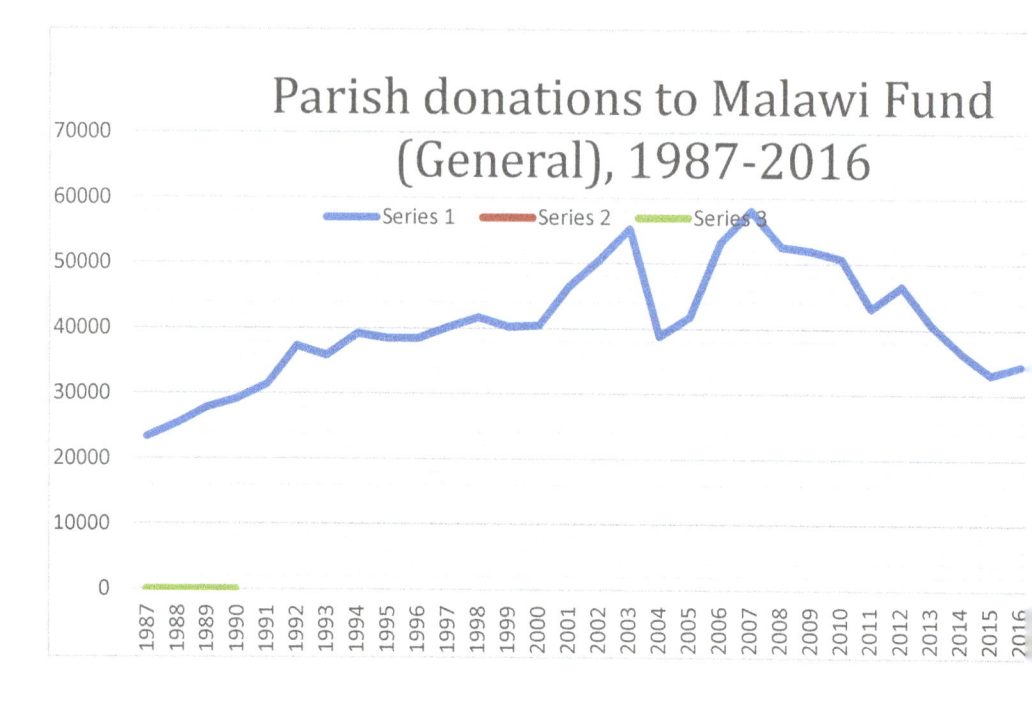

Parish donations to Malawi Fund (General), 1987-2016

---

[32] Paul Wilson, Diocesan Accountant, *Letter to Hugh Carslake, Martineau Johnson Solicitors, 26.9.1995*, and *Report to Bishop's Council, 3 October 1995*.

The chart above shows annual giving figures for 1987-2016. It can be seen that giving increased steadily; target figures for parish giving were set until 2014 and on occasion exceeded. General parish giving hit a high of £58,000 in 2007 but has declined quite sharply since then.[33] The decline in giving since 2007 can be put down to several factors. Most obviously, the financial crisis in the UK reduced the money that parishes could raise for Malawi. Another factor may be 'donor fatigue': the sense, however unjustified, that Birmingham money has gone to Malawi for 50 years, but the Church there is still not self-supporting, so the money may have been poorly used. There also appears to have been a shift of diocesan mission focus away from Malawi and towards mission at home and, to a lesser but significant extent, to the newer link with Bolivia. No serving Director of Finance has visited Malawi since 2011. The financial support base for Malawi seems to have narrowed: the number of parishes contributing to the General Fund dipped from 114 in 2007, to 89 in 2009, to 74 in 2016. In some cases, donations have also become less regular.

> "Accountability is arguably the most difficult issue in giving internationally. Cultural norms and understandings differ and can be the cause of misunderstandings that may threaten the sustainability of relationships ... Those who are making large donations from the West are governed by charitable giving and accounting law which require accounts and reports to be kept as public record. Accountability for funds given and received as understood in the cultural and legal terms of the highly bureaucratized West can be experienced as a lack of trust to those in communally based cultures in the Majority World."[34]

There have been delicate moments in the Partnership's history when such trust has been questioned, especially when dioceses or institutions

---

[33] A dip in 2004 and 2005 can be readily seen from the chart of parish donations. Very large sums were then being raised for the Malawi Wheels centenary appeal – see ch. 10 below – and this was no doubt a reaction.

[34] Janice Price, *World-Shaped Mission,* London: Church House Publishing, 2012, p. 63.

such as schools or hospitals have run into financial difficulty and Birmingham has been called on to help. More difficult still are cases where dishonesty has been alleged in the use of external funds. Such suspicions can be very destructive of the trust on which a partnership is based. Accountability has become an increasing problem since 2016: Birmingham has had to suspend grants to several dioceses when they were unable to produce audited accounts.

> "Can money be given without the receiver becoming dependent on a particular source? Dependency can destroy human dignity ... 'Dependency syndrome has little to do with wealth or poverty. It has to do with the mentality on the part of both local people and the outsiders who try to help.'"[35]

The large sums sent to Malawi down the years have largely been put to good use, but they have created a kind of inertia in the Partnership. This has long been recognized as a still unresolved problem which has made it difficult for the Partnership to move onto a more fully mutual basis. Sustainability was a key focus of the Partnership Review in 2014[36] and remains a major challenge.

The issue of the role of money is closely linked to that of decision making about its use. In the early years Birmingham, like others, wrestled with how to provide resources for the church in Africa whilst avoiding the colonial tendency to retain power; there was a sense of post-colonial guilt.[37] Successive bishops and diocesan officers in Birmingham were at pains to listen to Malawian bishops and help them to achieve their wishes and aspirations.[38] One of the major roles of the biennial consultations from the 1990s on was intended to be coming to a

---

[35] Glenn Schwartz, *When Charity Destroys Dignity: Overcoming Unhealthy Dependency in the Christian Movement,* Authorhouse, 2007, quoted in Price, *World-Shaped Mission,* p. 64.

[36] See ch. 12 below.

[37] Canon David Lee, interview, 23.11.2016.

[38] Canon Paul Wilson, correspondence, 20.2.2019.

common mind on the use of funds from Birmingham. From the mid-1990s into the 2000s attempts were made to fix the level of diocesan grants below the expected giving from Birmingham and to put the difference into a fund for agreed projects. After the increase from three Malawian dioceses to four the system fell into disuse. Birmingham may have been unwilling deliberately to lower the level of grant to leave headroom for project funding. One could also argue that management weaknesses at ACM and unwillingness on the part of the dioceses meant that it proved impossible to agree a priority list of projects.

The consultations were reportedly diminishing in effectiveness during the later 2000s; the last one was in 2009.[39] Since then the Partnership has suffered from the lack of a proper forum for Birmingham and the Malawian bishops to assess experience and discuss future plans. This makes it all the more regrettable that no face-to-face discussion of the 2014 Partnership Review proved possible.

James Tengatenga acknowledges the value of the money sent from Birmingham: "Diocesan admin. would collapse had it not been for Birmingham money." But he reflects on the partnership's shortcomings, some of which he puts on the Malawian side:

> "What I believe we did not do well is that we fought over this and did not think outside the box. We could have used Birmingham money to do greater things. We could pool it and do projects... Because we did not have a common mind and common cause, the money side has not benefitted us as much as it could have... The challenge has been the Malawian church not wanting to think beyond a shopping list mentality. Several link meetings identified this problem but we never surmounted it."[40]

Simply sending money became a substitute for the hard work of discussing together where the partnership was going and how money

---

[39] Very Rev Peter Howell-Jones, interview, 16.8.2018.

[40] Rt. Rev. James Tengatenga, correspondence with author, 13.10.2018.

could be most strategically used – and this is a fair criticism of Birmingham too:

> "It's more us than Birmingham money that got in the way. Money makes things work and is the 'easiest' to transact… All you need is a working banking system!!!!! But relationships are work. Thinking outside the box is work. Common cause is work."[41]

Andrew Kirk places the problem more on the donor's side:

> "A bad conscience about former patterns of relationship inclines sensitive Western mission agencies to respond by giving without accepting the responsibility of genuine consultation with the recipient."[42]

Specific Funds and Projects

The Malawi Church Trust was a charity set up in 1974 by David Potter, who had worked in the country and wanted to help meet the needs of the Anglican Church there. The Trust was administered by a UK board of trustees which included successive Bishops of Birmingham. It was decided to wind it up in 1994.[43] Most of the Marjorie Francis funds were transferred into the Diocese of Birmingham Malawi Fund in 1997.[44] The income was used initially for a secondary school and Sunday school work, but in due course sent to the dioceses annually roughly in proportion to the numbers of their schools.

---

[41] Ibid.

[42] Andrew Kirk, *What is Mission? Theological Explorations,* London: Darton, Longman and Todd, 2002, p. 192.

[43] The bulk of the Trust's funds were converted into Kwacha – shortly before a collapse of the currency, alas – and transferred to ACM; some went for the purchase of houses in Lilongwe to rent out. The Marjorie Francis funds had been left by a missionary school teacher and could not be transferred to Malawi for legal reasons.

[44] Canon David Lee, *The Marjorie Francis Endowment for Christian Education in Malawi,* diocesan paper, July 2000.

The Bishop Josiah Trust was an endowment fund launched by Bishop Mark Santer in 1996. Its purpose was to assist Christian leaders in Malawi with the cost of Biblical and theological training in Africa and so equip them for the mission of the church. Giving from parishes and individuals in Birmingham plus the excess over giving targets built up the Trust's assets over the following five years. The income was passed to the dioceses in fixed proportions and small grants were made to clergy and lay leaders.[45] The income never grew big enough to fully fund further in-service studies by clergy, and this limited its effectiveness. In course of time the distinctive stress on theological studies was lost and the income was applied, like that of the Marjorie Francis funds, to supporting church schools.[46]

Down the years funds have been raised for various specific projects, from Birmingham diocese as a whole or by specific parishes. In the 1990s ex-British army Bedford lorries were sourced in the UK, painted in the 'Anglican colour' of bright blue, filled with things asked for by Malawian parishes and bishops, shipped via Dar es Salaam and driven down to Malawi. The first went to DLM and DSM in about 1995, to be followed in 1999 by one for DNM. The Bedford trucks proved cheap to purchase but difficult and expensive to keep on the road. "They were fine for industry mechanics but not for diocesan employees to maintain, and parts took a long while to arrive from specialist suppliers in the UK." In response to complaints from Malawi Paul Wilson quickly raised £38,000 from selected parishes to finance their replacement in 2006 with four Japanese- or German-built lorries bought locally.[47]

Other projects included improvements to the lakeshore cottage at Kaphiridzinja; a parish hall for the Blantyre suburb of Ndirande, financed

---

[45] The Bishop Josiah Trust for Theological Education in Africa: Birmingham launch notice, 1996; Canon David Lee, *An Introduction, July 2000*.

[46] The values of the funds were: Marjorie Francis £55,243 in 1999 and £61,314 in 2015; Bishop Josiah Trust £57,451 in 2015.

[47] Canon Paul Wilson, *My Involvement with Birmingham Diocese Malawi Partnership,* note to author, 15.10.2018.

from sales of the first of several Malawi calendars produced from 2005 onward; the reconditioning of a fast boat enabling the bishop and other passengers from DNM to reach Likoma Island speedily; and the purchase and installation of sound equipment for the lakeshore church in Mpondas when it became the cathedral for DUS.[48] Big anniversaries have been the occasion for major project appeals: for the centenary of Birmingham Diocese, the Malawi Wheels appeal for motorbikes for clergy[49] and for the 50th anniversary of the Partnership, financing a classroom block in each diocese.[50] The rebuilding of two teachers' houses at Linga Primary School in Nkhotakota was paid for by St Michael's, Boldmere and from the proceeds of a sponsored 'Church Crawl for Malawi' on foot, by bike or by car in 2013. Birmingham has responded to many relief appeals down the years, often coming through ACM. A special appeal was launched in 1989 after natural disasters including cyclones, earth tremors and floods affected many parts of the country.[51] The famine relief appeal in 2002 was only the biggest of many.

Patterns and Structures of Support for the Partnership

Personnel and Malawi Committees

Since early days there has been a Birmingham committee [under various names] supporting the work of the partnership, raising its profile within the diocese, liaising with the Church in Malawi and performing financial functions. Fr Henry Burgess claimed to have been a committee member continuously until he stepped down in 2017 aged 96. At some stages it has included clergy who have served in Africa; one such was Rev John Weller, who had been principal of a theological college in Zambia before becoming Vicar of West Heath in 1971. He

---

[48] Ibid.

[49] See ch. 10 below.

[50] See ch. 10 below.

[51] Canon Bob Jenkins, *In Touch with the Warm Heart of Africa*, 1998, p. 11.

recalled those years, when the committee was chaired by Archdeacon Vernon Nicholls:

> "I think the three of us must have constituted the committee for a year or two at that stage, which means the committee was not a vast one. But I think you'll find ... that we met our [financial] target every year and we put out a certain amount of leaflets."[52]

The Malawi link had lost its initial impetus in Birmingham by the mid-1970s and needed revitalizing. Bishop Brown, remembering the impact on him of his visit to Malawi, encouraged Colin and Sylvia Bishop and Rev Bob Jenkins to visit Malawi in 1976. On their return they visited some fifty churches, colleges and schools putting flesh and blood on the companionship link.[53] Bob Jenkins joined the Malawi Support Group and stepped up to be chairman. He became a generous supporter of the link and a tireless advocate for it. He did some valuable work on its history and interviewed many significant figures. He used a Sabbatical in 1984 to study 'lessons in church growth from Malawi.'[54] Brenda Holloway, on her retirement as Bishop's Secretary, served as a very efficient secretary to the Support Group from 1978 to 1988.[55]

A working party in 1986 drew up a report "Faith in the World Church and its Mission." Diocesan Synod accepted its main recommendations, among them that a mission resource centre should be established. In the late 20th century, the structures supporting the Anglican mission societies were more elaborate and more ecumenical than more recently. The CMS shared its headquarters in Partnership House, large premises in Waterloo Road, London, with other Anglican mission agencies from 1966 until CMS' move to Oxford in 2007.[56] Following this

---

[52] Rev John Weller, interviewed by Canon Bob Jenkins, 12.5.1989.

[53] Bob Jenkins, *In Touch with the Warm Heart of Africa, 1966-96,* p. 7.

[54] Ven. John Cooper, *Report of the Visit to the Dioceses of Southern Malawi and Lake Malawi by the Archdeacon of Aston, June-July 1987,* p. 7.

[55] Jenkins, *In Touch with the Warm Heart of Africa, 1966-96,* p. 8.

[56] https://churchmissionsociety.org/our-history [25.10.2018].

pattern, a Birmingham mission resource centre opened in 1987, open to the public and serving the mission agencies, Christian Aid and the Malawi Link. This was initially at the PWM office in Carrs Lane in the city centre, then from 1992 at the diocesan offices in Harborne.[57] The diocese employed a succession of support officers working with the various Directors of Mission until 2010. There was also a full-time Diocesan [international] Development Officer in post for 5 years from 1978, in the person of Rev Martin Wilson, son of Bishop Leonard.[58]

The Support Group was chaired by Archdeacon Cooper from 1987 to 1993.[59] In 1995 Bishop Mark Santer was himself formal chair of the Malawi Coordinating Committee [as it had become].[60] The next chair was **Canon David Lee**, who was appointed Director of Mission in 1996 and stayed until 2004. He had taught 6 years in Uganda with CMS and been pastor to missionaries. He saw there how the Church in Africa intersects with the expectations of the West. He kept up a regular rhythm of annual working visits to Malawi and his co-working with Bishop Mark was particularly fruitful. A 'snapshot' of the Committee taken in 2003 shows that it was chaired by David Lee; it had 11 members and another 4 'in attendance'. Of these, 8 were Birmingham clergy, two others were diocesan staff including the Director of Education and the Diocesan Accountant, and one represented the MU. Two USPG staff were in attendance. All had visited Malawi once or more or had plans to visit. The committee met every two months - as it still does.

The Board of Mission was dissolved and David Lee's successor, **Canon Peter Howell-Jones** became Canon Missioner in 2004. He renamed the Committee 'Malawi Task Group', to indicate that he wanted doers on the committee, not just advisors.[61] He aimed to visit Malawi twice a year

---

[57] Interview by Canon Bob Jenkins with Rosemary Reynolds, who was employed at the centre 1987-94, 25.11.1998.

[58] Checked in Crockford's Clerical Directory, 2018-19, [8.5.2019].

[59] Interview with Canon John Cooper, 12.7.2019.

[60] Malawi Coordinating Committee, Membership list 1995.

[61] Canon Paul Wilson, correspondence, 23.11.2017.

for 2-3 weeks and make new contacts wherever possible. A great entrepreneur, he saw the need to increase exposure by Birmingham Christians to life in Malawi as a means of supporting the Partnership and developed the mission encounter and skills share programmes to this end.[62]

Rev Richard Tucker. On Peter Howell-Jones' departure from Birmingham in 2011, Peter and I drew up a job description for the role of Malawi Partnership Officer, which included chairing the Task Group. I was appointed in 2011 and retired in 2017. It was difficult for me to visit more than once a year alongside my parish responsibilities. However, I visited all four dioceses each year. Bishops have been strikingly generous with their time; I have had conversations on each occasion with finance and other diocesan officers and visited a wide variety of parishes, schools, colleges, lay training centres and hospitals. I have also made many deep and valued friendships. The Task Group was progressively slimmed down, from 15 in 2003 to 10 in 2013. It became markedly less clerical, with just one bishop and two other clergy. Andrew Watson, Bishop of Aston, was co-opted as a senior member.[63] It included 2 MU representatives and 4 other lay members. Finance was looked after by Paul Wilson in retirement; from 2014 on the Director of Finance, Melanie Crooks, had this responsibility.

Canon Paul Wilson. Paul as Diocesan Accountant [later Director of Finance] had dealt with Malawi from the outset, but became increasingly involved after Bishop Christopher Boyle persuaded him to visit Malawi after 2001. He then visited at least annually until shortly after his retirement in 2011 and became for some 'the face of Birmingham'. He was assiduous in persuading parishes to give to the Malawi Fund – it is no coincidence that the highest totals were raised during his years in office. He was creative in finding sources of money

---

[62] See chapter 10 below.

[63] Malawi Task Group, minutes of meeting on 11.7.2013.

for worthwhile projects he came across in Malawi and was also concerned to raise standards of accounting in the dioceses there.

Publicity, Prayer Topics, Open Meetings

From the outset the Link has been publicized as a means of supporting giving and prayer. In the late 1960s a 'Malawi Special' church newspaper was produced. This was followed by a series of publications to stir up church members' interest. Rev Alan Priestley was appointed as the diocese's first communications officer in 1976. 'Malawi on the Move' became 'Mirror on Malawi' in 1978; it was enlarged and transformed into a publication with world church issues in line with the recommendation of a working party in 1986.[64] Archdeacon Cooper's visit in 1987 was followed up by a four page 'Malawi Report' newspaper.[65] In the 1990s and early 2000s David Lee produced video reports on episcopal visits and the results of the 2002 famine appeal. 'Mission Matters', with a focus on world mission and Malawi, appeared three times a year later that decade. Its replacement in 2009 by 'Transforming Mission' reflected a change in diocesan focus from supporting world mission towards engaging in mission locally. The diocesan website has always had a Malawi area; at one point there was also a Malawi Partnership site. Prayer by Birmingham for Malawi was focused for several years by the diocesan four-monthly Praying Together booklets, each of which had 3-4 items of prayer for Malawi, some provided by Agnes Mkoko and Claire Laland.

Centrally located open meetings on world mission were held for several years; these were succeeded by meetings focused on Malawi, with speakers, displays and videos. One breakfast meeting was addressed by the International Development Secretary, Andrew Mitchell MP; at another, *nsima* was prepared and eaten in church.

It is always a challenge to raise the profile of Malawi in Birmingham Diocese among the great majority who have not visited but are asked

---

[64] Jenkins, *In Touch with the Warm Heart of Africa, 1966-96*, pp. 5,7,9.

[65] See ch. 4 above.

to give and pray. A Malawi Octave, eight days in March 2011, was proposed by Claire Laland, from her background of communications and agreed by the Task Group. A pack was sent to each parish in the Diocese including a CD-ROM 'The Heartbeat of Malawi' intended for showing in a service or meeting, story cards, prayer bookmarks, a facts and figures quiz sheet, recipes for Malawian dishes and ideas for children's activities. Meetings were held all over the diocese. The 25 minute DVD 'Matilda's Malawi' was professionally made in 2014 to prepare for the Partnership's 50th anniversary. It used a day in the life of a Malawian schoolgirl to illustrate aspects of life in Malawi and Birmingham's support. Malawian voices were heard wherever possible.

Parish Support

Grass-roots support for the Partnership has always been on a parish basis and has been very broad-based, even if in some cases support goes no deeper than contributing to the General Fund. Two surveys were conducted in the years 2007-10 covering support for Malawi. In 2007 Sally Bossingham, newly appointed world mission officer, conducted an audit of world mission engagement. Of 171 surveys sent to parishes, 97 were returned; of these, 53 parishes listed Malawi as one country they were involved with. [This understates the breadth of support: in 2007, 114 parishes contributed to the Malawi General Fund]. Parishes had a wide variety of other world mission links, notably with India, Pakistan, South Africa, Zambia, Zimbabwe, Rwanda and Kenya. In 2010 the 'Articles of Enquiry' sent annually by the Archdeacons included a question about parishes' partnership links with Malawi. In response, 106 parishes said they contributed to the General Fund and 4 more mentioned supporting specific projects; and 42 parishes said they already had links with a Malawian parish or project or through church members having visited Malawi.

Study and Training

One of the support structures in Birmingham, not only for the Malawi Partnership but for the development of the Church overseas generally, was the training formerly provided by the inter-denominational network of colleges in Selly Oak. The USPG College of the Ascension, which opened in 1923, was the venue for much-valued training courses for overseas clergy and lay leaders including a 'small but steady flow' from Malawi. This included bishops and future bishops: Peter Nyanja and Nathaniel Aipa in 1984 and James Tengatenga in 1990. In March 1993 it was reported that no less than four Malawians were studying at the College.[66] It became the United College of the Ascension [jointly with the Methodists] in 1996, but closed in 2006.[67] Its successor programme, Selly Oak Centre for Mission Studies [SOCMS] within the Queen's Foundation, continued the work on a much reduced basis. This decline reflects both the wider availability of mission training courses in Africa, and the combined pressures of finance in the UK and the increasingly onerous visa requirements for overseas students.

A further significant Birmingham-Malawi link was the ministry of Rt Rev Patrick Kalilombe at the Selly Oak colleges between 1980 and 1996. Kalilombe was a pioneering theologian and ecclesiologist and former Roman Catholic Bishop of Lilongwe. From 1987-96 he was Director of the Ecumenical Centre for Black and White Christian Partnership, a centre that aimed at building bridges of mutual understanding between the white-led, white-majority churches and black-led, black-majority churches of Britain and Europe.[68]

The Bolivia Link; Reviewing and Resourcing Intercultural Mission

The possibility of Birmingham setting up another companion link to complement that with Malawi, was considered as far back as 1999.[69] The initial suggestion was to link with a diocese in India or Pakistan.

---

[66] Donald Arden (ed), *Nkhani Zaulere,* March 1993.

[67] en.wikipedia.org/wiki/Selly_Oak_Colleges, [5.9.2018].

[68] Patrick A Kalilombe, *Doing Theology at the Grassroots, Theological Essays from Malawi,* Gweru: Mambo Press, 1999, p. 6 and pp. 39-40.

[69] Canon David Lee, *A Second Companion Link Diocese?* Paper for Board for Mission, September 1999.

However, an interchange of visits between Birmingham and Bolivia facilitated by Assistant Bishop Maurice Sinclair[70] over a period of 8 years led to a diocesan link with the Anglican Church there that was officially recognized when Bishop David visited in 2017. At the time of writing eight congregations in Birmingham were actively involved in this link, with Christ Church, Selly Park the most active.

Birmingham's links with Malawi and Bolivia are very different in character, reflecting the differences between the churches in those two countries. One similarity is that both countries are landlocked and underdeveloped by the standards of their respective continents. The Malawian Anglican Church in 1966 was served by white missionaries from the UK or USA and by poorly paid, poorly trained African priests; it had quite a large 'estate' of church buildings, schools and hospitals, but underfunding had led to their being badly neglected. Over the last 50 years the white missionaries have all but gone, the numbers of priests have increased and their training and pay have improved, but underfunding remains a problem. It is hardly surprising that money transfers have figured so largely in the Partnership.

The Anglican Church in Bolivia, by contrast, was founded only 40 years ago by Anglican missionaries invited from neighbouring countries by the Bolivian Evangelical Council. Its vision has been to minister to professionals and students, to raise up leadership, lay and ordained, and to develop stewardship to enable it to be self-supporting. Churches have been planted in four main cities of the country. Its bishop, Raphael Samuel, has a vision for intentional discipleship: focused on personal relationship with Christ, development of Christian character, growth in the knowledge of God and his purposes for the world, developing competence in specific ministries, and communicating the gospel cross-culturally. Four invited groups from Birmingham, largely clergy, have visited Bolivia since 2012. A party from Bolivia visited Birmingham in

---

[70] The information about Bolivia is derived from an interview on 18.1.2019 with Maurice Sinclair, an Assistant Bishop in Birmingham since 2002 and Presiding Bishop of the Southern Cone [of South America], 1995-2002.

2016 at the latter's expense.[71] The link includes a strong training element, and Birmingham has paid for several small-scale leadership training conferences in Bolivia. But the Bolivia link has "neither opportunity nor wish to subsidize the clergy"[72] and risk creating dependency.

In 2014 an independent review of the partnership was conducted by Canon Janice Price.[73] Unfortunately the review was not given proper discussion at the time, but its findings are still relevant. Alongside the review of the partnership, a group chaired by Bishop Sinclair was tasked with producing a 'Review of World Mission Engagement of the Church of England in Birmingham' at diocese, deanery and parish level. The group stressed the importance for the C of E Birmingham of engaging with world mission and recommended the appointment of a World Mission Officer.

A follow-up report 'Sharing the Gift: Developing fruitful Intercultural Training across C of E Birmingham'[74] was produced in 2016 by a group co-chaired by Bishop Sinclair and Archdeacon Simon Heathfield. Recognizing Birmingham's 'super-diverse' context, this stressed the need to integrate mission thinking locally and globally and to develop intercultural training for both contexts. It recommended the appointment of an 'Intercultural Missioner', with an ambitious range of responsibilities including oversight of the Malawi link. The diocese

---

[71] www.cofebirmingham.com/hub/world-mission/bolivia [18.12.2018].

[72] Bishop Maurice Sinclair, in conversation, 18.1.2019.

[73] Canon Janice Price, World Mission Adviser for the Archbishops' Council of the Church of England, *Review of the Link between the Diocese of Birmingham and the Malawian Anglican Church, Report of the Independent Reviewer*, April 2014. The review is described in ch. 12 below. A summary of the report prepared by the present author is at Appendix C.

[74] www.cofebirmingham.com/documents/view/sharing-gift-intercultural-training, [21.12.2018].

accepted the report and made an appointment to fill the multicultural part of the brief; its world mission responsibilities remain unfilled.

Chapter 10

Birmingham's Engagement with the Partnership, 2000-2016

Several new forms of engagement have arisen since about 2000, driven by the desire to move beyond the dominance of money to more varied interactions.

Parish Links

Many diocesan companion links encourage links between parishes in England and in the link diocese; some go further and arrange links between deaneries in the UK and link dioceses. The Partnership took the first steps towards parish links in 1999. Birmingham parishes were sent a PCC discussion pack including a video: its title, 'Joy and Heartache in Malawi', reflected the toughness of conditions when the HIV/AIDS crisis was at its height. To quote the introductory booklet : "Partnership means giving and receiving, sharing from strengths and receiving in our weakness... The Partnership gives high priority to transparent mutual accountability in the area of finance... If money is to be sent, the Diocese recommends that it is routed through the diocese in Birmingham to the appropriate diocese in Malawi with instructions for its [onward] transmission." As time has gone on, advice has been added that "Funding may be an element of the link, but it will not be the central feature." Friendship, prayer and personal contact, nowadays usually through email or WhatsApp, remain the essential foundations.

Applications can come from parishes in the UK or Malawi; they will always be agreed by bishops in each diocese. Some links have been 'project links' between parishes, schools or hospitals, running for a limited period and involving funding for a project. Others have been open-ended 'parish links', launched at intervals since 2000. These are highly significant to a few parishes and important to others, but the majority of Malawi-supporting parishes in Birmingham have opted not to develop one. There have always been more parishes in Malawi seeking a link than in Birmingham, so the willingness of the latter has been the limiting factor. It is hard to say how many are active, as they have proved vulnerable to changes in personnel at either end. Some links have faded and been revived; others have fallen into disuse.

A very active link is that between St Richard's, Lea Hall and Balaka, DUS. This began in 2010 and has been greatly strengthened by exchange visits. The priest at St Richard's, Rev Paul Bracher, visited Malawi in 2011 and spent 15 days in Balaka. Further visits have taken place in each direction: Fr Michael Malasa and his wife Carolyn spent three weeks in Lea Hall in 2012 and Fr Son Ali visited briefly in 2018. Paul visited again in 2015 and 2018. In 2017 Denese Ryan, a member of St Richard's congregation, stayed five days there with Fr Matthews Kachala.[1]

The link with Balaka has had profound effects. St Richard's is a poor congregation in one of the UK's most deprived areas, but the link has led to a remarkable outpouring of generosity. St Richard's has sponsored a number of young people, including children of priests, to attend secondary school [they are fee-paying]. The parish has also sponsored two young people through tertiary education – medical school and nursing college - and one young person through college to qualify as a tailor. Harvests were poor in the years 2015, 2016 and 2018, and St Richard's gave money for the purchase of fertilizer and seed before the start of the rainy season. Specific projects in Balaka have included the purchase of solar lamps for classrooms in the two church primary schools, the repairing of the head teachers` houses there, and the purchase of Bibles for the church congregation. St Richard's has helped with income earning projects: the construction of a waterproof roof to the community shelter at the main church site and the purchase of chickens. Many varied gifts have also been sent on the annual containers or taken by visitors.

After Paul`s first visit several personal friendships developed between people in Lea Hall and Balaka, especially where there was something in

---

[1] Rev Paul Bracher, *Parish Partnership: St Richard's, Lea Hall with Balaka*, 25.2.2019 – also source of the following paragraphs.

common, e.g., two garage proprietors were linked. St Richard's has also received from Balaka in various other ways. Gifts have included home-made palm crosses for distribution on Palm Sunday. Most significantly, St Richard's has no live musician but has used CDs of the Balaka singing group and of pupils in Malawian schools to help in worship.

The partnership has changed people at Lea Hall. Its joys have included expanding often very limited horizons there by reports and pen-friendships with Balaka; putting their own difficulties into perspective; reminding people that God is at work on a much bigger scale than we imagine; unlocking the generosity described above; and learning hospitality, not part of the local culture. On the downside, it has been found frustrating that between 2011 and the time of writing Balaka had four priests, one of whom was moved on just as he was about to visit Birmingham. By contrast, Paul Bracher has been priest at Lea Hall since 1993. Some priests have been better communicators than others. There has been a degree of episcopal interference in the partnership and problems with money transfers. Finally, it has not always been possible to know what pupil sponsorship is achieving, as school reports have either not been provided or been uninformative.

A link was set up in 2014 between St Mark's, Mzuzu, DNM and St Peter's, Hall Green. A group of seven from Hall Green was invited to Malawi in 2016. The vicar, Canon Martin Stephenson, wrote:

> "We had been warned! So many people who had been to Malawi told us to expect a warm welcome and to fall in love with this beautiful country and its people. They also told us to expect to be changed, and to be encouraged as Christians. They were not wrong."

The group felt they were being received by a community of faith and joy, living the gospel of love and the divine gift of hope. They received deep friendship in Christ and a reminder that 'everything is possible with God.'[2] Martin reported two years later that St Peter's prayed every week for the church life of St Mark's. They were raising funds to help

---

[2] Martin Stephenson, *Malawi - 'The Warm Heart of Africa.' Visit to Mzuzu*, July 2016.

finish the construction of the new church there and in particular the planned sound system – an example of a parish link underpinning project support. St Peter's had also supported a Sunday School day away to Likoma Island; they had collected and sent by container items such as autoclaves for clinics and sewing machines for the sewing workshops at St Mark's.[3]

Some very effective links have come about by unconventional routes. Glynis Gayton, a member of St Nicholas, Baddesley Ensor, a village in Warwickshire, tells a heart-warming story. She felt called to go to Malawi but did not qualify for the teachers' skills share trip. She was given the name of Stephen Drew of Medic Malawi, a charity which supports the community of Mtunthama, DLM, and Stephen agreed to arrange her trip there.

> "We have a bakery here at home, and on my first visit talking to Father Petro [parish priest of Mtunthama] he was sharing his vision for the future with me, he said he would like some units to be built ... to create employment and services, and I say 'what would you like your first one to be Father?' He said a bakery (he had no idea that we have a bakery). It was a divine moment for me, I knew why Malawi was calling me, I knew why I had been put on this earth. So excited but I never make a promise that I cannot keep, so I say I will see what I can do. So, I came home, and have raised £43,500 to cover the cost of purchasing the machinery and sending it to Malawi. I have made five more visits, one with a friend. The bakery has been built; the electric money has been sent ... The ripple effect from me going to Malawi, and building a bakery has been amazing, from old people's homes getting involved, schools, W.I. and so on. Everyone wanting to do their bit."[4]

Bishop Francis of DLM visited Glynis for a day when he came for the 50th anniversary in 2016. She invited people who had helped with the fundraising for the bakery, to meet the bishop for a meal in the church hall. Glynis has had to be very patient: the machinery has been

---

[3] Martin Stephenson, correspondence with author, 30.11.2018.

[4] Glynis Gayton, Survey reply, 13.3.2018 with subsequent additions.

dispatched from the maker in Lancashire, complete with coverage by the local TV news, transported by container and delivered. Funds for the installation of the three phase electric have been sent to Malawi, but at the time of writing the bakery remains unconnected. The whole episode is a small picture of how the Malawian economy is handicapped by an inadequate electricity supply.

From time to time efforts have been made to set up school-to-school links. Guidelines were issued in 2004 by the Education Department of C of E Birmingham. Links for the exchange of messages, greetings and information have tended to be fragile and short-lived, as few schools are on email and communication is not easy. Four links with Malawian schools were recorded in about 2008; I am not aware that any still operated at the time of writing. 'Project links' with schools have been set up for construction of classroom blocks, pit latrines or teachers' houses, some of them on the back of teachers' skills share trips.

Birmingham Children's Hospital/ Queen Elizabeth Central Hospital, Blantyre Link

Standards of maternal and child health in Malawi have long been poor, and maternal and child mortality rates high. The country suffers from a significant shortage of qualified paediatricians, children's nurses and other healthcare staff. It is estimated that in 2005 there were a mere 56 nurses per 100,000 people. This lack of qualified and motivated healthcare staff, combined with poor family planning, which was actually illegal until 1985, poverty, the HIV epidemic and lack of resources such as equipment and gloves meant that 1 in 10 children would die before their 5th birthday.[5] Clinics were lacking in the villages, and expectant mothers there often turned to untrained traditional birth attendants. Their lack of knowledge could lead to their giving traditional medicines too early in the birthing process, causing the womb to

---

[5] UNICEF estimate, quoted in correspondence from Dr Mandy Goldstein, BCH, 21.5.2019.

rupture with loss of mother and baby.[6] Obstructed labour and eclampsia were frequent.

In view of this, a Safe Motherhood Programme fully supported by the churches was launched in 1996. With the help of health professionals and volunteers, NGOs and churches, the rate of maternal mortality has been brought down from 952 per 100,000 in 1996 to 634 per 100,000 in 2015, still over twice the global average.[7] Neonatal mortality has been halved over the same period, from 44.1 to 23.1 per 1000 live births.[8]

Bishop Sentamu was keen to broaden the base of the Partnership to include areas of life beyond the churches. In 2004 he spoke at Birmingham Children's Hospital [BCH]. His comment "it takes a whole village to educate a child" resonated strongly with some staff who were acutely aware that the hospital did little for the health of children globally. As a result, a link was set up in 2004 between BCH and Queen Elizabeth Central Hospital [QECH] Blantyre. Bishop David visited QECH on his first visit to Malawi in 2009 and met two nurses from Birmingham!

QECH is a large government funded hospital and the regional referral centre for all of Southern Malawi. As a teaching hospital it supports undergraduate medical students, nurses and clinical officers. The children's department at QECH was run by the "incredible" Professor Elizabeth Molyneux, who had earlier worked briefly at St Luke's Hospital, Malosa and was pleased to support the partnership's evolution.[9]

---

[6] Salomi Kachusa, a nursing midwife based at the clinic at Chilambwe, DNM. This report was passed on by Rt Rev Christopher Boyle.

[7] www.knoema.com/atlas/Malawi/topics/Health/Health-Status/Maternal-mortality-ratio [24.5.2018]. The maternal mortality rate in the UK stood at around 9 per 100,000 in this period.

[8] www.knoema.com/atlas/Malawi/Neonatal-mortality-rate [24.5.2018].

[9] Correspondence with Dr Mandy Goldstein, BCH, 21.5.2019.

A group from BCH headed by consultant paediatrician Dr Mandy Goldstein visited Blantyre in 2004 with the aim of helping develop health professionals in Malawi to provide for the future health of the nation's children. Dr Goldstein approached Dr Sentamu for help, and Birmingham Diocese funded a full assessment of the potential of the partnership, including a second visit in 2005 by Dr Goldstein and the Assistant Director of Nursing, Rosy Rogers. They proposed a scheme of education that crossed national and professional boundaries.[10] The overriding aim was to develop an effective and sustainable partnership for education of health care staff. It should improve the health of children in Malawi and patients and staff in each participating hospital should benefit. Specifics included:

- Facilitate links for nurses and non-medical staff
- Develop teaching skills for those who would train the healthcare staff
- Develop the training of children's nurses in Malawi
- Support the medical education programme in Malawi
- Act as a catalyst to increase the resources of the community served by the hospital

These objectives have been achieved with the help of other external sources of support, local and international. Other objectives successfully delivered over the ensuing years included: continuing education for consultants and postgraduate nurses, support and training for laboratory, radiology, therapy and administration staff, resuscitation and child protection training for doctors and nurses.

Over its 15+ year life the link has contributed to the sustained development, recruitment and retention of Malawian healthcare staff.

---

[10] Dr Mandy Goldstein, *Birmingham Children's Hospital – Blantyre, Malawi Partnership, Development of an Effective, sustainable and Appropriate Partnership to Support the Education Programme for all Grades of Paediatric Health Care Professionals*, 1.9.2005.

The children's department head and more than half the consultants at QECH were Malawian at the time of writing. As many as 41 doctors from BCH have visited Malawi. A BCH trained consultant paediatrician, Dr Joe Langton, lived and worked in Blantyre as head of the children's department for nearly 3 years; she has remained a tireless advocate for the link. BCH medical registrars have spent 6-12 months in Malawi and provided regular bedside teaching for medical students as well as providing medical care to the patients. A variety of other BCH staff have offered their skills, including 27 nurses. "For years BCH nurses have worked alongside their Malawian colleagues on the wards in QECH leading by example and teaching at the bedside, thus over time benefiting hundreds of student nurses and qualified nurses."[11]

In their turn, 29 nurses and 14 doctors from QECH have visited Birmingham. Most have been able to attend formal training courses of up to 3 weeks, run by BCH for nurses or nationally for doctors. One doctor did an acclaimed conference presentation. The attachments at BCH are highly valued. One Malawian A&E Sister commented: "We do not have as much equipment but the exchanges mean we learn new skills and they provide us with the ability to use what we have."

Since 2008 BCH has used the Birmingham containers to send medical equipment and supplies, including tubes for feeding small, sick or premature babies, equipment for blood taking and giving fluid and antibiotics intravenously, and wound dressings. Items of clothing, bedding including blankets for the smallest babies, play equipment and other gifts have also been sent.

A BCH Malawi partnership charitable fund was established from the outset. BCH staff have been very generous with their time and resources. The nurses and junior doctors have gone for 6-12 months unpaid from the UK, usually with a grant towards travel and subsistence. For many of the shorter secondments BCH staff have used their annual leave. The partnership charity has met costs including travel and visas for Malawian doctors and nurses training at BCH, who

---

[11] Correspondence with Dr Mandy Goldstein, BCH, 21.5.2019.

are accommodated by a Birmingham family. The partnership is now recognized as a national leader in paediatric global health. One A&E Sister from Malawi summed up its value: "We feel we are not alone; I beg you to continue."[12]

Mission Encounter and Skills Share

The Malawi link has always been about people as well as money. As the Birmingham pioneer in Malawi, John Parslow, said: "It doesn't matter very much to [Africans] to say, 'Birmingham put that school up'. That's alright, it's bricks and mortar, but you want to know people. This is the African approach, it is not intellectual, it is not theoretical, it is not intuitive, it is warm, it is personal. This is where links are important, not in schemes and projects."[13]

This gave great significance to the visits from Birmingham to Malawi. However, with some significant exceptions, until about the year 2000 these were carried out largely by male clergy. Bishops made infrequent official visits to Malawi; selected clergy made working visits there. Bishops from Malawi came to confer and fundraise, clergy came to train in Birmingham and to be attached to a parish. The exceptions included youth groups: a series of visits to and from Malawi took place during the 1990s and early 2000s, and the Youth Encounter programme built on these. The visits to Malawi led by Bishop Santer in 1991 and 2000 included lay parishioners; the one led by Bishop Sentamu in 2003 was confined to diocesan staff. But there was no scope for interested adults to visit Malawi except by invitation.

Bishop Sentamu considered it a priority to get more lay Christians to visit Malawi as one aspect of combatting the clericalism of the Partnership. Peter Howell-Jones developed ambitious plans for groups of lay Christians to visit Malawi to have a 'mission encounter' with the

---

[12] Correspondence with Dr Mandy Goldstein, BCH, 21.5.2019.

[13] Interviewed by Canon Bob Jenkins, 19.10.1988.

local church or to offer their skills. These came to fruition from 2006 onwards, after Bishop Sentamu's departure for York.

The mission encounter visits were seen as "a great way for people to step out of their comfort zones, to engage, learn and listen"[14]. They were self-financed and self-selecting, and appealed especially to interested professionals and business people, who visited Malawi in parties of up to 15 led by diocesan staff. The trips fed ongoing interest in the country and its welfare, and led to some repeat visits, including by a couple who spent several months in Malawi as doctor and diocesan planner. They had a catalytic effect on local church life in Birmingham: in one parish giving to Malawi went from £150pa to £1500pa.[15] There was always a tension between participants seeing these visits as 'mission', bringing the necessary patience and openness to Malawian ways, or as a form of sanctified ethical tourism, with European expectations of comfort and scheduling. Mission encounter groups visited Malawi between 2006 and 2011.

The skills share visits were of two types: general and teachers'. The general skills share trip in 2006 was valuable but the format was not repeated. A large team of 16, varying in age, background and skills, was gathered and carefully prepared by two leaders for their encounter with each other and with Malawians. This included time spent with families in Blantyre and a week doing practical work at Chilema. Team leader Rev Philip Swan reflected:

> "Overall, it's been quite an amazing experience of communion – 16 people from different parishes, of different ages, different outlooks, and we have come, we have stayed together, we have laughed, done battle with mosquitoes, dealt with water problems, worked, ate, drank wine or Kuche Kuche [Malawian beer] and laughed a bit more...."[16]

---

[14] Very Rev Peter Howell-Jones, interview, 16.8.2018.

[15] Ibid.

[16] Rev Philip Swan, *Some Reflections from our Visit to Malawi,* 31.11.2006.

Team members' skills, notably that of water engineer, were put to good use. But the greatest benefit to the Partnership proved to be the group members' ongoing involvement, including with the container team and as Task Group secretary.

There were five teachers' skills share trips between 2006 and 2015. Their basis has been for teachers from Birmingham [not only from church schools] to take part in interactive in-service training for Malawian primary school teachers, whose initial training is scanty and in-service training non-existent. The idea was born in discussion between Birmingham and the Bishop of Northern Malawi and his staff. Peter Howell-Jones got Jim Carr on the phone to discuss the idea and Willy Musukwa 'liked the man Jim even before I met him'.[17] The first training courses in 2006 were in DNM, including one on Likoma Island. For the subsequent trips in 2009, 2011, 2013 and 2015, all the dioceses nominated teachers to attend the workshops which took place in the lay training centres at Malosa, DUS, and Nkhotakota, DLM. For Jesman Seva, Nkhotakota LTC has been a 'neutral playground' for the church leadership training sessions led by Rev Emma Sykes in 2017 and the skills share programme. The pattern has been for two sets of workshops to be held, with 35 teachers at each. The Birmingham teachers have funded themselves and some Malawian costs, and the trip included a holiday/tourism element. Birmingham diocese provided modest financial help but had no sustained involvement in terms of recruiting teachers for the programme or raising funds to supply the basic needs of schools there.[18]

Jim and Liz Carr, who co-led the first four skills share trips, commented:

> We did our best to pass on some practical ideas, skills and strategies for teachers in Anglican schools, bearing in mind the huge differences in class sizes, buildings and resources as well as the Government's provision of teacher training – or lack of it. We always tried to make the

---

[17] Interview, 21.6.2018.

[18] A view expressed by Jim and Liz Carr in response to survey from author, 26.3.2018.

> Skills Share workshops a genuine **sharing** – and have continued to recognize just how much teachers in both countries do have in common … We and our UK teacher colleagues on all four visits have vowed never to complain again about classroom and teaching conditions at home![19]

On more recent trips, issues of school leadership were discussed alongside training in subject teaching. In 2019, senior Malawian teachers made up half the leadership team and took a big share in leading workshops.

In September 2011 a group of lay Malawians including professionals and business people came for a self-financed visit called Mission Encounter to Birmingham. The four dioceses nominated three participants each, and the team was led by Canon Christopher Mwawa, General Secretary of ACM. All the group stayed in Christians' homes, and the Birmingham hosts arranged an ambitious programme of targeted visits to local companies, accountancy and legal firms, schools etc. The visit included a day trip to Stratford-on-Avon; the visitors appreciated the sense of history. This was reckoned to be a successful visit, but there were doubts as to whether it repaid all the work needed on the part of the hosts and organizers.

Visits to and from Malawi by Bishops, Clergy and Diocesan Officers

Established patterns of episcopal visiting continued in the years after 2000. Birmingham Bishops visited Malawi at irregular intervals: Bishop Sentamu visited in 2003 with a team of diocesan staff; Bishop David visited in 2009 for what turned out to be the final biennial consultation; Andrew Watson, Bishop of Aston, went to Malawi for the consecration of Fanuel Magangani in Mzuzu in 2010. Bishop Andrew went again the following year to represent Birmingham at the celebrations for the 150th anniversary of the Anglican Church in Central Africa, attended by the Archbishop of Canterbury. Bishop David made a week-long visit in 2014 to the dioceses of Lake and Northern Malawi, accompanied by a

---

[19] Response to survey from author, 26.3.2018.

Mothers' Union group and the team which produced the DVD 'Matilda's Malawi.' A visit by Anne Hollinghurst, Bishop of Aston, followed in 2017. She and a small team visited Lake Diocese and the two southern dioceses. Bishop Anne's husband Steve, a theological teacher, led a much-appreciated seminar in Blantyre for DSM clergy on Christian mission past and present.

Malawian bishops paid regular working visits to the UK to confer with USPG and other personal links as well as visiting Birmingham; this was especially true of Bishop Christopher with his Birmingham roots. I made every effort to take bishops and other visitors into church primary schools to lead assemblies as a means of mutual learning, and showed a PowerPoint of Malawian life for the children's benefit. All four bishops were invited for the centenary of the diocese in 2005 and again in 2016 to mark the 50th anniversary of the Partnership.

Before 2000 clergy visits to Malawi had been largely official or representing the diocese. During the following decade 'encounter' visits were encouraged. A Birmingham ordinand, Alexandrina Mann, who had visited Malawi on a youth exchange, did a placement with Fr Eston Pembamoyo in 2002. Another ordinand, John Bleazard, did a month's summer placement in Malawi in 2007, spending about half that time at Leonard Kamungu Theological College. Rev Philip Swan and his family had a month's stay with his family on Sabbatical in 2002 and did a placement in Mwanza, DUS; Philip went on to chair the Malawi Task Group from 2004 to 2010. Rev Peter Smith and his family visited Malawi in about 2007 and his daughter Lois returned for a year's service in the country. Rev Matthew Rhodes visited as a representative of USPG. Rev Adrian Leahy accompanied me on a visit on Sabbatical in 2012.

Malawian priests no longer come to Birmingham to train. Some senior priests have visited the UK at the invitation of other bodies, universities or charities. Recent visits by younger Malawian priests have been largely been to take part in the 'Canterbury courses' to introduce younger clergy to the workings of the Anglican Communion. Priests have been invited to Birmingham for a few days at the course's conclusion.

Diocesan officers visited Malawi too. Mary Edwards, Diocesan Director of Education, visited in 2000 as part of Bishop Mark's party. The Ven. Hayward Osborne, Archdeacon of Birmingham, and his wife Sandy went in 2005, visiting Anglican parishes, schools and colleges, and in Sandy's case, a nursing college as well. In these ways, and in regular annual visits by the Director of Finance, the partnership was supported by the institutional engagement of the diocese.[20] Budgetary and other constraints have prevented Malawian officers from visiting Birmingham, other than one visit by the General Secretary of ACM. Visits from Birmingham and email contact have had to suffice.

Containers

Launching the Birmingham Malawi Containers was my own small distinctive contribution to the Partnership. I visited Malawi on Sabbatical in 2007 and was shocked by the lack of school resources. On return it became clear that I must appeal for a range of resources and organize containers to send them on the diocese's behalf. I took advice from CART [Christian Africa Relief Trust] who had long experience of sending charity containers. I then set up what became a very committed team including Paul Wilson, who arranged financial support from the diocese, Judith Grubb, who became responsible for donor relations, and Jan Beare as treasurer. The first container went in January 2008 and the team continued to give generously of their time and effort for several years. A full-size shipping container is 40 ft. [12.2m.] long, with a capacity of some 2600 cu.ft. or 75 m^3. Carefully loaded, it takes a lot of gifts; loading has been done by teams of volunteers. All gifts must be labelled with a description and the sender's and recipient's details. To be exempt from customs duty, gifts must be secondhand and destined for use in a school, hospital, community project or church.

By June 2019 14 containers had been sent. Quality used gifts have included school books, supplies and furniture, medical equipment and supplies, hospital bedding, computer equipment, sewing machines,

---

[20] The phrase is that of Peter Howell-Jones, 16.8.2018.

bicycles, woodworking and other tools, clothes for children or adults and clergy robes. Amongst the more unusual gifts sent have been 12 hospital beds for St Anne's Hospital, Nkhotakota and two canoes for a charity in Nkhata Bay, DNM. Alongside Birmingham Christians and the Children's Hospital, senders have included a variety of UK charities supporting churches and communities in Malawi; all have paid a uniform charge of £6 per cu.ft. A key partner since 2009 has been the Roman Catholic parish of Corpus Christi in Tonbridge, Kent, who have had a very active twinning project with Malawi headed by Brian Wilkins. A lorry load of gifts and skilled packers have come to Birmingham for each container and so helped to ensure it is financially viable.

Containers were sent initially to DUS and DSM, with access to DLM and DNM soon added. The regular drop-off points have been Blantyre and Lilongwe, but one container was sent in 2013 direct to Mtunthama, DLM, filled with furniture from a church school in Chelmsley Wood which was relocating. The consignee for most containers until 2016 was Fr Eston Pembamoyo. The consignee is the legal recipient of the contents, and needs to arrange with the Malawi Revenue Service for them to be received duty-free [provided they qualify as used gifts] and collected by the addressees promptly in orderly fashion. Eston's reports reflected the stresses of climate change and a deteriorating economic situation. He described the containers' sending as "the Gospel in practice":

> "When we break the body of Christ in the Eucharistic service — the Holy Communion - the breaking of the wafer is in reality the causing of pain in the body of Christ, and all who partake in that one broken body are actually sharing in the pains of the broken body as one and united people. When the broken body gets healed in the resurrection, we who are many and partake in that one healed body get healed too and are commanded to go out to witness the living Christ in us into the world... Many Malawians... regardless of their faiths or creed are supported above all by people they do not visibly know but believe they love them

to an extent that they are willing to share with them in the agonies of their poverty and economic hardships..."[21]

Senders in Birmingham churches share in the joy of giving:

"We've always used the container to send as much as we can in the way of school books and stationery items, given by a range of supporters ... In addition, we've sent a good many boxes of children's clothes and toys, and our Knit and Natter Group at Church currently supports Agnes Mkoko by sending at least 4 or 5 boxes per year containing wool, fabrics, knitting patterns, knitted baby clothes, etc."[22]

"... There is always a good response from Mothers' Union and church members. I cannot emphasize enough the importance of the container. It keeps the link very much alive and more personal. People love to see photos from Malawi of the gifts being used."[23]

Birmingham Diocesan Centenary, 2005, and 50th Anniversary of the Malawi Partnership, 2016

As the celebrations for the centenary of Birmingham Diocese in 2005 were planned, it was clear that the Malawi Partnership must have a high profile. Bishop Sentamu and his party were struck on their visit to Malawi in 2003 by the huge difficulties faced by clergy in travelling to distant churches. The bishop proposed to the Malawian bishops that every parish should be provided with a motorbike. 'Malawi Wheels' was made the Birmingham Lent Appeal for 2004 – see the handbill below - and fundraising continued into 2005.[24] A stock of suitable unsold motorbikes was discovered at the then British-owned Stansfield Motors Ltd in Blantyre. Peter Howell-Jones and Paul Wilson struck up a close

---

[21] Fr Eston Pembamoyo, Birmingham Container 7 Report, 3.4.2013.

[22] Liz and Jim Carr, reply to survey from author, 26.3.2018.

[23] Canon Claire Laland, correspondence, 2.8.2018.

[24] Letters from Bishop Sentamu to Malawian bishops, 12.12.2003; to licensed clergy in the diocese, 6.2.2004 and 19.11.2004.

and beneficial business relationship with Stansfields that lasted until they retired or moved on.[25]

The final sum raised was enough to buy 58 Yamaha motorbikes with crash helmet, registration and motorcycling lessons. At the Malawi Wheels service in June 2005 "A motorbike roared up the main aisle of Birmingham Cathedral ... to hand over more than £115,000 ... to a visiting delegation of Malawian bishops and lay representatives ..."[26] The Malawian dioceses ensured that clergy and parishes were careful about maintaining the motorbikes, and some of them were still on the road 13 years later.

Bishop Sentamu and Peter Howell-Jones heard Ndirande Anglican Voices, from a shanty town parish in Blantyre, sing at a dinner in Blantyre in 2003 and recognized their special quality. Their singing expresses the joy and trust in God, even in the face of adversity, that is at the heart of Malawian Christian experience. It was proposed to bring the choir to Birmingham for the centenary; the Board of Education were persuaded to make a grant towards the costs of bringing them.[27] Their arrival at Birmingham Airport was delayed as choir members and Alison Bownass, who was to meet them, were questioned closely and at length. However, Claire Laland had asked MU members living near the airport to come along with welcome banners, some made by two of Claire's grandchildren. It was a big hit at the airport, especially when the choir were finally allowed through and sang to everyone in thanksgiving.[28]

Alison worked closely with Peter Howell-Jones to organize an action-packed schedule which included 13 events at schools and 18 in churches

---

[25] Very Rev Peter Howell-Jones, interview, 16.8.2018; Canon Paul Wilson, *My Involvement,* 15.10.2018.

[26] Centenary Newsletter, Diocese of Birmingham, November 2005, p. 6.

[27] £25,000 towards a total net cost of just over £30,000. Source: Canon Paul Wilson, Director of Finance, 20.7.2005.

[28] Claire Laland, correspondence with author, 2.8.2018.

Malawi Wheels
help get the Malawian Church moving

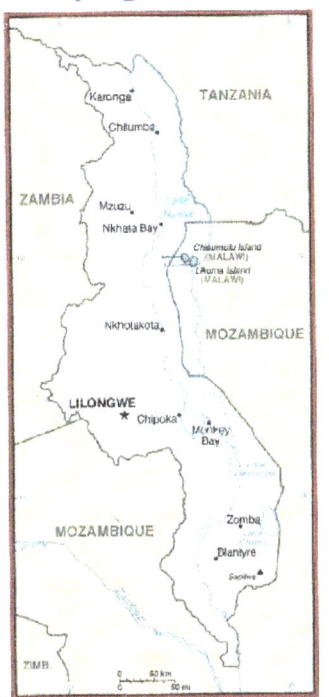

Some parishes have 10 churches

Some priests travel 10 miles to one of their churches

Most priests walk

Yamaha AG100 - choice of Malawian Church - widely used in Malawi: tyres, parts and servicing are easily available

Lent 2004
Diocese of Birmingham Lent Appeal

To celebrate the Centenary of the Diocese, we are raising funds for 65 motorbikes for parish transport. £2,000 buys a motorbike, crash helmet & tuition. The Fund-raising begins with the 2004 Lent Appeal.

Every gift counts - Will you play a part?
Contact Michele Gillmore at the Diocesan Office: 0121-426-0423
Please make cheques payable to *Diocese of Birmingham Malawi Fund*

over a period of 3½ weeks. They had special sets of brightly-coloured printed t-shirts made for them.[29] The choir featured at the Malawi Wheels service and linked up with the City of Birmingham Young Voices, the city's foremost young people's choir. The choir's visit really raised the profile of Malawi and had wider benefits: "Before then, Malawi had been a place of poverty and discontent, but the choir showed Malawi as a vibrant culture."[30]

The four Malawian bishops were invited to the UK again in May 2016 to mark the 50th anniversary of the Partnership. The bishops attended a Round Table meeting in London of the main charities and agencies supporting the Malawian Anglican church. Nine parishes in Birmingham hosted them for their busy 8-day visit to the city. They took a full part in the parishes' life as well as having meetings and visits arranged by the diocese. They shared two Bible studies with Bishop David and Bishop Maurice Sinclair.[31]

On the Day of Pentecost in the Cathedral a celebration service took place, at which a Memorandum of Understanding was signed by the five bishops of Malawi and Birmingham. This stated: "We give thanks together for fifty years of the Malawi Birmingham Partnership ... We acknowledge the partnership in the gospel of Jesus Christ and our sharing in the bonds of unity that link us within the worldwide Anglican Communion. We recognize with joy the spiritual riches that we find in each other and that are unlocked as we share them together." It went on to express thanks for Birmingham's practical support in the areas of education, health, 'ministries' including clergy and youth visits and provision of vehicles, and administration including budgetary support. The benefits to Birmingham included: "the blessings of being able to give support and offer mutual prayer and thanksgiving for each other's needs and joys. We recognize the need to infect the next generation with the joy we have discovered in this Partnership." The core principles

---

[29] Alison Bownass, correspondence with author, 5.9.2018.
[30] Very Rev Peter Howell-Jones, interview, 16.8.2018.
[31] C of E Birmingham Annual Report 2016.

under which each side sought to operate the Partnership were stated to be sustainability, trust and accountability, and relationship.[32]

The Partnership's 50th anniversary gave another opportunity for a special appeal. The possibility of Birmingham financing a student hostel on the LKTC site in Zomba as an income generating project was discussed between the partners. It was discarded when it became clear the cost would be well beyond what could be raised in Birmingham. Instead, it was agreed that Birmingham should contribute to solving the universal problem of a lack of classroom blocks for the burgeoning school population. Each diocese chose a site for a single storey two-classroom block, built to one of two standard designs: for DLM, the primary school at Ntchisi in the hills of the Central Region; DNM, the primary school at Msomba near Chintheche on the lake shore; DSM, Trinity Anglican Secondary School near Blantyre; and DUS, the secondary school at Matope, long established as a mission station on the river north of Blantyre. A total of £44,000 was raised for their building. The classroom block at Msomba stands next to a girls' boarding hostel financed by USPG: a practical example of how the different agencies can complement each other's work. The block at Ntchisi, the first to be completed, was opened at a joyful ceremony in 2017 by Anne Hollinghurst, Bishop of Aston, and Bishop Francis Kaulanda.

UK Partners – MACS, USPG, Mothers' Union

Birmingham has always been aware of working alongside many other charities to serve the Malawian Anglican Church and its mission. In 2011 the links between the largest four such charities or mission agencies were formalized in the Malawi Round Table, which has shared member bodies' news and thinking and coordinated action for the Malawian Church. Face-to-face meetings have taken place about twice-yearly,

---

[32] Malawi Birmingham Partnership: A Memorandum of Understanding signed by the Bishops of Birmingham, Lake Malawi, Northern Malawi, Southern Malawi and Upper Shire, Pentecost, 15.5.2016.

usually in London. Malawian bishops have taken part when visiting the UK.

Malawi Association for Christian Support [MACS] has been working in Malawi since 1993. It works in partnership with local people on education, health and community projects in the rural areas, where the needs are greatest. Most of the Board of Trustees including the Chair, Tony Cox, have lived and worked in Malawi. MACS has had a UK Projects Officer, Eileen Eggington, and a Malawian local representative, Grafiud Tione, formerly employed by the Ministry of Finance. It majors on building projects in DLM and DUS, particularly for schools and hospitals; it has strong links with particular communities including Nkope Hill, DUS. It also offers bursaries for secondary school fees. In 2009 12 hospital beds were sourced by the author and sent by Birmingham container to St Anne's Hospital, Nkhotakota at MACS' expense.

USPG, which since 2016 stands for United Society Partners in the Gospel, is the successor mission agency to UMCA, which sent missionaries to Malawi for more than a century. Mothers' Union is a key strength of every Anglican parish in Malawi. Other charities, not Round Table members, specialize in supporting the development of particular communities. Of these, Birmingham has worked most closely with Medic Malawi, which supports Mtunthama, DLM. Its director was briefly a member of the Task Group.

Chapter 11

Developments in the Malawian Church, 2002-2016, and Birmingham's Role

The nation of Malawi faces formidable challenges, many of them common to all regions and dioceses. The climate is prone to extreme events – storms, floods and drought – and population density is high for a nation largely dependent on rain-fed agriculture. Climate change is making the country increasingly vulnerable to natural disasters. In recent years the densely populated south has been particularly hard hit.

The urban economy is fragile, with companies closing and unemployment increasing. Giving in the urban parishes that usually bear the burden of supporting rural ones through the high assessment to the diocese is affected by salaries failing to keep pace with inflation. The Church has quite a large infrastructure to maintain and 'income generating projects' often do not manage to generate income.

Malawian politics and society, like those of many African nations, are marked, or marred, by neopatrimonialism. This is described as a system whereby rulers use state resources for personal benefit and to secure the loyalty of clients in the general population.[1] Corruption is a natural result of such a system. On occasion the Church, too, has fallen into neopatrimonial ways, with a bishop as dispenser of favours to those loyal to him and withholder of favours from others.

Developments in the Malawian Church over this period are covered very briefly. The four dioceses are described in turn, then the important topic of training, both ordination and lay, and ACM. Brief biographies of Malawian leaders who have been particularly engaged with the Partnership follow. While Birmingham's role has not always been

---

[1] Description: *Neopatrimonialism in Africa and Beyond,* ed. Daniel C. Bach, Mamoudou Gazibo. Routledge, 2012. See Gifford, *African Christianity: Its Public Role*, London: Hurst & Company, 1998 pp. 5-8.

obvious, its officers, Task Group members and others have kept in continuous contact and offered support and resourcing founded on careful discussion and prayer.

Diocese of Southern Malawi

Bishop James Tengatenga moved to Blantyre to found the diocese in 2002. It covers the southern part of the Southern Region of Malawi. It includes Blantyre and nearby Limbe, the main commercial centres of the country, which enjoy modest prosperity by Malawian standards. It also covers rural areas of deep poverty in the Shire and Ruo valleys suffering badly from climate change, with repeated extremes of flooding and drought.

The new diocese had to start from scratch; it acquired some fairly basic office buildings in Limbe, and a bishop's house in Blantyre was built with help from USPG. The new diocese had few schools and no secondary ones; a school on the edge of Blantyre was purchased and reopened as Trinity Anglican Secondary School. The school buildings have required a lot of investment to bring them up to standard and allow for expansion; the school was chosen as the location for the Birmingham 50th anniversary classroom block.[2]

Bishop Tengatenga needed somewhere peaceful to complete his PhD dissertation;[3] Bishop Santer opened the doors for a visiting fellowship in 2003 at Clare College, Cambridge, where he had been Dean of Chapel. Bishop James served on the Standing Committee of the Anglican Consultative Council from 2002 and as its Chair from 2009, travelling extensively in that capacity. He resigned from the diocese in 2013, and since 2014 has been Distinguished Visiting Professor of Global Anglicanism at the School of Theology at the University of the South, Tennessee, USA.

---

[2] See ch. 10 above.

[3] The resulting book was published by Kachere in 2006 as *Church, State and Society in Malawi, the Anglican Case*.

The 150th anniversary of the Anglican Church in Malawi was marked by a visit to Southern Malawi by the Archbishop of Canterbury, the Most Rev Rowan Williams. Archbishop Rowan was preacher at a service on 8 October 2011 at Magomero. Many international mission partners were represented; the Birmingham party was led by the Bishop of Aston, the Rt Rev Andrew Watson, and included his wife Beverly and a mission encounter group.

Bishop James was succeeded by Alinafe Kalemba, one of many Malawian priests to have been profoundly influenced by the Birmingham Partnership.[4] Alinafe was elected Bishop in 2013. His consecration took place at short notice, and no bishop from Birmingham was free to attend. The diocese was represented by Canon Paul Wilson, who brought greetings and the gift of a pectoral cross. In view of the acute poverty affecting rural areas, while industry and commerce support modest prosperity in urban areas, Bishop Alinafe agreed with his clergy that they should be given posts alternately in urban and rural areas as a matter of fairness.

---

[4] Alinafe Kalemba was born in 1967 as the son of a nomadic fisherman and evangelist; he accompanied his father when evangelizing and church planting. He began an engineering degree but transferred to Zomba Theological College for priestly formation, gaining his diploma in 1993. He served in several parishes in DSM. In 1999-2000 he studied for a Master's degree at Durham University and spent his vacations in various parishes. In December 1999 he stayed two weeks with Rev Philip Swan at the Lickey in SW Birmingham; it was the beginning of a deep friendship. In 2001 Bishop James made Alinafe his training chaplain at Malosa, and took him with him the following year to Blantyre. In 2005 Alinafe was chosen to be Dean of Leonard Kamungu Theological College [LKTC]. He resigned in 2011 as Dean after disagreements with Bishop Brighton Malasa. He was found a parish in DSM in Chirimba, near Blantyre, and combined his parish work with an evangelistic ministry. The details of Bishop Alinafe's life and work are derived from an interview with him on 18.6.2018.

All four dioceses produced profiles for the 50th anniversary visit of their bishops to Birmingham in 2016. The DSM profile reported that: "Much of our area is prone to natural disasters like floods and drought, particularly in the past two years. Even now living conditions are still very difficult. The area has high levels of poverty, illiteracy, infant mortality and health related problems - HIV/AIDS, malaria, eye problems, poor water and sanitation."

Diocese of Upper Shire

The diocese covers the northern part of the Southern Region plus the district of Ntcheu, Central Region, a largely rural but densely populated area at the southern end of the lake and in the Shire valley. When the Diocese of Southern Malawi was split in 2002, most of its assets – diocesan headquarters and bishop's house on the Malosa site, hospitals, clinics, schools etc. –fell in the Upper Shire area. The church of SS Peter and Paul, by the lakeshore at Mpondas near Mangochi, became its cathedral. On the creation of the diocese, Archbishop Bernard Malango became its first bishop 'on transfer' from Zambia while continuing to serve as Archbishop.[5][6] He has been described as "very hardworking, ambitious, an achiever, but egocentric. He

---

[5] Bernard Malango came from Kayoyo, Ntchisi District in the Central Region of Malawi. After training in Tanzania and Zambia he was ordained in 1965. He occupied several important positions in the Diocese of Southern Malawi from 1970 onwards, including Warden of Chilema and Archdeacon of Blantyre. He obtained his Master's Degree in Ecumenical Studies at Dublin in 1981 and finally his DD. In 1988, the Central African bishops' meeting for the Lambeth Conference in England elected Malango as Bishop of Northern Zambia. In 1999 he was elected Archbishop of Central Africa.

[6] Henry Mbaya, *Raising African Bishops in the Anglican Church in Malawi 1924-2000*, uir.unisa.ac.za/bitstream/handle/10500/4483/Mbaya.pdf.S.12 [11.2.2019].

demanded hard work and absolute loyalty from those around him"[7] and his leadership style was described as "autocratic."[8] He retired in 2007.

The Anglican Communion was plunged into crisis following the consecration in 2003 of an open homosexual, Gene Robinson, as bishop of New Hampshire, USA. Archbishop Malango, together with others such as Archbishop Peter Akinola of Nigeria, proved a vigorous defender of the traditional Christian sexual ethic against liberalist tendencies;[9] in this he was followed publicly by some other Malawian bishops. The views of Birmingham Anglicans on the ordination of homosexuals probably ranged at this time over a scale somewhere between African conservatism and American liberalism. As in the case of women's ordination, it was seen by both sides as very important to maintain the friendship despite strongly-held differences of view or practice. There have been tensions in Birmingham, but no near-breakdown of relations such as occurred in the link between Nigeria and the C of E Diocese of Guildford.

Malango's successor, Brighton Vita Malasa,[10] was appointed bishop by the House of Bishops in 2008. Birmingham was represented at Bishop Brighton's installation in 2009 by Bishop Sinclair and Canon Howell-Jones. Under Bishop Brighton the drive towards self-sufficiency was publicly endorsed: "The Anglican Diocese of Upper Shire is to be financially self-reliant, spiritually and socially well developed with

---

[7] Fr Eston Pembamoyo, who served as Malango's Provincial Secretary, in interview, 20.6.2018.

[8] Fr Alinafe Kalemba, quoted in report by Rev Richard Tucker, 6.2007.

[9] Mbaya, *Raising African Bishops in the Anglican Church in Malawi 1924-2000,* uir.unisa.ac.za/bitstream/handle/10500/4483/Mbaya.pdf, S. 12 [11.2.2019].

[10] Brighton Vita Malasa came from the Mangochi area and is a member of the Yao tribe on his father's side. He was ordained in 2000 and priest at Magomero from 2001. From 2004 he was Bishop Malango's chaplain and acting Provincial Secretary, and from 2006 Dean of Mpondas Cathedral.

improved infrastructure and communication channels."[11] However, the diocese embraced the 'aid route' of pursuing progress via large inputs of external capital. An ambitious and costly diocesan strategic plan was drawn up with the help of Simon Morgan, then a member of St John's, Harborne, who made two stays of several months there. The episcopal New Year letter for 2011 majored on external support from Vancouver, Birmingham, MACS and USPG, with only one project out of 11 covered by local funding. In the subsequent experience of the diocese and of St Luke's Hospital, Malosa, large-scale plans have often been undermined by poor or defective financial management. In recent years the diocese has been conflict-ridden, to the extent that I do not believe I can yet write a reliable account of the diocese and its relations with Birmingham.

Diocese of Lake Malawi

The diocese covers the Central Region, barring one district, and includes the nation's capital, Lilongwe.

The death of Bishop Peter Nyanja from cancer in 2005 brought to an end an episcopate of 27 years. With that death began a 5-year period described as 'terrible' by his successor. In the Province of Central Africa, bishops are elected by diocesan electors but must then be confirmed by the bishops of the province. Bishop Nyanja had been appointed by the President [not elected] in 1978; so in 2005 the diocesan electors had no experience, and Archbishop Malango failed to give them proper information about the procedure.[12] Rev Nicholas Henderson, Vicar of All Saints', Ealing, and St Martin's, West Acton, in London, was elected in July 2006; however, the bishops of the province refused to confirm his election. Objections were lodged by five Anglicans from the Nkhotakota region.[13] Disorder broke out: groups came to parishes to tell the electors

---

[11] DUS Diocesan Development Board, *Concept Paper, August 2009*.

[12] Rt Rev Francis Kaulanda, interview, 14.6.2018.

[13] www.churchtimes.co.uk/articles/2005/9-december/news/uk/elected-bishop-is-vetoed-as-unsound [8.2.2019].

to stand their ground – without even notifying the parish priests! Physical fights took place in Nkhotakota Cathedral. Disputes and court injunctions delayed matters until Archdeacon Francis Kaulanda was elected and confirmed in 2009 and consecrated in 2010.[14] The Bishop of Birmingham decided after his visit in 2009 that it would not be right to intervene in the politics of the election,[15] and during these difficult years Birmingham was no more than a regretful and prayerful bystander.

Three separate factors seem to have been mixed up in this sorry business:

Mr Henderson's theological liberalism and his alleged pro-gay views [always denied by him], which were out of sympathy with the Archbishop's well-known conservative stance and objected to by a conservative Catholic faction in the diocese;

Regional jealousies between Nkhotakota, lakeshore seat of the cathedral, and Lilongwe, capital and location of the diocesan offices; and

The choice between a Western priest who had reportedly worked with the diocese for 18 years, helping raise £250,000 for religious, social and humanitarian projects[16] and who might be expected to bring more external money into the diocese; and an African leader rooted in the culture and spirituality of the diocese who could help it discover its own resources.

The first of these was the 'presenting factor'; the last was, I reckon, the most important, and on this basis the diocese surely got the right bishop in the end.

---

[14] Rt Rev Francis Kaulanda, interview, 14.6.2018.

[15] Interview with Rt Rev David Urquhart, 18.7.2019.

[16] www.christiantoday.com/article/malawi.sees.huge.protests.over.appointment.of.progay.anglican/3737.htm [8.2.2019].

Francis Kaulanda became Bishop of Lake Malawi in 2010.[17] His first challenge on becoming bishop was to reunite the diocese. He claims to have done so within 6 months, but found Nkhotakota to be the most troublesome place.[18] One of his strengths has been his determination to appoint on merit, not on favour; he had to persuade people this was the case. The production of a diocesan strategic plan in 2011 after extensive consultation was a sign that the diocese was taking full responsibility for itself. The benefits of leadership that was firm, wise and transparently fair were soon showing. In 2016 the whole Christian Church in Malawi was growing, with all the Anglican dioceses expanding, bigger churches being built and new parishes opened; but the effect was particularly pronounced in DLM.

The bishops see the Church in Malawi as fulfilling the threefold ministry of our Lord:

1. Teaching and Education – primary and secondary schooling, and tertiary education in lay training centres, the nursing college, and the two ministry colleges.

2. Healing and Health, with the Christian Churches together providing 40% of the nation's health provision and running HIV/AIDS and malaria control programmes.

3. Evangelism.[19]

---

[17] Francis Kaulanda was born in 1959 on Likoma Island [like many Anglican clergy including his predecessor Josiah Mtekateka]. His education was on Likoma and on the mainland. He trained at Zomba Theological College and was made Deacon in 1986, serving in various parishes in the Central Region. From 1992 he was youth coordinator and in 1998 led a group of 12 young people to Birmingham on a youth exchange. From 1998 he was Archdeacon, first of Nkhotakota, then from 2001 of Lilongwe.

[18] Rt Rev Francis Kaulanda, interview, 14.6.2018.

[19] Rt Rev Francis Kaulanda, at a meeting with Canon Janice Price and the author, 10.1.2014.

All four dioceses set up development arms to face the challenges faced by the country. DLM's development work has operated in four areas: health and 'cross cutting issues' such as water and sanitation, malnutrition and family planning; education, particularly for girls, who have historically been disadvantaged; agriculture, food security and climate change; and youth and women's empowerment, including anti-gender-based violence campaigns.[20]

Diocese of Northern Malawi

The description and history of the diocese to the resignation of Bishop Boyle are told in detail in chapter 7. Rev J. Scott Wilson of the Diocese of Fort Worth, Texas, was initially the sole candidate to succeed Bishop Christopher, but withdrew.[21] Canon Fanuel Magangani[22] was elected in due course and was consecrated in Mzuzu on a baking hot day in November 2010. Birmingham was represented by the Bishop of Aston, Andrew Watson, Canon Paul Wilson and the author. In his early years Bishop Fanuel was happy to be mentored by his predecessor. In more recent years he studied for a doctorate at the Anglo-Catholic seminary of Nashotah House, Wisconsin, USA.

At his first diocesan synod Bishop Fanuel chose to confront the diocese's endemic problem of dependency syndrome, asking 'What is in our hands?'- An echo of God's question to Moses in Exodus 4. He attacked the fatalistic 'spirit of poverty' and 'the spirit of being an orphan' that was always looking for outside help. He pointed out that the diocese was 97% dependent on well-wishers overseas, including in Birmingham

---

[20] ADLM diocesan profile, 2016.

[21] *Church of England Newspaper*, churchnewspaper.com, 2.7.2010.

[22] Fanuel Emmanuel Magangani was born in Ntcheu district in 1972. He was ordained in 2000; he recalled that Bishop Santer preached at the ordination and said: "I see great men here ... one of you may be something one day." [Source: interview with Fanuel as Bishop-elect on 6.11.2010]. He brought the famine of 2001-2 to Bishop Christopher's attention while serving as parish priest at Chilumba. He has served as Dean of St Peter's Cathedral, Likoma.

and the USA. He challenged the diocese to learn to give, and parishes and diocesan departments to become more self-sufficient.[23] This has proved no easy task, as the diocese has been hit by repeated droughts and floods, lowering parish giving capacity.

Under Bishop Fanuel as under his predecessor, the main focus of the diocese has been on Christian formation, capacity building and social services to the communities within it. To this has been added a new focus on achieving a solid financial base through local income generating activities including a printing press and the development of an office complex in Mzuzu projected in 2016.[24] One notable instance of the new spirit of self-sufficiency has been the rebuilding of St Mark's Church, Mzuzu. This is now a very large building, fitted to serve as a pro-cathedral for the diocese on the mainland. The diocese, link parish and well-wishers in Birmingham have supported the rebuilding on a modest scale, but it has been largely financed from the giving of the local faithful.

Theological and Lay Training[25]

The Anglican Church in Malawi is in the unfortunate position of having two colleges for ministerial/ordination training when it would struggle to afford even one. Zomba Theological College, shared between the Anglicans and the CCAP, had been set up in 1972 as an initiative of Archbishop Donald Arden, but ecumenical relations in the college were deteriorating in the 1990s. Bishop James Tengatenga commented that:

"Ecumenism works well when those engaged know who they are and can engage with confidence and none claiming superiority. Anglican identity is a great contribution to the ecumenical movement. Our

---

[23] Rt Rev Fanuel Magangani, *What is in Our Hands: Let us Move on,* Sixth Diocesan Synod Charge, 28.6.2011.

[24] DNM diocesan profile, 2016.

[25] This section complements that in ch. 2 by Rt Rev James Tengatenga on theological training and priestly formation.

Presbyterian partners have never acknowledged that and have made no secret of their intentions to eclipse our contributions."[26]

In 1996 the Anglicans were demoted to be associate members of the college on the grounds of their not showing enough practical commitment to its staffing and the development of its buildings.[27] The Anglican bishops wrote to Birmingham that year about the plans they were beginning to lay for a separate Anglican theological college in Zomba. The Birmingham side urged renewed commitment to the existing college[28]; they expressed serious doubts at the 1996 consultation about the wisdom of setting up a separate college and its viability.[29] The plans continued to be developed: Alinafe Kalemba was chosen in 2005 to be Dean, and Leonard Kamungu Theological College [LKTC] was opened in Zomba in September 2006. Birmingham's single 'generic' skills share group was present for the opening.

The college has never had more than 30 students and has always struggled for viability, particularly as some dioceses have defaulted on their contributions. Up to 2016 It was always focused on ordination training, and its flavour reflects the distinctive history and ethos of the Malawian Anglican Church. I was among the visitors from Birmingham; I taught there for a week on sabbatical in 2007 and was warmly welcomed by staff and students. I reported that: "Academic standards so far are fairly basic. The teaching is in English, but some students struggle with English academic vocabulary." Given this, it was surprising that "the college is trying to operate a traditional 'academic' curriculum model, with the more able students learning Hebrew or NT Greek."[30]

Another Birmingham visitor in 2007 was John Bleazard, a Birmingham ordinand and former Community Regeneration Officer. John was

---

[26] Rt Rev James Tengatenga, correspondence with author, 14.10.2018.

[27] Canon David Lee, Interim Report of the Visit to Malawi, 1996, n.d.

[28] Letter from Rt Rev Mark Santer to all three Malawian bishops, 7.5.1996.

[29] David Lee, Anglican Consultation in Malawi, 17.8.1996, draft record.

[30] Richard Tucker, Leonard Kamungu Theological College *Zomba,* 6.2007.

disappointed by "the apparent lack of contextualization or inculturation [use of African cultural and musical elements] of worship and liturgy in the Malawian Anglican Church;" he felt this was being perpetuated at the college. His other comments revealed the depth of the cultural divide from the UK:

> "I was given insights into a different definition of Anglicanism. To the ordinands at LKTC and others, to be Anglican was to uphold a narrow, Anglo-Catholic, Victorian and very counter-cultural view of church... Attempts by me to even try and explain to the ordinands at LKTC the nature of, and issues involved in, the contemporary debate in the West/North about homosexuality brought outright hostility – without my even stating a personal opinion... It was a sobering eye-opener for me to see how... the Malawian understanding of what it meant to be Anglican was fundamentally different to that found in England. "[31]

Alinafe began to stress all-round preparation for rural parish life and community leadership: the college had vegetable gardens, fishponds and banana trees. A library was built with the help of a Festina loan. The interest on this was paid out of the income from a legacy from Mark Green, Bishop of Aston 1972-82. The library was stocked with donated books, some of which were sent from Birmingham by container. For some years after Alinafe's resignation in 2011, the college lost its focus, in his view and mine. More recently it has become part of Malawi Anglican University, but it remains beset with problems of low student numbers, resources and buildings, exacerbated by the effects of the COVID-19 pandemic on the finances of the church. The current and former bishops who have worked at the college expressed optimism about its survival and future prospects;[32] I confess to a degree of scepticism.

As the plans for LKTC began their long gestation, parallel plans were being laid for a college in Lilongwe. The College for Christian Ministries

---

[31] John Bleazard, *Report on Summer Placement 2007*, 3.8.2007.

[32] Professor James Tengatenga in correspondence, 19.2.2019; Rt Rev Alinafe Kalemba in interview, 18.6.2018.

was the vision of an American, Esther Miller; plans developed from 1997 on with support from Bishop Peter Nyanja. The college opened in 2003 as a DLM institution, offering a certificate in theology, with plans for a diploma.[33] A small number of ordinands have trained at CCM, especially from DLM. Attempts were made to incorporate the Anglican learning institutions, including a projected college of nursing at Nkhotakota, into a Malawi Anglican University. However, the initial opportunity for this, and for rationalizing Anglican ordination training, was lost when the Board of LKTC declined the offer to join with CCM to be part of the new institution. As a result, the institution was launched as Lake Malawi Anglican University; it was visited by Bishop Anne Hollinghurst and a Birmingham party in 2017.

The lay training centres at Chilema, DUS, and Nkhotakota, DLM, are described above.[34]

Anglican Council in Malawi [ACM][35]

The history of ACM goes back to the division of the Diocese of Malawi in 1971. In earlier years all of Birmingham's financial support for the dioceses was routed through ACM; more recently this has gone direct to the dioceses. ACM has coordinated many visits from Birmingham down the years.

ACM is active in the public health area. A national AIDS coordinator, Matilda Chiutula, was appointed in 2005 and worked with Rev Dr Anne Bayley on AIDS prevention.[36] It has been the contact point with Episcopal Relief and Development for their anti-malaria 'Nets for Life'

---

[33] Lilongwe: College for Christian Ministries, Newsletter no. 1, 2006

[34] The setting-up and role of Chilema in ch. 4; the use of the LTC's for teachers' skills share courses and the generic skills share trip from Birmingham in 2006 in ch. 10.

[35] This section complements that in ch. 2 by Rt Rev James Tengatenga on Anglican Council in Malawi and 'The Anglican Church in Malawi'.

[36] See ch. 6 above.

programme. It has coordinated support for health measures from agencies such as USPG and MACS, and it worked with USPG on their 'Hands on Health' programme launched in 2011. With USPG support it runs the Community Integrated Intervention Programme, coordinated by Tamara Khisimisi. This addresses education for girls, protecting livelihoods, management of the environment, and hygiene and sanitation and has a focus on gender equality, hygiene and AIDS.

In 2012 ACM launched a Gender Policy document arising from ecumenical work since 2006. This reflected and to some degree affirmed the conservative and patriarchal outlook of Malawian society. It candidly admitted the existence of gender-based violence in church and society, but aimed to enable progress in emancipation and towards gender equality.

ACM's finance and administration manager, Erasto M'baya, had long had a concern for higher standards of accounting and auditing in the diocesan offices and institutions. He saw a need for staff to be trained in accounting procedures and made the case to Paul Wilson; Birmingham then supported the costs of training workshops in 2013. After retiring from ACM, Erasto conducted internal audits on a contract basis, paid for collectively by the member bodies of the Malawi Round Table.

In the period to 2016, ACM disappointed the hopes of mission partners that it might grow into an effective executive secretariat for the Church. This may be because bishops feared for the loss of their independence and so withheld authority from ACM, or because it was held back by weaknesses in management; or it may be a chicken-and-egg situation where one factor aggravated the other. The aspirations of the Malawian Church for ACM's future role are articulated by James Tengatenga.[37]

---

[37] See ch. 2 above.

Friendships

Close friendships are as essential to any companion link as close working relationships. Many leaders in Malawi and Birmingham, bishops and others, have formed such friendships. Alongside Agnes Mkoko (see ch. 8) I would mention the following, representing a far larger number in Malawi:

Fr Eston Pembamoyo

Eston was born in 1965;[38] his father was a Malawian Muslim working in Zimbabwe and his mother was from a CCAP background. His parents separated and he was brought up by an Anglican uncle and aunt. He became a young Christian leader and qualified as a teacher. He trained for the priesthood at Zomba Theological College from 1993-96 and his wife Joyce did a 3-year TEEM course in Chichewa, her choice of language. Alongside being a parish priest, he was youth chaplain of DSM and led the very successful youth visit to Birmingham in 2001.[39] He was hosted by St Margaret's, Short Heath, and this led to a link with Likwenu parish and a friendship with the late John and Pauline Healy. They left money for work in Malawi and their name lives on in the Trust established by Eston.

Eston had long wanted to teach theology, and in 2003-05 he had a scholarship to study African Christianity in South Africa and Ghana. In 2005 Archbishop Malango asked Eston to help him in the demanding post of Provincial Secretary for two years. On the arrival in 2008 of Bishop Malasa, Eston was dismissed to the small rural parish of Jali, near Zomba. Malawian bishops have the absolute right to move clergy. Like many other priests in DUS, Eston was subjected to the diocesan practice of frequent moves of parish, often at short notice, that have been disruptive to clergy, their families and their parishes. Meantime, he

---

[38] This profile is based on interviews with Eston on 20.6.2018 and 4.7.2018.

[39] See ch. 6 above.

acted as consignee for numerous containers, from Birmingham and other UK charities.

Eston is part of the movement for permaculture, a set of design principles for creating sustainable human environments. "When applied to agriculture, it is a design framework that farmers can use to mimic nature and to allow natural processes to play their part in the farming process."[40] Eston and Joyce visited the UK for a month in 2015 to attend a permaculture conference, visit friends and parishes in Birmingham and Huddersfield and see the container charity CART. Faced with the unwanted division of his parish of Mchenga, Eston took four years' unpaid leave in 2016 and at the time of writing was studying for a PhD at Stellenbosch, South Africa.

Oscar Mponda

Oscar was born in 1963 in Mozambique.[41] His parents, both Anglicans, came to Malawi as refugees. Oscar studied education from 1984-87 at Chancellor College and then taught until 2003. He came to Birmingham in 2001 as joint team leader of the youth exchange with Eston Pembamoyo. A return team led by Alexandrina Mann came to Malawi; she and Oscar worked hand in hand exchanging ideas on how to promote ideas of evangelism among the Birmingham youth, not all of whom were "fully engaged in evangelism"!

From 2003-2009 he was in government service with the Ministry of Education, working on managing construction projects with international partners. He found there was too much interference from politicians and left to work with an overseas partner. In 2014 he was approached by Bishop Francis to support projects, although DLM could not match salaries elsewhere. He saw this as "a chance to give back to God what God had given me," and accepted. I worked closely with him

---

[40] Anne Bayley and Mugove Walter Nyika, *More and Better Food,* Oxford, UK: Strategies for Hope Trust, 2011.

[41] Interview with Oscar Mponda on 14.6.2018.

on plans for the classroom block at Ntchisi, which was the first to be started, first to be completed, and most trouble-free of the four.

Fr Edward Kawinga

Edward is another priest in DUS who has received several visitors from Birmingham. As parish priest of St George's, Zomba he was placement host of John Bleazard in 2007. John describes a visit to a seriously ill church member in a noisy and smelly hospital ward.

> "After talking to the woman's relatives, praying for her, and anointing her body with oil, Edward strode to the middle of the ward and called for silence. Dressed in his white cassock, and surrounded by people, he just stood still and prayed for everyone in that ward for about 5 minutes. You could have heard a pin drop in what had been a hubbub of noise and crying."[42]

John's immediate feelings were of inadequacy and he questioned whether this prayer could be answered in any meaningful way. He then felt challenged to trust God and emulate Edward's boldness in prayer.

St George's is a well-supported parish, and when John visited, a large office block was being constructed on the church site to augment parish income. John commended the project, and Edward asked Birmingham for help to raise funds to complete it. Paul Wilson found a sponsor in the form of St George's, Edgbaston.

Fr Edward was subsequently parish priest at Mangochi, which has had a longstanding parish link with Amington near Tamworth. He visited Birmingham for two weeks in 2010 and stayed in homes in Amington. At a meeting in the Cathedral where he was asked to speak about the Partnership, despite feeling unwell he sang a hymn composed by himself in his local language of Yao. In successive parishes he has run a clerical tailoring business alongside his parish duties to help pay his children's school fees; Birmingham friends have helped him with supplies.

---

[42] John Bleazard, *Summer Placement 2007 – Malawi*, full report, p. 9.

Fr Baird Mponda

Baird was a young man completing his ordination training at LKTC when I first visited there in 2007. In February 2009 he was made priest in Dwambazi parish, DLM. In a bold move, Bishop Kaulanda appointed him Acting Dean of All Saints Cathedral, Nkhotakota less than two years after he was priested, at the end of 2010 when 'factions were still hot' there.[43] Baird unified the cathedral congregation, galvanized and transformed its life and hugely increased the giving. Canon Janice Price and I spoke to him in the course of Janice's fact-finding visit for the 2014 Partnership Review. Impressed by his candour and theological grasp, we arranged for him to visit the UK later that year and speak at the PWM conference in Swanwick. Since then, Baird's ministry has developed an international dimension, including forming a link between the cathedrals in Nkhotakota and Chester. Janice returned to Nkhotakota for two weeks in 2016 to teach and to experience pastoral work among many groups including the needy and dying. In 2014 I became godfather to Elite, son of Baird and his wife Grief. In 2019 Baird was appointed Archdeacon of Lilongwe North.

Fr May Machemba

May was born in 1968 in Nkhotakota and studied at Zomba Theological College from 1993 to 1996.[44] All of May's ministry has been in DLM. Unusually, he spent his first 15 years of ministry in one parish, Dedza. This had 3 outstations in 1996 and 9 by 2011. They were very widely spread, including one in Mozambique! Getting a Birmingham motorbike in 2005 made a big difference to May – he no longer needed to cover great distances on a pushbike or spend a night at an outstation. The church started numerically small, so May had scope to be also on district council committees, including the AIDS committee.

Birmingham has had a big impact on Fr May's ministry. He first went there in 2001 for 3 months to train at Crowther Hall. He was attached

---

[43] Interview, 15.6.2018.

[44] Profile based on an interview on 23.6.2018.

to three parishes: the then vicars of two of them, Philip Swan and Peter Smith, have visited him in Malawi and stayed in touch with him. I have also visited him, in 2007 and subsequently. May was the parish priest at Ntchisi in 2017 when the first Birmingham classroom block was dedicated by Bishops Francis and Anne.

Jesman Seva

Jesman was born in 1982 in Nkhotakota. He grew up in a broken family and both his parents died before he completed secondary schooling. His impoverished childhood gave him great sympathy for those struggling to meet their secondary school fees. He studied at the University of Livingstonia, where his leadership gifts became obvious in several voluntary commitments. He joined the staff of Bishop Mtekateka Secondary School in Nkhotakota in 2009 and his ability rapidly impressed: he was invited to be acting Headmaster within a month of his arrival! Under his leadership the school has become well known for its students' performance and discipline. Its facilities have been developed with help from UK partner MACS. In 2013 he was also appointed Acting Director of Nkhotakota LTC, the venue for teachers' skills share sessions.

The first Birmingham visitors met by Jesman were Jim and Liz Carr, when they came to Nkhotakota leading the 2009 teachers' skills share group. Their friendship has deepened and he became almost like an adopted son to them. For Jesman, the Partnership is "God's planned initiative for members of the church in England to reach out to the poor people in Malawi." Having received well-targeted support from Birmingham and MACS for his school and his own higher studies, he stresses that "Malawian people need to be involved … in deciding and planning for the support which is to be directed to them."[45]

---

[45] Correspondence with author, July 2018.

Chapter 12

Evaluation

The 2014 Review of the Partnership

The Review of the Partnership conducted by Canon Janice Price in 2014 looked towards its 50 years celebration in 2016. The review's terms of reference, agreed by the bishops in Birmingham and Malawi, were to consider "the overarching question of how it could be a relationship that was mutually beneficial and equipped each partner for their common participation in God's mission in the world."[1] It combined celebration of what had been achieved, assessment of current activities and recommendations for the future. The mutuality of the partnership was shown in the varied ways in which each side supported the other.

The Malawian Church offered hospitality and the challenge of seeing, hearing and learning about living with faith amidst challenges. This should prompt prayer for one another. Prayer by Birmingham for Malawi has been focused by 'Praying Together', but there has been no organized means of prayer by Malawi for Birmingham. The DVD 'Matilda's Malawi' was produced to bring to life the challenges of life in Malawi.

Birmingham's activities discussed in the review were grant support to dioceses, support for schools, hospitals and other projects, the teachers' skills share programme; containers of gifts; and group and individual visits in each direction. In addition, the value of the hospital link and the various parish links should be stressed.

The key issue identified in the review was the challenge of self-sustainability, an aim widely aspired to but hard to achieve. Self-

---

[1] Canon Janice Price, World Mission Adviser for the Archbishops' Council of the Church of England, *Review of the Link between the Diocese of Birmingham and the Malawian Anglican Church, Report of the Independent Reviewer*, April 2014. A summary of the report is at Appendix C.

sustainability included the capacity to give, and to endure. "Essentially self-sustainability means the re-balancing of means from a primary reliance on outside funders to a primary reliance on internal giving to sustain ministry and mission."[2] The inherited form of financial support was under strain arising from the increase of one Malawian diocese to four and potentially five dioceses. The recommendations were for both partners to engage in a journey towards self-sustainability, with a particular focus on the Church and Community Mobilisation Process [CCMP]. Self-sustainability in Malawi remains a challenge when the economy is weak. One Malawian bishop expressed the view that issues of self-sustainability in Birmingham needed to be addressed too. ACM and the dioceses have begun to move in the direction of CCMP, but other agencies such as Mothers' Union have gone further.

The review highlighted three issues that could only be addressed together across global cultures: climate justice, inter-religious living and gender-based violence. Working together to mitigate the causes and effects of climate change, and the challenge of living in harmony alongside significant numbers of Muslim neighbours, continue to be challenges both to Birmingham and Malawi and would seem to be possible future directions for the partnership.

Is the Malawi Birmingham Partnership a True Partnership?

Throughout this book I have referred to the relationship between Malawi and Birmingham as a partnership. Partnership is recognized more widely as valuable in North-South relations. One of the Sustainable Development Goals agreed internationally in 2015 is Partnerships for the Goals [Goal 17]. "The SDGs can only be realized with a strong commitment to global partnership and cooperation." What characteristics does a companion link need to have to warrant the

---

[2] Richard Tucker summarizing Report by Janice Price, *Review of the Birmingham Malawi Link and Responses to it,* 2014, at Appendix C.

title of partnership? Andrew Kirk and Phil Groves[3] both offer helpful checklists. Kirk explores in depth what 'sharing in partnership' means and could mean.[4]

> "Within world Christianity, 'partnership' expresses a relationship between churches based on trust, mutual recognition and reciprocal interchange. It rules out completely any notion of 'senior' and 'junior', 'parent' and 'child', or even 'older' and 'younger'... It implies a relationship in which two or more bodies agree to share responsibility for one another, in which each side meaningfully participates in planning the future of the other. Put in this way, partnership is an ideal to be aimed at. In practice... there are real difficulties in the way of a truly equal partnership."[5]

Partnership, as a translation of the Greek word *koinonia,* is a term with a good New Testament pedigree; it is explored particularly in Philippians and 2 Corinthians. Following Kirk's and Groves' headings I shall assess how far the Malawi Birmingham Partnership matches up.[6]

Sharing in a Common Project [7]

The 'common project' has been largely implied rather than explicit. No Memorandum of Understanding [MoU] was drawn up at the Partnership's launch in 1966. Biennial consultations, participating in planning the future together, took place between 1991 and 2009, but without an agreed overarching framework and with a shifting agenda. They ceased in 2009, arguably because neither side had sufficient

---

[3] Phil Groves, *Global Partnerships for Local Mission,* Cambridge: Grove Books Ltd, 2006, pp. 15-19.

[4] Andrew Kirk, *What is Mission? Theological Explorations,* London: Darton, Longman and Todd, 2002, ch. 10, pp. 184-204.

[5] Ibid, p. 184.

[6] In a presentation in 2010, the Rt Rev Chad Gandiya listed seven 'ingredients of a true partnership'. These are quoted at length in Janice Price, *World-shaped Mission,* London: Church House Publishing, 2012, pp. 54-56

[7] Cf. Phil. 1.5&7, 4.15.

commitment to making them work or to implementing in Malawi what had been decided together.[8] The MoU agreed in 2016 laid down principles, but with no intention to return to regular consultations.

Sharing of Gifts [9]

Historically, Birmingham has been by far the better resourced partner. Missionaries to Malawi have included Tony and Helen Cox, Keith and Gill Gale, and above all, Bishop Christopher Boyle. The Selly Oak colleges drew many Malawians to Birmingham to train, and to enrich and learn from the life of the diocese while doing so. More recently the skills share programme has been all about sharing of gifts and mutual learning. Some of the gifts of the Malawian church to Birmingham have been musical: the sharing of worship resources since the 1990s and with Lea Hall and especially, the visit by Ndirande Anglican Voices in 2005.

The Malawian church has also offered gifts to the Anglican Communion and the world church. Adrian Hastings' book 'Christian Marriage in Africa'[10] was commissioned during Donald Arden's Primacy as a resource for the contentious matter of marriage. The Council of Anglican Provinces in Africa was promoted by Arden and established in 1979 at a meeting in Chilema. Its aim is to coordinate and articulate issues affecting the Church and communities across the region, and it has become an increasingly significant force. The Anglican Consultative Council has benefitted from the presence of Bernard Malango and James Tengatenga on the Standing Committee and James' work as Chair from 2009-2016, while Bishop of Southern Malawi and afterward. And Harvey Kwiyani , a Malawian theologian currently based in the UK, is making important contributions to mission thinking.

---

[8] A view expressed by Very Rev Peter Howell-Jones, interview, 16.8.2018.

[9] 1 Cor. 12.7; Eph. 4.11-13.

[10] Adrian Hastings, *Christian Marriage in Africa: a Report,* London: SPCK, 1973.

Sharing of Material Resources[11]

This has been a wide seam running throughout the Partnership's 50 year history. Given their disparity, the sharing of material resources has been overwhelmingly from Birmingham to Malawi. A full discussion of the role of money is at ch. 9 above. It would be generally agreed that the partnership's history has inclined it to stress transfer of material resources at the expense of giving or receiving other forms of support.

Sharing in Suffering [12]

"In reality [Paul and his readers] are all sharing in the sufferings of Christ, which continue in the sufferings of his body, which is the Church. In many ways this is the most profound and difficult of all manifestations of partnership."[13] Such sharing in suffering, of course, goes beyond the aid that Birmingham has generously provided in the natural disasters that have frequently befallen Malawi. In my view, the Partnership's two finest hours have been times of stress and suffering. In 1992-94, Birmingham played a partly hidden role as part of the ecumenical, international effort to prise the country from President Banda's authoritarian grip.[14] And Birmingham led the way on famine relief for several months in 2002.[15] It is fortunate that the Bishop of Birmingham in these two great hours of need was deeply committed to the welfare of Malawi. In the latter case, a former Birmingham priest serving as a bishop in Malawi was also able to sound the alarm in Birmingham, use his profile there to raise relief funds, and convene a highly effective team on the spot to meet the urgent need.

---

[11] 2 Cor. 8-9; Rom. 15:26-7.

[12] 2 Cor. 1.7 and 4.8-12; Phil. 3.10.

[13] Andrew Kirk, *What is Mission? Theological Explorations,* London: Darton, Longman and Todd, 2002, pp. 190-1.

[14] See ch. 5 above.

[15] See ch. 7 above.

The Covid-19 pandemic in 2020 again brought out the best in both partners. Birmingham raised large sums to make Malawian schools Covid-safe and provided scientifically based advice to counter myths. Malawi offered prayer support to communities in Birmingham with high rates of infection.

Power and Powerlessness

"Partnership is undoubtedly linked to questions of power. A truly mutual relationship cannot exist between two parties who possess unequal power."[16] Groves speaks of the need for partners to have equal status and mutual respect.[17] The Malawian Church in 1966 was undoubtedly far weaker than Birmingham, but it has grown greatly in numerical strength, resources and confidence. Birmingham is still materially better resourced; but the decline in confidence that comes from reduced participation – churchgoing etc. - and with it, a decline in influence, should not be overlooked. Malawian dioceses also have links in other parts of the world, particularly North America, some of them with deeper pockets than Birmingham. All this makes the comparison more complex than it might appear.

Other key elements of partnership on Groves' list include:

A Common Basis of Belief and a Shared Theological Tradition

Anglican theology and tradition provide the basis for the Partnership, but there will always be differences and mutual learning: "In fact complete agreement is not possible and we need to understand that our 'truths' will be enlarged and enlivened by contact with 'truth' in other contexts."[18] Companion links can provide a platform for internationally shared study and discussion. The Malawian bishops studied the Bible together with Bishop David and Bishop Maurice

---

[16] Andrew Kirk, *What is Mission?* p. 194.

[17] Phil Groves, *Global Partnerships for Local Mission,* Cambridge: Grove Books Ltd, 2006, pp. 15-16.

[18] Ibid, p. 16.

Sinclair in 2016. A discipleship conference in Birmingham with Malawian and Bolivian bishops present was planned for just before the postponed Lambeth Conference of 2020. Such discussions, and the Partnership generally, are a precious contribution to the global unity of a Communion riven by theological tensions.

'The Partners are Individually United'

Where, as in Malawi, a church community has four dioceses that prize their degree of autonomy, there will never be uniformity, nor indeed, perfect coordination. But it is not this, but divisions within the church, which are in mind. Groves asserts: "Partnership with a divided community inevitably leads to a partner taking sides and identifying with one group over another."[19] This need not be so: Bishop David declined to intervene in the election dispute in DLM, partly so that no such impression could be given. Disputes over the integrity and authority of bishops raise more difficult issues; Birmingham needs to seek to ensure that its donated funds and interests are safeguarded, but again, it cannot take sides or speak out publicly.

Regular Contact – 'Eager to Keep in Touch'

In today's world, email, social media etc. make it extremely easy to stay in touch. But making an effective link usually requires initial face-to-face contact. A great deal of travel over the 50 years has aimed at making contact and cementing friendships. There is less currently than say, 10 years ago, partly because less stress is put on official or Sabbatical travel from Birmingham to Malawi, and partly because increasingly onerous and expensive immigration procedures make it harder to come from Africa to the UK. The loss of personal contact makes the Partnership poorer.

I would conclude that the Malawi Birmingham partnership, for all its imperfections and shortfalls, merits the description of 'partnership' and should continue to be known as such.

---

[19] Ibid, p. 17.

The Value of Companion Links

The Malawi Partnership was one of the first of about 90 such links to be formed between Church of England dioceses and Anglican dioceses or provinces abroad. Their official title is the rather more neutral 'companion links'[20] and their value, not least to the Church of England dioceses involved, is as great as ever. A recent research project[21] found that:

There is a strong link between growth in discipleship for church communities and individuals and international encounters.

Two observable changes in perception can happen when positive international, cross-cultural encounter occurs – the world shrinks, and perceptions of God expand. These can have transformative effects on prayer, worship, engagement with the Bible and Christian service.

While friendship is the dominant expression of companion link relationships, they can imperceptibly move into becoming donor recipient relationships.

The cycle of gift giving – giving, receiving and returning – offers a way of understanding giving gifts as an alternative to donor-recipient relationships.

Many of these benefits have been reaped within the Malawi Birmingham Partnership, but there is always scope for more. The warning about donor-recipient relationships is very telling.

This book has been an attempt to illustrate the Malawi Birmingham Partnership in its strengths and weaknesses, joys and sorrows. The Partnership has proved its durability: the bishops recommitted themselves to it at the 50th anniversary in 2016. However, its continued

---

[20] A list may be found at www.churchofengland.org/more/church-resources/world-mission/diocesan-links [12.8.2019].

[21] Conducted by Canon Janice Price, Archbishops' Council World Mission Adviser. The report "The Nature and Extent of Companion Links in the Anglican Communion," www.churchofengland.org/sites/default/files/2018, [2.8.2019]

existence and effectiveness should never be taken for granted. Existing and inherited patterns, particularly of financial support, need to evolve with changing circumstances. The partnership continues healthy and active, but has seen little development or innovation in recent years. Birmingham and Malawi alike need to exercise creativity and imagination. I would suggest it has suffered from a lack of episcopal interest and support in Birmingham. The partnership's future direction of travel is unclear, but it still has great potential.

A Malawi Partnership Prayer

Heavenly Father, we thank you for our fellowship with each other
in and through the family of your church.
We pray that you will continue to pour your Holy Spirit on us
in Malawi and Birmingham and enable us to grow in holiness and love.
Support, sustain and help us share in each other's needs and blessings,
joys and sorrows, and reach out to those who know not your love.
We ask this in the name of Him who lives and reigns with you and the
Holy Spirit, one God for ever and ever. **Amen.**

Source: Father Henry Burgess

Appendices

Appendix A: Statistics for Malawi and Birmingham

Malawi

Land Area:	94,552 km^2. [118,484 km^2 including lake]. For comparison, the UK is 242,495 km.^{2} Both countries are a similar distance north to south.
Population [2018 census]:	17,563,749
Of which, Northern Region:	2,289, 780
Central Region:	7,523,340
Southern Region:	7,750,629
Population density:	198/km^2 or 512/sq. mile, 5½ times the average for Africa
Rate of increase [2018]:	2.6% p.a.[1]
GDP/head [2020]:	$625.3[2]
Human Development Index ranking:	171 of 189 countries. HDI value increased by 40%, 1990-2017.

Religious Affiliation[3]

Roman Catholic:	18-22%
Protestant [exc. Pentecostal]:	22-27% (of which CCAP 18%)

---

[1] Knoema.com/atlas/Malawi [29.11.2019].

[2] data.worldbank.org/indicator/NY.GDP.PCAP.CD?locations=MW [16.8.2021].

[3] Estimates vary widely, so a range of figures is given. Sources: www.thearda.com/internationalData/countries/Country_138_1.asp; www.worldatlas.com/articles/religious-beliefs-in-malawi.html; www.indexmundi.com/malawi/religions.html.

Pentecostal:	20.8%
Anglican:	2.6-13%
Seventh-day Adventist:	6.9%
Sunni Islam:	12-13% [one estimate 19%]
Traditional/ Animist:	6%

Birmingham Diocese

Area:	290 sq. ml. or 750 sq. km.
Population [2018][4]:	1,588,000
Population density [2018]:	5410/sq. mile

Religious affiliation[5]	**2001**	**2011**
Christian:	63.8%	50.6%
Muslim:	10.8%	17.0%
'Religion, other':	5.4%	8.3%
	[Sikh, Hindu, Buddhist, Jewish, others]	
Religion not stated:	7.9%	6.5%
No religion:	12.2%	19.7%

Diocesan [C of E] worshipping community [2018] 20,500.

---

[4] Church of England Statistics for Mission 2018, **Error! Hyperlink reference not valid.**.

[5] Source: UK census figures, 2001 and 2011, collated and supplied by Dr Ken Eames, Research and Statistics, Church of England.

Appendix B Bishops in Malawi and Bishops of Birmingham

Malawi

Bishops of Nyasaland/Likoma*:

Charles Frederick Mackenzie, 1861-62

William George Tozer, 1862-74

Edward Steere, 1874-83

Charles Alan Smythies, 1883-92

Wilfrid Bird Hornby, 1892-95

Chauncy Maples, 1895*

John Edward Hine, 1896-1902*

Gerard Trower, 1902-10*

Thomas Cathrew Fisher, 1910-30

Gerald Wybergh Douglas, 1930-36

Frank Oswald Thorne, 1936-61

Bishops of Malawi

Donald Seymour Arden, Nyasaland 1961-64, Malawi 1964-71, Southern Malawi 1971-80

Josiah Mtekateka, Suffragan 1965, Lake Malawi 1971-78

Peter Nathaniel Nyanja, Lake Malawi 1978-2005

Dunstan Daniel Ainani, Suffragan 1979, Southern Malawi 1981-87

Benson Nathaniel Aipa, Southern Malawi 1987-97

Jackson Cunningham Biggers, Northern Malawi 1995-2000

James Tengatenga, Southern Malawi 1998-2013

Christopher John Boyle, Northern Malawi 2001-09

Bernard Amos Malango, consecrated 1988, Upper Shire 2002-08

Brighton Vita Malasa, Upper Shire 2009-date

Francis Frank Kaulanda, Lake Malawi 2010-date

Fanuel Emmanuel Magangani, Northern Malawi 2010-date

Alinafe Kalemba, Southern Malawi 2013-date

Source: ed. James Tengatenga, *The UMCA in Malawi: a History of the Anglican Church,* Zomba: Kachere, 2010, p. viii, updated

Birmingham

Charles Gore, 1905-11

Henry Russell Wakefield, 1911-24

Ernest William Barnes, 1924-53

John Leonard Wilson, 1953-69

Laurence Ambrose Brown, 1969-77

Hugh William Montefiore, 1978-87

Mark Santer, 1987-2002

John Tucker Mugabi Sentamu, 2002-05

David Andrew Urquhart, 2006-2022

Appendix C

Review of the Birmingham Malawi Link: Summary of the Report by Canon Janice Price, Independent Reviewer, April 2014[6]

1. 'If one part suffers, every part suffers with it; if one part is honoured, every part rejoices with it.' I Corinthians 12:26. For nearly 50 years the Partnership has expressed what Paul describes. Janice expresses thanks to the bishops in Malawi and Birmingham and to others who have helped in the review's production.

2. The agreed Terms of Reference were:

"The purpose of the Review is:

1. To help both parties look towards the 50 years celebration of the Partnership in 2016
2. To celebrate what has been achieved in the last 50 years of the Partnership
3. To consider the current characteristics and activities of the Partnership
4. To make recommendations as to the Partnership's future purpose and shape

The overarching question to be considered in the Review is how the Partnership can be a relationship that is mutually beneficial and equip each partner for their common participation in God's mission in the world."

The preparation of the Review included fact-finding visits to the four dioceses in Malawi in January 2014 and to Birmingham in February 2014.

3. The theological and Biblical roots of the Partnership include the key concepts of 'one body, many members, in Christ' [1 Cor. 12] and Christ's love commandment. The depth of commitment to the partnership is

---

[6] Produced by the author for a Birmingham Diocesan Synod meeting in 2015.

evident from statements from bishops in Birmingham and Malawi. Bishop David has said: 'Living in partnership with the Anglican Church in Malawi is a vital part of mission here in Birmingham'.

4. Alongside the Malawi Review a task group has been at work to review Birmingham's engagement with the world church at every level. The group has produced ten reasons why engaging with world mission is important for the C of E in Birmingham. These include gratitude, generosity, bringing a healthy broader perspective, obedience to the Great Commission, participation in what the Spirit is doing, and its transformative effect. World Church engagement also forms and informs those doing cross-cultural relations in Birmingham.

5. Two characteristics of world mission today are that the church is both global and local, and that all mission is cross-cultural. The review highlights three cross-cultural issues that can only be addressed together: climate justice, inter-religious living and gender-based violence.

6. The mutuality of the partnership is shown in the varied ways in which each side supports the other. The Malawian Church offers hospitality and the challenge of seeing – or hearing and learning about – living with faith and trust amidst challenges. The Birmingham Church gives grant support to dioceses running at £10,000 each in 2014, and supports hospitals, schools and other projects; runs the Skill share programme that takes Birmingham teachers to Malawi to train interactively with Malawians; and sends annual containers of gifts. Group and individual visits take place in each direction.

7. The key issues identified include the strain on the inherited form of financial support arising from the increase of one Malawian diocese to four, and potentially five dioceses.

"Essentially self-sustainability means the re-balancing of means from a primary reliance on outside funders to a primary reliance on internal giving to sustain ministry and mission." Self-sustainability can also be seen as the capacity of a church to give to others from its own resources; and the capacity to endure. The journey to self-sustainability includes realizing the gifts God has given to the Malawian Church and the development of a mixed approach that includes both small scale income generating activities and teaching on stewardship at parish level. The movement towards self-sustainability needs to be an aim publicly acknowledged and shared by all partners. A self-sustaining church needs to develop flexible and entrepreneurial leadership.

8. Recommendations

1. In the time leading up to the 50th anniversary of the partnership the Bishops in Birmingham and Malawi discern together whether God is calling them to engage in the journey towards self-sustainability. As part of this process of discernment the dioceses in the partnership be called to prayer for the partnership and for God's mission in Malawi and Birmingham.

2. If this is discerned to be the way ahead, working with the Council of Anglican Provinces in Africa as well as other Anglican mission agencies, Bishops in both dioceses embark on an exposure visit to a part of Africa where the Church and Community Mobilisation Process [CCMP] has been implemented with a view to implementation in Malawi.

3. A small number of parishes in Malawi and their parish links in Birmingham pilot a local CCMP process.

Bibliography

Anderson-Morshead, A.E.M. *The History of the Universities' Mission to Central Africa, 1859-1909*, London: Universities' Mission to Central Africa, 1897-1909, www.archive.org/details/historyofunivers00ande.

Chadwick, Owen, *Mackenzie's Grave*, London: Hodder & Stoughton, 1959.

Comaroff, John, *Of Revelation and Revolution*, vol. 1, Chicago: Chicago University Press, 1991.

De Gruchy, John, *Christianity and Democracy: A Theology for a Just World Order,* Cambridge: Cambridge University Press, 1995.

Englund, Harri (ed), *Christianity and Public Culture in Africa,* Athens, Ohio: Ohio University Press, 2011.

Gifford, Paul, *African Christianity: Its Public Role*, London: Hurst & Company, 1998.

Groves, Phil, *Global Partnerships for Local Mission*, Cambridge: Grove Books Ltd, 2006.

Hastings, Adrian, *African Christianity: An Essay in Interpretation*, London & Dublin: Geoffrey Chapman, 1976.

Hastings, Adrian, *Christian Marriage in Africa: A Report,* London: SPCK, 1973.

Hastings, Adrian, *A History of English Christianity, 1920-1985,* London: Collins/Fount Paperbacks, 1987.

Jenkins, Bob, *In Touch with the Warm Heart of Africa, 1966-96.* Privately published, n.d. [c.1998].

Kalilombe, Patrick A., *Doing Theology at the Grassroots, Theological Essays from Malawi,* Gweru: Mambo-Kachere, 1999.

Kambalu, Samson, *The Jive Talker,* London: Jonathan Cape, 2008.

Kirk, J. Andrew, *What is Mission? Theological Explorations.* London: Darton, Longman and Todd, 2002.

Mbaya, Henry, *Raising African Bishops in the Anglican Church in Malawi*

Mbaya, Henry, *1924-2000*, uir.unisa.ac.za/bitstream/handle/10500/4483/Mbaya.pdf, 2007.

Mbaya, Henry, *The Making of an African Clergy in the Anglican Church in Malawi with Special Focus on the Election of Bishops (1898-1996)*, n.d. researchspace.ukzn.ac.za/jspui/handle/10413/2883.

Mbaya, Henry, *Resistance to Anglican Missionary Christianity on Likoma Island, Malawi: 1885-1961*, n.d. uir.unisa.ac.za/handle/10500/4222.

McCracken, John, *Politics and Christianity in Malawi, 1875-1940: The Impact of the Livingstonia Mission in the Northern Province*, 2nd ed. Zomba: Kachere, 2000.

Moriyama, Jerome T., *The Evolution of an African Ministry in the Work of the Universities' Mission to Central Africa in Tanzania, 1864-1909*, University of London, 1984.

Newell, Jonathan, "There Were Arguments in Favour of Our Taking Arms': Bishop Mackenzie and the War against the Yao in 1861," *The Society of Malawi Journal*, 45, no. 1, 1992, pp. 15–45.

Price, Janice, *World-Shaped Mission, Evolving New Frameworks for the Church of England in world mission,* London: Church House Publishing, 2012.

Price, Janice, *The Nature and Extent of Companion Links in the Anglican* Communion, www.churchofengland.org/sites/default/files/2018.

Reijnaerts, Hubert, Ann Nielsen and Matthew Schoffeleers, *Montfortians in Malawi: Their Spirituality and Pastoral Approach*, Zomba: Kachere, 1997.

Ross, Andrew C., *Blantyre Mission and the Making of Modern Malawi*. Zomba: Kachere, 1996.

Ross, Kenneth R., ed., *Christianity in Malawi: a Source Book.* Gweru: Mambo-Kachere, 1996. Revised and enlarged edition Mzuzu: Mzuni Press, 2020.

Ross, Kenneth R., *Gospel Ferment in Malawi: Theological Essays,* Gweru: Mambo-Kachere, 1995 (Mzuzu: Luviri Press, 2018)

Ross, Kenneth R., *Malawi and Scotland: Together in the Talking Place since 1859,* Mzuzu: Mzuni Press, 2013.

Ross, Kenneth R. and Klaus Fiedler, *A Malawi Church History 1860-2020,* Mzuzu: Mzuni Press, 2020.

Sanneh, Lamin, *Encountering the West: Christianity and the Global Cultural Process: The African Dimension,* London: Marshall Pickering, 1993.

Sanneh, Lamin, *Translating the Message: The Missionary Impact on Culture,* 2nd ed., Maryknoll: Orbis, 2009.

Sanneh, Lamin, and Carpenter, Joel A. (ed), *The Changing Face of Christianity*, Oxford: OUP, 2005.

Shepperson, George, and Thomas Price, *Independent African: John Chilembwe and the Nyasaland Rising of 1915*, Edinburgh: Edinburgh University Press, 1987.

Stuart, John, *British Missionaries and the End of Empire: East, Central and Southern Africa, 1939-64*, Grand Rapids, Mich. and Cambridge, UK: Eerdmans, 2011.

Tengatenga, James, *Church, State and Society in Malawi: The Anglican Case.* Zomba: Kachere Series, 2006.

Tengatenga, James. "The Good Being the Enemy of the Best: The Politics of Frank Oswald Thorne in Nyasaland and the Federation, 1936-1961," *Religion in Malawi*, no. 6, 1996, pp. 20–29.

Tengatenga, James, *The UMCA in Malawi: A History of the Anglican Church, 1861-2010,* Zomba: Kachere, 2010.

Wakelin, Brian, *Money-Master or Servant in Church to Church Partnerships?* Cambridge: Grove Books Ltd, 2017.

Waller, Horace, *The Last Journal of David Livingstone in Central Africa from 1865 to his Death, 1866-1868*, vol. 1, London: John Murray, 1874.

Weller, John C., *The Priest from the Lakeside. The Story of Leonard Kamungu and Zambia, 1877 – 1913,* Blantyre: CLAIM, 1971 - openlibrary.org/works/OL51780W/The_priest_from_the_lakeside.

Index of Names and Subjects

'Make Poverty History' campaign, 95
'Matilda's Malawi' [DVD], 113, 165, 181, 210
'Trojan Horse', 2014, 147
50th anniversary, 12, 38, 111, 113, 160, 165, 173, 182, 185, 188f, 192, 194, 217, 226
accountability, 89, 93, 155f, 170, 189
Accountant, Diocesan, 154, 162f
accounting, 109, 155, 164, 204
ACM, see Anglican Council in Malawi
African Lakes Company, 23f
Afro-Caribbean, 43
Agreed Statement, 1996, 94
agriculture, 89, 104, 109, 191, 199, 205
Ainani, Dunstan, 31, 65, 222
Aipa, Benson Nathaniel, 47f, 67, 69, 77, 80, 89f, 92f, 166, 222
Akinola, Peter, 195
Ali, Son, 171
All Africa Council of Churches, 140
All Saints Cathedral, Nkhotakota, 21, 89, 138, 197, 207
Amanze, James, 31, 90
AMECEA [the Episcopal group for East African Churches], 72
Amington, 207
Amnesty International, 78f
Anglican Communion, 5f, 8, 33, 45, 81, 182, 188, 195, 213, 216f, 228
Anglican Consultative Council, 5, 33, 59, 192, 213
Anglican Council in Malawi (ACM), 32-34, 88, 93f, 140, 154, 157f, 160, 181, 183, 191, 203f, 211
Anglicanism, 5, 21f, 99, 192, 202
Anglo-Catholic, 38-40, 46, 86, 99f, 142, 199, 202
Anti-retroviral [ARV] treatment, 88
ARCIC, the Anglican-Roman Catholic International Commission, 149
Arden, Donald, 5, 14, 28, 30, 32f, 38, 44, 46-53, 56, 61, 63-65, 74, 80, 90, 101f, 120, 140, 148, 166, 200, 213, 222
Arden, Jane, 7, 47f, 50f, 120, 140
Arora, Arun, 105
Association for the Advancement of Women in Malawi (CCAM), 138
Aston, 35, 67
Aston, Archdeacon of, 48, 62f, 89, 141, 161

Aston, Bishop of, 50, 57, 60, 91, 102f, 113, 144, 163, 181, 189, 193, 199, 202
Austin, John, 91, 103, 114
bakery, 173
Balaka, 171f
Banda, Aleke, 73
Banda, Hastings Kamuzu, 13f, 27, 45, 53f, 70-72, 77f, 80, 83, 92, 117, 214
Banda, Margaret Marango, 138f
Barnes, Ernest, 39
Barton, John, 141
Bayley, Anne, 7, 84, 88f, 114, 203, 205
BCH, see Birmingham Children's Hospital
Beare, Jan, 183
Berlin Conference [1884], 22, 25
Biggers, Jackson, 8, 38, 54, 99-101, 222
Birkenhead, Bishop of, 150
Birmingham Children's Hospital, 83, 174-178, 184
Birmingham City Council, 149f
Birmingham Council of Christian Churches, 73
Birmingham diocesan centenary [2005], 12, 38, 133, 141, 160, 185

Birmingham Diocesan Synod, 68, 75, 87, 118, 161, 224
Birmingham Evening Mail, 105
Birmingham, Bishop of, 12, 39, 41, 62f, 67, 133, 148-150, 197, 214
Birmingham, Diocese of, 7, 35, 43, 58, 62, 70, 79, 81f, 105, 145f, 148f, 151, 153, 168, 186, 210
Birmingham, Peter de, 35
Birmingham, RC Archdiocese of, 37
Birmingham, University of, 39
birth attendants, traditional, 174
Bishop Josiah Trust, 94, 159
Bishop Mtekateka Secondary School, Nkhotakota, 209
Bishop, Colin and Sylvia, 161
Bishop's Croft, Harborne, 7, 39, 65
Black and Asian communities, 146
Black-led churches, 43
Blantyre, 12, 17-19, 24f, 47, 49, 51, 53, 67, 74, 77, 84, 91, 98, 102, 109, 140, 143, 159, 176f, 179, 182, 184-186, 189, 192-194
Blantyre Mission, 17, 228
Blantyre Synod CCAP, 24, 51, 77
Blantyre, Dean of, 81
Bleazard, John, 182, 201f, 207
Blessitt, Arthur, 151
Board of Enquiry [DSM, 1995], 90

Boldmere, 111
Bolivia, 155, 166-168
Booth, Joseph, 26
borough, incorporation as a, 37
Bossingham, Sally (Hayden), 165
Botswana, 30, 33, 90
Boulton, Matthew, 36
Bournville, 39
Bownass, Alison, 186, 188
Boyle, Christopher, 7, 14, 82, 87f, 99-105, 110-114, 116-118, 125, 133, 163, 175, 182, 199, 213, 222
Bracher, Paul, 7, 171f
Brennan, Loretta, 105
Brocklebank, Jackie, 8, 127, 134f, 137
Brocklebank, Ralph, 137
Broomfield, Gerald, 30
Brown, Laurence, 102, 147, 161, 223
Burgess, Henry, 7, 48f, 101f, 160
Burrup, Henry, 15, 18
business development, 134
Called to Care, 88f
Cambridge, 15f, 64, 148f, 192, 212, 215
Campbell-Smith, Claire, 114f
canals, 36
Canterbury, 18, 22, 101, 116, 182

Canterbury, Archbishop of, 15f, 73, 146, 150, 181, 193
Carr, Jim, 8, 111, 127, 136f, 180, 185, 209
Carr, Liz, 8, 111, 127, 136f 180, 185, 209
CART [Christian Africa Relief Trust], 183, 206
Castle Bromwich, 137
Catholic social teaching, 71
CCAP, see Church of Central Africa Presbyterian
CCBI, 74-77, 79
Central Africa, Archbishop of, 38, 53, 194
Central Africa, Province of, 30, 32f, 59, 62, 73, 138, 140, 143, 181, 196
Chama, Albert, 33
Chamberlain, Joseph, 37
Chancellor College, University of Malawi, Zomba, 56, 91, 206
Charles Janson [ship], 20
Chauncy Maples [ship], 20, 28, 31
Chelmsley Wood, 184
Chester Cathedral, 208
Chichewa, 56, 58, 62, 80, 87, 102, 117, 132, 138, 205
Chikwawa, 15, 19
Chilema, 28, 31f, 51, 65, 69, 80, 90, 179, 194, 203, 213

232

Chilema Ecumenical Lay Training and Conference Centre, 28, 51
Chilembwe, John, 26f, 229
Chilumba, 104, 199
Chinkwita, Emmanuel, 76
Chintheche, 111f, 189
Chipembere, Henry, 53
Chiradzulu, 18
Chirwa, Matilda, 130. See 'Matilda's Malawi'
Chirwa, Orton, 73, 78
Chirwa, Vera, 78f
Chitumbuka, 118, 139
Chiutula, Matilda, 88, 203
Chiwowa Chisala, 113
Christ Church, Selly Park, 167
Christendom thinking, 42
Christian Council of Malawi, 75
Christian Health Association of Malawi, 83
Christian Literature Association in Malawi (CLAIM), 28
Christian Service Committee, 27f
Church and Community Mobilisation Process [CCMP], 134, 211, 226
Church Mission Society (CMS), 29, 41, 93, 96, 161f
Church of Central Africa Presbyterian (CCAP), 13, 23, 25, 29, 46, 77, 51, 53f, 70, 73, 77, 81, 138, 200, 205, 221
Church of England, 5f, 13, 35, 37, 39, 45, 59f, 74, 76, 82, 146, 149f, 152, 168, 195, 199, 210, 217, 221, 225, 228
church, organic growth of, 52
Churches of Christ, 51
Circles without Centres' [church building] appeal, 42
city of a thousand trades, the, 36, 145
City of Birmingham Young Voices, 188
civic education, 77, 80
Civic Gospel, 37
classroom blocks, 111, 160, 174, 189, 192, 206, 208
climate change, 6, 89, 109, 184, 191f, 199, 211, 225
coal industry, 40
Cole, George, 50
Cole-King, Susan, 45f, 48, 84- 86, 88, 120
Coleshill, 35
College for Christian Ministries, Lilongwe, 202f
College of the Ascension, Birmingham, 32, 48, 50, 69, 91, 103, 140, 166
Collins, Martyn, 101

Colorado, Diocese of, 47
comity agreements, 22, 25f, 92
community development, 134
companion links, 6, 8, 13, 45, 100, 166, 170, 204, 211, 217
condoms, 86
consultations, 33, 59, 63f, 81, 92f, 156f, 181, 198, 201, 212f
containers, 135, 141, 171, 173f, 177, 180, 183-185, 190, 202, 205f, 210, 225
Cooper, John, 7, 48, 62f, 69, 81, 93, 122, 161f, 164
Corpus Christi parish, Tonbridge, Kent, 184
Council of Anglican Provinces in Africa [CAPA], 213, 226
Council of Churches for Britain and Ireland (CCBI), 74-77, 79
Covid-19, 146, 215
Cox, Dr Helen, 56
Cox, Tony, 7, 56, 59, 65, 77, 190, 213
Crooks, Melanie, 163
Crossley, Elizabeth, 110
Crowther Hall, Birmingham, 208
cultural misunderstandings, 97
Dakilira, Chrispin, 127
Darwin, Erasmus, 36
decline in churchgoing, 41, 152
Dedza, 208

demonstration garden, 113, 125
denominationalism, 25
dependency, 62f, 88, 100, 136, 156, 168, 199
development, 27, 35, 51, 58, 65, 71, 78, 80, 82, 84, 88, 93, 95, 103, 112, 132, 134, 162, 165, 176, 190, 196, 199f, 220, 226
DfID, 95, 164
Diocesan Communications Committee [Birmingham], 141
Diocesan President, MU, 133-135, 141f
diocesan synod, 199f
Disasters Emergency Committee, 106
DLM, see Lake Malawi, Diocese of
DNM, see Northern Malawi, Diocese of
doctors, 45, 176f
Dowa, 132
Drew, Stephen, 173
DSM, see Southern Malawi, Diocese of
Dube, Cecilia Hasha, 33
DUS, see Upper Shire, Diocese of
Dutch Reformed Church, 22, 24f, 132
Dwambazi, 207
Dwangwa, 57

ecumenism, 26, 32, 72, 76, 78, 81, 141, 161, 200, 204, 214
Edgbaston, 39
education, 21, 23, 27, 30, 32, 39, 71, 76, 80-82, 85, 94f, 103, 110, 117, 135, 147, 158, 171, 176, 188, 190, 198f, 204, 206
Education, Board of, 186
Education, Diocesan Director of, 95, 162, 174, 182
Edwards, Gill, 8, 137
Edwards, Mary, 8, 95, 182
Eggington, Eileen, 140, 190
Elston, Philip, 7
Emmanuel, Wylde Green, 101
Episcopal Church, 47
Episcopal Church [US] Relief and Development, 112, 203
ethnicity, 26
Evangelism, Decade of, 151
expatriate staff [in Malawi], 59
external influences, 13
Faith in the City of Birmingham [1988], 146
Faith in the City report [1985], 146
Famine Appeal [2002], 105-109
famine of 2002, 83, 103, 112
famine relief [2002], 109, 160, 214
Federation of Rhodesia and Nyasaland, 29
Festina loan, 101f

Fiedler, Klaus, 7, 13, 17, 20, 23-27, 29, 55, 70, 77, 82, 229
Finance, Director of [Birmingham], 154f, 163, 183
financial support, 80, 82, 94, 155, 183, 203, 211, 218, 225
First World War, 39
flour, vitamin-enriched [Likuni phala], 108f
food security, 112
Fort Worth, Diocese of, 100f, 105, 199
Francis, Marjorie, 158f
Friends of Bishop Christopher, 87, 103, 110, 112f, 116, 119
Fulford, Margaret, 142
G8 Nations, 94
G8 Summit, 94f
Gabriel [DNM boat], 101
Gale, Dr Gill, 57f
Gale, Keith, 7, 57-59, 64, 213
Gayton, Glynis, 173
gender-based violence, 199, 204, 211, 225
General Synod [of the Church of England], 60, 97
generosity, 96, 114, 116, 118, 136, 153, 171f, 225
Germany, 90
Ghana, 205
Gilmore, Michele, 123

giving, monetary, 153, *See* money, role of
Goldstein, Dr Mandy, 129, 174-178
Gordon, Ronald, 50
Gore, Charles, 37-39
Graham, Billy, 151
Great St. Mary's, Cambridge, 16
Green, Bryan, 44
Green, Mark, 57, 60, 102, 202
Groves, Phil, 60, 212, 215f, 227
Grubb, Judith, 8, 127, 135, 183
Guildford, Diocese of, 195
guilt, post-colonial, 156
Hall, Christopher, 56
Handsworth riots, 1985, 147
Harare, 30, 34
Harborne, 39, 162
Hastings, Adrian, 152, 213, 227
Hayden, Sally (Bossingham), 118
health, 71, 80, 83, 85f, 88f, 103, 134, 174-176, 188, 190, 194, 198f, 203
health, maternal and child, 83
Healy, John and Pauline, 205
Heathfield, Simon, 168
Henderson, Nicholas, 196f
High Church, 29, 39f, 112
High Commission, British, 95, 112

HIV/AIDS, 14, 70f, 80, 83-89, 103f, 110, 112f, 134, 137, 170, 174, 194, 198, 203, 208
Hollinghurst, Anne, 131, 144, 181f, 189, 203, 208
Hollinghurst, Steve, 182
Hollingsworth, Paula, 96, 143
Holloway, Brenda, 161
homosexuality, 195, 197, 202
Hope, David, 16
hospitality, 67, 114, 117, 136f, 172, 210, 225
hospitals [Anglican], 24, 49, 59, 62, 74, 82, 156, 163, 167, 170, 190, 194, 210, 225
Houghton, Josephine, 7
housing estates, 41, 146
Hoverd, Christine (Sister), 55
Howell-Jones, Peter, 7, 118, 123, 157, 162f, 178-180, 183, 185f, 188, 195, 213
Human rights, 78
Hunt, Jo, 93, 96f
Hunter, Rodney, 31, 142
IMF, 104
immigration, 42, 147, 216
income generating activities, 200, 226
income generating projects, 82, 93, 134, 191
inculturation, 202

infant mortality, 194
initiation rituals, 85
Inman, Dr Clive, 58
intentional discipleship, 167
International Development, Department for, 95
International Development, Secretary of State for, 95
Islam, 21f, 221
J John, 151
Jaguar Land Rover, 145
Janson, Charles, 20
Jehovah's Witnesses, 54, 99
Jenkins, Bob, 5, 8, 33, 44-48, 50, 52, 59, 64f, 67, 84, 97, 101f, 153, 160-162, 178, 227
Jenkins, Wendy, 8
Jepson, Rachel, 97,122
Jerusalem Trust, 141
Jewish, 148, 221
Johnson, Percival, 20
Johnson, Susan, 67
Jubilee 2000 [debt campaign], 94f, 151
Kachala, Matthews, 171
Kachebere Major Seminary (RC), 31
Kalaile, Mr Justice James, 8
Kalemba, Alinafe, 8, 32, 64, 100, 116f, 130f, 193, 195, 201f, 223
Kalilombe, Patrick, 54, 166, 227

Kambalu, Samson, 132
Kamungu, Leonard, 31
Kapeni, Chief, 19, 24
Kaphiridzinja, 159
Karima, Emmanuel, 31
Karonga, 103f, 110, 135
Kaswaya, Constantine, 31, 80
Kaulanda, Francis, 8, 96f, 131, 137, 173, 189, 196-198, 206-208, 223
Kaulanda, Nellie, 137
Kawinga, Edward, 8, 207
Kayoyo, 16, 194
Khisimisi, Tamara, 204
Kilekwa, Petro, 31
Kingston-on-Thames, Bishop of, 64
Kirk, Andrew, 212, 214f, 227
Kishindo, 28
Kiungani Boys School, 19, 31
Kumpolota, Matthews, 8, 33, 123
Kwiyani, Harvey, 213
Lake Malawi Anglican University, 55, 203
Lake Malawi, Bishop of, 57, 63, 142, 198
Lake Malawi, Diocese of (DLM), 18, 32-34, 47f, 53, 55, 57, 63, 73, 89, 96, 99, 105, 108, 148, 159, 161, 173, 180f, 184, 189f,

196, 198f, 202, 206-208, 216, 222f
Laland, Claire, 8, 133f, 141f, 164f, 185f
Lambeth Conference, 64, 138, 194
Langton, Dr Joe, 177
language, 117
Lay Training Centre, 32, 163, 180, 198, 203, 209
Leahy, Adrian, 182
Leake, John, 51
Lee, David, 8, 90f, 93, 100f, 105f, 108f, 122, 156, 158f, 162, 164, 166, 201
Leicester, Diocese of, 118
Leonard Kamungu Theological College (LKTC), 31f, 116, 182, 189, 193, 201-203, 207
Lichfield diocese, 57
Likoma, 15, 20, 22, 30f, 52f, 68, 87, 99f, 111, 148, 160, 173, 180, 198f, 222, 228
Likwenu, 28, 61, 205
Lilongwe, 16, 33, 53f, 57f, 64, 91, 93, 99, 104, 153, 158, 184, 197f, 202f
Lilongwe, Archdeacon of, 58, 99
Lilongwe, RC Bishop of, 54, 166
Limbe, 192
Literacy and Financial Education Programme [LFEP], 134

Livingstone, David, 15-18, 21, 23f, 27, 229
Livingstonia, 17, 23, 25, 209, 228
Liwaladzi, 127
London, 30, 39, 45f, 61, 79, 97, 101, 133, 141, 152f, 155, 158, 161, 188, 190f, 196, 212-214
Longbridge, 145
Lords, House of, 148, 150
lorries, 58, 93, 104, 159, 184, 188
Low Church, 39
Lunar Society of Birmingham, 36
Lutheran, 90
M'baya, Erasto, 8, 204
Machemba, May, 8, 208
Mackenzie, Charles, 15, 17-19, 68, 222, 227, 228
Macmillan, Harold, 29
Magangani, Fanuel, 8, 103, 111, 131, 181, 199f, 223
Magomero, 15f, 18f, 27, 68, 193, 195
Mainga, Bernard, 8, 116f
maize, 104f, 108f
Makanjira, 21f
Makawa, Peter, 97
Malango, Bernard, 28, 31, 33, 123, 142, 194-196, 205, 213, 222
malaria, 18f, 194, 198, 203
Malasa, Brighton Vita, 8, 33, 131, 193, 195, 223

Malasa, Michael and Carolyn, 171
Malawi against Polio [MAP], 58
Malawi Association for Christian Support (MACS), 46f, 52, 140, 189f, 196, 203, 209
Malawi Broadcasting Corporation, 138
Malawi Church Trust, 158
Malawi Coordinating Committee, 162
Malawi Council of Churches, 28, 75
Malawi Development Group, 80
Malawi Fund, Diocese of Birmingham, 154, 158
Malawi General Fund, 154, 165
Malawi Human Rights Network, 79
Malawi Law Society, 78
Malawi Octave [2011], 165
Malawi Partnership Officer, 5, 163
Malawi Round Table, 188-190, 204
Malawi Support Group, 161f
Malawi Task Group, 118, 133, 141, 162f, 165, 180, 182, 190, 192
Malawi Wheels appeal [2004-5], 155, 160, 185f, 188
Malawi, Diocese of, 32, 47, 50, 153, 203
Malindi, 16, 20f, 69, 140

malnutrition, 83, 199
Malosa, 33, 47, 50f, 56, 59, 61, 143, 180, 193f, 196
Malosa Secondary School, 51, 56, 59
Manchester, 35
Manchester, Dean of, 42, 45
Mandala House, Blantyre, 25
Mangochi, 20, 25, 194f, 207
Mankhokwe, Henry, 96
Mann, Alexandrina, 182, 206
Mapapa, Charles, 28
Maples, Chauncy, 21f, 222
Maputwa, Fr, 28
Marsh, Laura, 105
Mary Sumner House, London [MU world headquarters], 133
Matope, 20, 189
Mayes, Stephen, 84, 97
Mbweni, 19f, 22
Mchenga, 206
Media Awareness Project [MAP], 141
Medic Malawi, 173, 190
Memorandum of Understanding [2016], 188f, 213
Methodists, 36, 43, 166
Midlands Enlightenment, 35
Miller, Esther, 203
Miller, Janice, 67, 133

Mindolo Ecumenical Centre, Kitwe, Zambia, 32
mission encounter, 163, 178f, 181, 193
Mission England [1984], 151
mission resource centre, 161f
missionaries, 12f, 15-21, 23-26, 28-30, 46f, 52-54, 64, 92f, 117, 162, 167, 190, 228f
Mitchell, Andrew, 164
Mkamwera, Franklin, 127
Mkata, Frank, 54
Mkoko, Agnes, 8, 33, 126, 133, 140, 142, 164, 185, 205
Moir brothers, 23f
Molyneux, Elizabeth, 175
money, role of, 14, 45, 48, 60f, 67, 71, 100f, 104f, 142, 152-159, 163, 166f, 170f, 178, 197, 204f, 214
Montefiore, Hugh, 62, 64f, 102f, 114, 121, 145, 148, 223
Montfort Missionaries (RC), 25
Morgan, Simon and Margaret, 126, 196
Mothers' Union [Birmingham, UK], 67, 133-135, 140-142, 162f, 181, 185f, 189
Mothers' Union [Malawi], 10, 14, 61, 89f, 95, 125, 132-136, 138-140, 142f, 190, 211

motor industry, 145
motorbike, 12, 185f, 208
Mozambique, 18-20, 22, 67, 206, 208
Mpassou, Denis, 28
Mponda, Baird, 8, 65, 138, 208
Mponda, Oscar, 8, 97, 206
Mpondas, 21, 28, 31, 47, 160, 195
Msekawanthu, Dean, 50
Msini, Irene, 97
Msomba, 111, 126f, 189
Mtekateka, Josiah, 30, 52-54, 63, 65, 99, 120, 148, 198, 209, 222
Mtunthama, 105, 130, 173, 184, 190
MU, see Mothers' Union
Mua, 25
Muluzi, Bakili, 77, 80
Muslim, 22, 25, 65, 75, 77, 109, 147, 205, 211, 221
Muslim Association [of Malawi], 75
Musukwa, Willy, 8, 110f, 117, 180
Mutual Responsibility and Interdependence, 45
mutuality, 46
Mwanza, 141, 182
Mwawa, Christopher, 31, 33, 181
Mzimba, 123
Mzuzu, 7, 72, 98f, 101, 112, 135, 172, 181, 199f

Nashotah House, Wisconsin, 199
natural disasters, 67, 160, 191, 214
Nazism, German, 40
Ndirande, 159, 186, 213
Ndirande Anglican Voices, 12, 98, 124, 136, 186, 213
Ndomondo, George, 28, 31, 80
neopatrimonialism, 191
Nets for Life, 203
New Street station, 36, 146
Newman, John Henry, 37
Newsome, David, 8, 76, 79-81
Nicholls, Vernon, 161
Nigeria, 195
Nkhata Bay, 68, 113, 184
Nkhoma Synod, CCAP, 24
Nkhotakota, 15f, 21, 24, 32, 53, 55, 63f, 68, 148, 160, 180, 190, 196-198, 203, 208, 209
Nkope Hill, 31, 190
nonconformity, religious, 35
Northern Malawi, Bishop of, 14, 38, 54, 101, 118, 133, 180
Northern Malawi, Diocese of (DNM), 23, 34, 87-89, 96, 99-101, 103, 105, 108, 110, 114f, 119, 134f, 159f, 172, 175, 180f, 184, 189, 199f, 222f
Northern Zambia, Bishop of, 33, 194

nsima, 137, 164
Ntaba, Hetherwick, 73
Ntcheu, 25, 90, 194, 199
Ntchisi, 16, 24, 63, 189, 194, 206, 208
nurses, 174-177
Nyanja, Peter, 27, 31, 33, 55, 57, 63-65, 68f, 75, 108, 121f, 166, 196, 203, 222
Nyasaland, 46f, 52
Nyasaland, Diocese of, 22, 47
Nyika, Mugove Walter, 89, 205
Omar, Dr Sofia, 129
ordination of women, 44, 139, 142f, 195
Osborne, Hayward and Sandy, 182
Oxford, 15, 32, 38f, 89, 149f, 161, 205
paediatrics, 176-178
Paget, Bishop, 30
parish links, 94, 165, 170, 173, 207, 210, 226
parish visitations, 111
Parker, Erica, 95
Parliament, 17, 37, 40, 139
Parsee [Zoroastrian], 141
Parslow, John, 47, 49, 178
Partners in Mission (PIM), 59, 64
partnership, 5-7, 12-14, 38, 44f, 47f, 56, 59-62, 71, 75, 92f, 101, 109, 111, 114f, 118, 132f, 136,

138, 145, 150, 152f, 155-157, 159f, 163-168, 170-172, 175-179, 182f, 185, 188-191, 193, 207, 209f, 211f, 214-217, 224-226
Partnership for World Mission (PWM), 60f, 162, 208
Partnership Review [2014], see Review of the Partnership
Pastoral Letter of RC bishops [Lent 1992], 71-73, 76
paternalism, 45, 49
patriarchal [society], 85, 132, 204
Pembamoyo, Eston, 8, 84, 97, 98, 132, 182, 184, 195, 205f
Pembamoyo, Joyce, 205
Pentecostal, 43, 221
permaculture, 89, 135, 205
Phelps-Stokes Commission [1924], 27
Polesworth, 35
political prisoners, 78
poor nutrition. *See* malnutrition
Pope, 71
Porter, David, 50, 158
Powell, Enoch, 43
Prayer Book of 1927, 40
Praying Together [Birmingham], 141, 164, 210

Price, Janice, 8, 45, 59, 136, 153, 155, 168, 198, 207, 210-2012, 217, 224, 228
Priestley, Alan, 164
Priestley, Joseph, 36
primary schools, church, 44
Public Affairs Committee [PAC], 27, 75, 78
publicity, 164
Queen Elizabeth Central Hospital (QECH), Blantyre, 45, 83, 174-177
Queen Elizabeth II, 28
Queen's Foundation, Birmingham, 166
Race, Christopher, 8, 69, 73f, 76f, 79, 81
racial prejudice, 42
railways, 36
referendum [on a multi-party system], 75
Reformation, 26, 35
regionalism, 80
Review of the Partnership [2014], 6, 157, 168, 208, 210f, 224-226
Rhodes, Matthew, 8, 182
Robinson, Alison, 8, 51
Robinson, Gene, 195
Roche, John, 72
Rogers, Rosy, 176

Roman Catholic, 12, 25, 31, 36f, 39, 51, 54, 70f, 74f, 79, 117, 132, 142, 149, 166, 184, 220
Ross, Andrew, 54, 228
Ross, Kenneth R., 13, 17, 20, 23-27, 29, 54f, 70f, 73, 76f, 143, 228f
Rowley Regis, 91
Runcie, Robert, 15, 139
Ruo, River, 18, 192
Ryan, Denese, 171
Safe Motherhood Programme, 175
Samuel, Raphael, 167
Sandwell, Borough of, 38
Sangaya, Jonathan, 51
sanitation, 85
Sanneh, Lamin, 117
Santer, Henriette, 67
Santer, Mark, 8, 67-69, 72-74, 76, 80, 87, 91, 95, 106, 121, 133, 139, 149, 159, 162, 178, 182, 192, 199, 201, 223
savings group, community, 134
Schofield, Rodney, 31
school links, 174
Scotland, 13, 29, 54, 73, 76, 78f, 95, 97, 150, 228
Scotland, Church of, 17, 24, 46, 70, 73f, 78f

Scotland, Free Church of, 17, 23, 138
Second World War, 40-42
self-support, 155, 167
self-sustainability, 200, 210f, 225f
Selly Oak colleges, 32, 50, 91, 166, 213
Sentamu, John, 113f, 123f, 133, 147, 149, 175f, 178, 181, 185f, 223
Sentamu, Margaret, 123, 133
Seva, Jesman, 8, 180, 209
Shire, River, 16, 18f, 21, 192, 194
Short, Clare, 95
Silver Jubilee, 1991, 67
Sim, Fr Arthur, 15, 21
Sinclair, Maurice, 131, 167f, 188, 195, 216
skills share, 115, 163, 178-180, 201, 203, 213
Slater, Terry, 7, 35-44, 62, 145, 148f, 151, 153
slave trade, 16-19
Smethwick, 43
Smith, Guy, 57
Smith, Peter, 182, 209
Smythies, Charles, 20
soil fertility, 104, 113
Solihull, 35, 38, 146
South Africa, 24, 29, 32, 58, 116, 165, 205f

South Lunzu, 125, 141
Southern Malawi, Bishop of, 5, 65, 67, 84, 92, 213
Southern Malawi, Diocese of (DSM), 32, 47f, 53, 63, 73, 77, 80, 84f, 88-90, 97f, 109, 140, 143, 159, 161, 182, 184, 189, 192-194, 205, 222f
SS Peter and Paul, Mpondas, 194
St Agnes Guild, 133, 140
St Anne's Hospital, Nkhotakota, 49, 55, 68, 129, 183, 190
St Chad's RC Cathedral, Birmingham, 37
St Columba's, Sutton Coldfield, 98
St Gabriel, Weoley Castle, 101
St George's Cathedral, Cape Town, 18
St George's, Edgbaston, 207
St George's, Zomba, 206f
St James', Aston, 43
St John's, Harborne, 196
St Leonard's, Marston Green, 49
St Luke's Hospital, Malosa, 51, 175, 196
St Margaret's, Short Heath, 205
St Mark's, Mzuzu, 101, 172f, 200
St Martin's Hospital, Malindi, 21
St Martin's in the Bull Ring, 35, 44, 81, 93

St Mary and St Margaret, Castle Bromwich, 102
St Mary's College, Oscott, 37
St Mary's, Biwi [Lilongwe], 91, 99, 153
St Matthew's, Smethwick, 56
St Michael and All Angels, Blantyre, 24
St Michael's, Boldmere, 160
St Nicholas, Baddesley Ensor, 173
St Paul's Cathedral, Blantyre, 18, 53, 84, 102
St Paul's, Balsall Heath, 97
St Peter's Cathedral, Likoma, 20, 68, 89, 100, 111f, 138, 199
St Peter's Major Seminary, Zomba, 31
St Peter's, Hall Green, 172f
St Peter's, Lilongwe, 16, 50, 54, 58, 99
St Philip's Cathedral, Birmingham, 12, 38, 50, 186, 188, 207
St Richard's, Lea Hall, 171f, 213
Steere, Edward, 20, 222
Stephenson, Martin, 8, 172f
Stepney, Bishop of, 150
stigma, 86f
Stone, Geoffrey, 93
Stourton, Ed, 105
Stowe, Kate, 7

Strategic Grain Reserve [SGR], 104f
Sunday schools, 44
sustainability, 61, 155f, 189, 210f, 225f
Sustainable Development Goals [2015], 211
Sutton Coldfield, 50, 94
Swan, Philip, 8, 179, 182, 193, 209
Swanwick, 208
Swanwick Conference [1987], 78
Swanwick Conference [1993], 76, 79, 139
Sykes, Emma, 8, 143, 180
Takilima, Francis, 127
Tanzania, 20, 22, 30f, 63, 194, 228
Taylor, Humphrey, 7, 48, 50, 54, 59
teachers' skills share, 110, 115, 137, 173f, 180, 203, 209f
TEEM [Theological Education by Extension Malawi], 32, 140, 205
Tembo, John, 70
Tengatenga, James, 5, 7, 13, 15f, 21, 28-31, 33, 46f, 51, 54, 67, 69, 70-72, 77f, 83f, 86-92, 157, 166, 192, 200-202, 204, 213, 222f, 229
Tengatenga, Josie, 91, 98, 143
Texas, Diocese of, 47

theological training, 31, 69, 94, 112, 159, 193, 198, 200f
Thindwa, Bester, 135
Thorne, Frank Oswald, 28-30, 222, 229
three selfs, 92
Tione, Grafiud, 190
Tirola, 113
Tovey, Ronald, 54
Tozer, George, 19f, 23, 222
training, ordination, 191
Trinity Anglican Secondary School, DSM, 189, 192
Trower, Gerard, 22, 222
Tucker, Laetitia, 7
Tucker, Richard, 5, 32, 163, 195, 199, 201, 211
Tutu, Desmond, 151
ubuntu, 132
Uganda, 60, 96, 149, 150, 162
uniformed organizations [church], 44
Universities' Mission to Central Africa (UMCA), 15-18, 20-24, 28-30, 46f, 65, 69, 100, 142, 190, 223, 227-229
Upper Shire, Diocese of (DUS), 21, 89, 109, 140, 142, 160, 171, 180, 182, 184, 189f, 194-196, 203, 205f, 222f

Urquhart, David, 7, 113f, 126, 131, 150, 152, 167, 175, 181, 188, 197, 215f, 223, 225
USA, 5, 26, 32, 39, 47, 51, 56, 167, 192, 195, 199f, 215
USPG [United Society Partnership in the Gospel], 7, 15, 30, 32, 48, 51, 53-55, 57, 59, 61f, 80, 93, 101, 110, 143, 162, 166, 182, 189f, 192, 196, 204
Venn, Henry, 29, 92
Viner, Len, 7
violence, domestic, 134
Wakefield, Henry, 39
Wakeling, Catherine, 7
Waller, Horace, 19, 23
Warm Heart of Africa, the, 33, 44, 50, 52, 59f, 67, 96, 114, 153, 160f, 164, 172, 227
Warwickshire, 38, 173
Water Orton, 84
Watson, Andrew, 8, 113, 126, 163, 181, 193, 199
Watson, Beverly, 193
Watson, David, 151
Watson, John, 50
Watt, James, 36
Weller, John, 160f
Wesley, John, 36
West Heath, 160
Westcott House, Cambridge, 148f

White Fathers [Catholic religious order], 25, 74, 79
Wilkins, Brian, 184
Williams, Rowan, 16, 193
Willow, George, 33
Wills, Julie, 96
Wilson, J. Scott, 199
Wilson, [John] Leonard, 5, 41-46, 48-50, 84, 120, 147, 162, 223
Wilson, Martin, 45, 84, 162
Wilson, Paul, 8, 42, 154, 156, 159, 162f, 183, 185f, 193, 199, 204, 207
wind of change, 29
Windrush generation, 42
women's rights, 134
Worcester diocese, 37
Worcester, Bishop of, 37
Worcestershire, 38
Workman, John, 33, 59
workshop of the world, the, 36
World Bank, 95
World Council of Churches, 28, 51, 79, 140
World Food Programme, UN [WFP], 106
Wylde Green, 49, 102
Yao, 18f, 195, 207, 228
Yardley, 35
York, Archbishop of, 15f, 28, 133, 150

youth exchanges, 93, 96, 98, 122, 138, 182, 198, 205, 206
Zambezi, 18
Zambia, 31, 33, 85, 88, 160, 165, 194
Zanzibar, 15, 19f, 22, 31
Zimbabwe, 33f, 58, 60, 85, 90, 165, 205

Zingani, Willie, 28
Zomba, 28, 31, 53, 56, 81, 189, 201, 205
Zomba Theological College, 31f 59, 74, 81, 84, 90f, 142f, 193, 198, 200, 205, 208

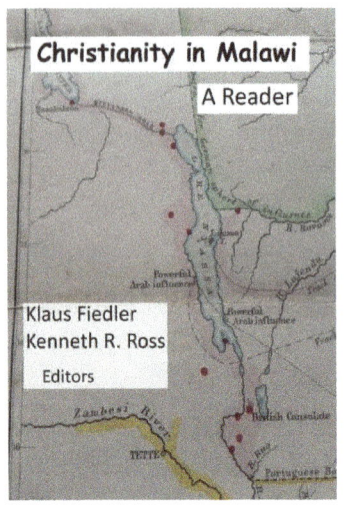

Klaus Fiedler and Kenneth R. Ross (Eds), *Christianity in Malawi. A Reader*, Mzuzu: Mzuni Press, 2021, 501 pp.

This book assembles some of the best writing about Malawi's church history. Drawing on more than 50 years of scholarship, it brings together chapters from books that are now out of print and articles that have receded far into the back numbers of the journals in which the were first published. It can also serve as a companion reader to Kenneth R. Ross and Klaus Fiedler, *A Malawi Church History*, Mzuzu: Mzuni Press, 2020

Kenneth R. Ross (ed), *Christianity in Malawi. A Source Book,* Revised and Enlarged Edition, Mzuzu: Mzuni Press, 2020, 308 pp.

The perfect companion for the study of Malawi Church History. It presents 32 original documents from all periods of the Church's history in Malawi. By bringing forward a selection of key primary sources, this book provides the opportunity to read the story of Malawian Christianity "from the inside." It allows some Malawian Christians to speak for themselves so that church history might be formed by listening directly and critically to voices from the past.

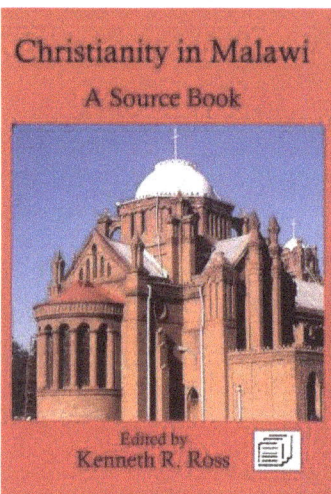

Kenneth R. Ross & Klaus Fiedler,
A *Malawi Church History 1860-2020*,
Mzuzu: Mzuni Press, 2020, 500 pp.

This is the first attempt to comprehend the whole of Malawi's church history in a single volume. The focus of this book is about documenting the religious experience which was at the centre of founding the new nation of Malawi as we have come to know it. The book strikes a balance in covering issues pertaining to both mission activities and African agency. In many instances interesting pieces of evidence have been marshalled to corroborate or emphasize some of the conclusions reached

"... a must-have book for institutional and personal libraries in Malawi and for all those interested in the impact of Christianity in Africa."

Prof Isabel Apawo Phiri, Deputy General Secretary, World Council of Churches

"The significance of this book cannot be over-emphasised ... a one-stop account for understanding Malawi's church history ... captivating and refreshingly informative."

Wapulumuka O. Mulwafu, Professor of Environmental History and Dean of Postgraduate Studies, Chancellor College, University of Malawi.

James Tengatenga, *Church, State and Society in Malawi. An Analysis of Anglican Ecclesiology*, Zomba: Kachere Series, 2006, 227 pp.

Missionary history in Africa asserts that political history on the continent cannot be understood without an in depth understanding of the workings of the missions: missionary activities and ideologies were central to political consciousness. The Anglican Church was involved in society, education, health and politics rights from its first foray into Malawi. This study considers the nature of the involvement of that Church in society, and how it engaged with the State from its genesis in the colonial period through the post-independence period to the new post-Banda political dispensation in 1994. It illustrates how the Church was involved on both sides of the independence struggle; and interrogates why it fell conspicuously silent thereafter.

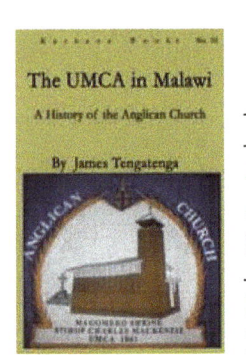

James Tengatenga, *The UMCA in Malawi. A History of the Anglican Church*, Zomba: Kachere Series, 2006, 238 pp.

In keeping with the work done by A.E.M. Anderson-Morshead, this book is a reproduction of the history of the UMCA and the Anglican Church in Central Africa. Bishop James Tengatenga rewrites the story of the Anglican mission that started at Magomero in 1861. The book lays out the origins, development and growth of Anglicanism that was facilitated by the work of the early UMCA missionaries, volunteers, local clergy and ordinary people.

Kenneth R. Ross, *Friendship with a Purpose. Malawi and Scotland for Sustainable Development*, **Mzuzu: Mzuni Press, 2021, 48 pp.**

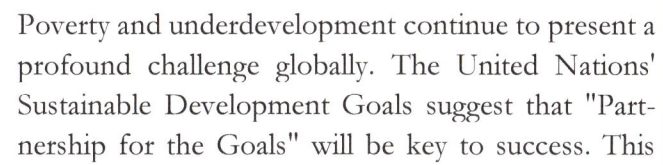

Poverty and underdevelopment continue to present a profound challenge globally. The United Nations' Sustainable Development Goals suggest that "Partnership for the Goals" will be key to success. This booklet explores the innovative people-to-people partnership developed by Malawi and Scotland during the 21st century. This is a model that invites emulation and challenges Malawians and Scots to be ambitious as they work together for sustainable development.

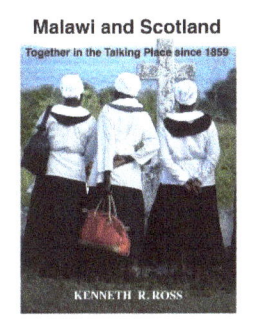

Kenneth R. Ross, *Malawi and Scotland in the Talking Place since 1859*, **Mzuzu: Mzuni Press, 2013, 242 pp.**

This pioneering and fascinating book is the first to tell the story of the remarkably enduring bonds between Malawi and Scotland from the time of David Livingstone to the flourishing cultural, economic and religious relationships of the present day. Why should there be any significant relationship between one small nation on Europe's north-western seaboard and another in the interior of Africa? How did it reach the stage where in 2012 Fiona Hyslop, Cabinet Secretary for Culture and External Affairs in the Scottish Government, could describe Malawi as Scotland's "sister nation"? This book attempts an answer.

Lightning Source UK Ltd.
Milton Keynes UK
UKHW021828270822
407820UK00005B/39